Healthy Pleasures

Healthy Pleasures

Robert Ornstein, Ph.D. and David Sobel, M.D.

Addison-Wesley Publishing Company
Reading, Massachusetts   Menlo Park, California   New York
Don Mills, Ontario   Wokingham, England   Amsterdam   Bonn
Sidney   Singapore   Tokyo   Madrid   San Juan   Paris
Seoul   Milan   Mexico City   Taipei

Library of Congress Cataloging-in-Publication Data

Ornstein, Robert Evan.
  Healthy pleasures / Robert Ornstein and David Sobel.
    p. cm.
  Includes index.
  ISBN 0-201-12669-9
  ISBN 0-201-52385-X (pbk)
  1. Health.   2. Pleasure principle (Psychology)
I. Sobel, David S. (David Stuart)   II. Title.
RA776.076   1989   88-34454
613—dc19   CIP

Cover design by Hannus Design Associates
Text design by Joyce C. Weston
Set in 10½-point Meridien by DEKR Corporation, Woburn, Massachusetts

0-201-48925-2

9 10 11 12-DOH-9998979695
Ninth printing, March 1995

To some of life's healthiest pleasures:
Sally, Judy, and Matt

And in memory of Phyllis,
who appreciated life's small pleasures

Contents

CONTENTS

Part Two: The Virtues of Sensuality

Acknowledgments

We'd like to thank our tireless editor, Jane Isay, for unflagging enthusiasm, encouragement, and good advice. Another healthy pleasure at Addison-Wesley has been William Patrick, whose advice animated the book's progress.

A lot of background research went into preparing this book. Special thanks to the generous contributions of Sharon Sokowitz, Nancy Bruning, Melanie Scheller, and Sarah Berkowitz.

Many people have also given us the benefit of their time and readings. Sally Mallam helped redirect us away from throat-clearing qualifications, and David Widdicombe contributed social and historical insights. Other readers, including Brent Danninger, Evan Neilsen, Doris Burgess, Don Bardole, and Laura Keranen contributed their insights and corrections to the manuscript. We thank you all.

And a special thanks to Doris and Alan Burgess for providing a room with a view in which to finish the book.

Preface

Many people today are concerned about living longer, feeling better, and having more energy, so there is a continuing demand for good health advice. Still, something is missing from all these recommendations, be they about nutrition, exercise, surgery, drug therapy, meditation, or stress-relief: the vital role of pleasure.

Healthy Pleasures proposes a new approach to the way women and men manage their health. We believe that it can be done better with less effort and with much more fun. We'll guide the reader through the maze of myths and misconceptions that stand in the way of health. We hope that you feel a great sense of relief—that health is not insured by a corporation, or delivered by a large medical complex, but streams naturally from within.

Here you will find scores of practical suggestions, based on recent scientific discoveries, on how to live life in a way that enriches, rather than just maintains, health: ways to mobilize positive beliefs, expectations, and emotions—from cognitive therapy, relaxation training, and successful behav-

ior modification practices. We draw on some surprising research about eating, drinking, and sleeping, education,
exercise, and sex to make suggestions about living.

But this is not another manual of simple practices; it is a
book about making real, lasting and attainable changes.
These important changes happen when they are approached
naturally and pleasurably, and not through a program of
difficult regimens. Because people are naturally drawn by
the pleasure principle to many of the things which promote
health, we believe that a program of healthy pleasures will
be easy to follow.

Being healthy and robust is much easier and more fun
than we had imagined. And we invite you to see why.

Robert Ornstein
David Sobel
November 1988

ONE

· · · · · · · · · · · · · · ·

The Pleasure Principle

1

The Pleasure Principle

Imagine the world without pleasure. Life would appear colorless and humorless. A baby's smile would go unappreciated. Foods would be tasteless. The beauty of a Bach concerto would fall on deaf ears. Feelings like joy, thrills, delights, ecstasy, elation and happiness would disappear. The company of others would not bring comfort and joy. The touch of a mother would not soothe, and a lover could not arouse. Interest in sex and procreation would dry up. The next generation would wait unborn.

Fortunately, life is not like that. Nerve pathways speed satisfying sensations to the brain. Packets of chemicals stand ready to transmit pleasure signals from one nerve cell to another. There is a pleasure machine within our head, in which several brain centers respond to gratifying stimulation.

All this didn't happen by accident; the human desire for enjoyment evolved to enhance our survival. What better way to assure that healthy, life-saving behaviors occur than to make them pleasurable? From eating to reproduction, from attending to the environment to caring for others, pleasure guides us to better health. Doing what feels right and feeling good are beneficial for health and the survival of the species.

So through evolution, health-promoting acts are biologically connected to positive feelings—pleasure. Although there are exceptions in the modern world, pleasure—enjoying food, sex, friends, work, and family—is the universal innate guide to health. People recognize what is healthful by the joys of life, by their pleasurable feelings—a delicious nap, a sated stomach, or the satisfaction of sexuality. These sensations signal our brain that we are on the right track and should continue.

It took us a long time to embrace this new kind of "Pleasure Principle." Pleasure rewards us twice: first in immediate enjoyment and second in improved health.

Joie De Vivre

Think about the healthiest, most robust people you know. What makes them so vital? It is this seemingly simple question that completely changed our minds about health and led us to the Pleasure Principle. We discovered that the most hardy people we know do not follow all the "correct" advice about health. Their health secrets don't lie in the proscriptions and prescriptions that leap from almost every magazine and television program. Some assault the government's dietary guidelines at nearly every meal. They salt their foods, savor fatty fare like steak and fried potatoes, and don't fill their plates with fiber-rich foods. They even love dessert.

The only exercise some pick up (to paraphrase Mark Twain) is as pallbearers at the funerals of their overactive friends. A drink now and then, even a couple of glasses of wine every day, is not unknown to them.

They're keenly aware of their senses and relish nearly every opportunity to indulge in sensory pleasures: savoring a tasty meal, listening to favorite music or bird songs, staring into the embers of a fire, or marveling at the fall foliage.

Many forgo regular medical checkups—no annual physicals, yearly Pap smears, prostate examinations, or EKGs.

Some of these hardy women and men have chronic diseases, but they manage to prevail in spite of them. They demonstrate daily that there is a healthy way to live with a disease.

These people don't lead bland, stress-free lives. They are no strangers to sleepless nights, deadlines, moving to new jobs, and raising children. Some brave extreme adversity—poverty, war, and loss of loved ones—and overcome these obstacles. Boredom seems to be their enemy. So they seek new challenges and novelty.

They aren't necessarily rich or famous. But the way they live and *envision* their lives nourishes their life itself.

They expect good things of the world. They expect that things will work out well; they expect that their world will be orderly; they expect that other people will like and respect them. And most important, *they expect pleasure in much of what they do.*

The positive moods and pleasurable expectations of healthy people were so striking to us that we began to collect experiences of what these people were like. As a rule, they were optimistic and happy and seemed to feel that things would work out no matter their difficulties. They enjoyed small, simple pleasures and stolen moments: witnessing the sunrise, building a model classic car, or indulging in silly talk with their spouses, kids, and pets. Surprisingly to us, they highlighted minor things that pleased them; a shotgun collection, playing the violin passionately (though terribly), or cooking their favorite meals. These pursuits seemed somehow to absorb some of the troubles of their active lives.

We met one man whose life and career were destroyed in the famous anti-communist tirade of the 1940s. We were surprised that he was so charming and so free of bitterness; one would never guess that he had been through such a devastating experience. His son once made a comment in passing about his father: "He was a happy State Department official, and now he is a happy paper salesman." How did he get through it? By reading the classics for hours each day. He didn't stop for anything, even during the agony of his trial. It gave him a continuing interest in life, a solace and a respite from the events of his life. He's in his eighties now, and still vital.

Most of the people we studied were passionate about their work, families, and hobbies. Once, we were in a tough meeting with one of our healthy friends when her secretary rushed in, tense, with an urgent note. She left quickly. We wondered what had happened: Did her child suddenly take sick? Did she get fired? Finally, she returned, smiling, and said, "Sorry, but the Celtics were just about to win the championship. I was taping it, but I just had to watch the final moments!"

These people also seemed to be immune to life's little troubles. When his car was stolen, one said, "Can you drive me home? I wanted to talk more to you this afternoon anyway."

We were visiting midwestern grain farmers when an unexpected hailstorm decimated the corn crop. A party had been planned weeks earlier for that evening, so we began to call people to cancel. One of the farmers stopped us saying, "Hell, no! Now's the time to party more than ever."

There was a type of optimistic unreality to these robust people that began to impress us. They were confident in the face of business losses, job setbacks, and family disappointments. Somehow things would work out. They seemed to feel that they were special—protected. They focused on a bright future rather than worrying about their pasts.

For instance, Ronald Reagan's overpowering optimism served him well for both votes and health. When he was shot, he said that his mistake was that he had forgotten to duck; before his operation, he asked his surgeons whether they were Republicans. When asked about his colon cancer surgery, he said with characteristic healthy denial, "I didn't have cancer. I had something inside me that had cancer inside *it*, and *it* was removed." He, like others, even mixed up the truth—in this case about his physiology—when it was advantageous. The more we considered healthy people, the more important to health this kind of amiable and unrealistic perception seemed to be.

Many robust people seem to maintain a vital sense of humor about life, enjoying a hearty laugh, more often than not at their own expense. Others bring an unbridled enthusiasm to everything they do and everyone they touch. They're deeply committed to someone or something outside of themselves. They care more for people, pets, political causes, or volunteer organizations than for micromanaging their blood chemistries or fiber intake based upon the latest headlines and health advice. They're ardent about life itself, not every little step they need to take to preserve their health. And they see themselves as a *part of life*, rather than *apart from life.*

These healthy, robust people have their weirdnesses, quirks, and eccentricities—which seems surprisingly important. Indeed, English eccentrics are said to live long lives. Good health is one result of *joie de vivre*. In contrast to the self-absorption of the health fanatic, these people are absorbed in life.

In short, the healthiest people seem to be pleasure-loving, pleasure-seeking, pleasure-creating individuals.

Don't get us wrong. We recognize well that exercising, not smoking or drinking to excess, wearing seat belts, and avoiding extreme sunburn all contribute to a long, healthy life. Even so, the sum total of all these good health habits still doesn't add up to as much as you might believe, and doesn't explain the essential vitality of some people.

The missing ingredients lie not only in your genes, which you can't change, but in your thoughts, which you can. Good health is much closer to home, much simpler (and more enjoyable) than we had imagined. It derives from a pursuit of healthy pleasures.

2

• • • • • • • • • • • • •

Civilization and Its Displeasures

If pleasure is so enjoyable, and apparently health enhancing, then why do we give ourselves such a bad time about feeling good? The connection between pleasure and health is loaded with guilt. No one tries to prove to cats that they really should nap, purr, and chase mice, or point out to puppies the pleasures of romping, sniffing, or gnawing on a bone, or instruct children how to play, laugh, or cuddle. Yet, many of us have a surprising and deeply rooted resistance to anything that smacks of simply having a good time. Our culture seems to have lost a vital perspective on what is natural for a human being to do, be, and feel. And our health, as well as our quality of life, suffers greatly as a result.

Many of us are inhibited and don't allow ourselves free rein to experience pleasure: to savor a sunset, hang out with friends, enjoy a wild dance now and then. We lament that we don't have time for such leisurely pursuits, given the demands of work, family life, or even time-consuming health regimens. Many people point to the rampant problems of drug addiction, obesity, and sexual disease, and caution that pleasurable indulgence will surely lead to ruin.

In our modern society, despite the visible excesses and

conspicuous consumption of so-called pleasure-seekers, we have not really learned to enjoy ourselves.

Or, more accurately, we have forgotten.

The Rise of Work and the Fall of Pleasure

Let's look back at our preindustrial ancestors. Even though craft and farm work could be strenuous at certain times, there were also marked alternations between periods of intense effort and moments of complete idleness. For most of the year, work was near home and family. The farmer might strain during planting and certainly during harvest, but there was little urgency in the fallow times. He could live long parts of the year at his own tempo—playing with the kids, watching geese fly, soaking up the morning sun, listening to the call of birds, and taking (literally) a roll in the hay in the middle of the afternoon.

For most workers today, the routine of rising early at 6:45 each weekday, traveling to the office on the 7:22, and returning home on the 5:36 is taken entirely for granted. We forget how alien this regimentation was to our ancestors, and we pass over the tremendous conditioning effort needed to curb our forebears' pleasures to prepare them for the industrial age.

In the eighteenth century, with the Industrial Revolution in full sway, the British Parliament passed laws requiring faster and faster production from domestic workers. Factory life became commonplace. But our ancestors did not go forth with a happy heart and leap joyously to give up control over their bodies.

Historical records of the era show that people simply hated the idea of going to work and taking up a tethered, regulated life. They were appalled, and they rebelled accordingly. They stopped work when it pleased them, were

absent more than a third of the time, and often came in only
to get their wages. Natural urges to seek pleasure had to be
subjugated to the appetites of the industrial machine. Factories became, in part, schools for the new way of life as the
"labor discipline" was pounded into workers' heads.

However, even well into the nineteenth century, workers
continued to celebrate a weekly holiday of their creation
that has somehow vanished. It was called "Saint Monday"—
a day of leisure shanghaied in the alehouse. One farmer
filled his diary with these notes: "All hands drunk; Jacob
Ventling hunting; molders all agree to quit work and went
to the beach. Peter Cox very drunk and gone to bed. . . .
Edward Rutter off a-drinking. It was reported he got drunk
on cheese."

Shoshanna Zuboff describes early work life in the book
In the Age of the Smart Machine.

> The ship's carpenter in one New York shipyard describes
> the typical workday: cakes and pastries in the early morn-
> ing and again the late morning, a trip to the grog shop by
> eleven for whiskey, a big lunch at half past three, a visit
> from the candyman at five, and supper, ending the work-
> day, at sundown. He recalled one worker who left for grog
> ten times a day. A cigar manufacturer complained that his
> men worked no more than two or three hours a day; the
> rest of the time was spent in the beer saloon, playing
> pinochle. Coopers were famous for a four-day work week;
> and the potters in Trenton, New Jersey, immigrants from
> Staffordshire, were known to work in "great bursts of
> activity" and then lay off for several days.

Against this background, the "civilizing" forces of modern
society began to oppose the "animal" aspects of human
nature. Many acts of eating, eliminating, and procreating
that we now consider disgusting were routine as late as the
nineteenth century. The display of intimate bodily functions,

free expression of powerful emotions, and violence were accepted parts of human life. The fork, the handkerchief, or the nightgown, and the new sense of disgust about bodily functions like defecating and spitting all moved us to distrust bodily delights.

Each generation comes into the world unaware of what has come before. We learn from our parents what to inhibit and what to exhibit but we don't learn much of what happened centuries or even decades before. It seems perfectly normal, obvious, and almost inborn for us to avoid blowing our nose on someone, to use eating utensils, and to live collectively; clothed, cleansed, and considerate. Most of us are so well socialized into a civilized routine that we don't realize that such civilization arises at the expense of physical and mental pleasures.

We are by no means arguing for a return to snot on the sleeve, neglect of daily hygiene, or unbridled violence. We are merely pointing out that with the restriction of some of these "animal" activities and the preeminence of the work ethic has come an almost involuntary dismissal of healthy sensuality and play. We have so learned to delay sensual gratification and curb our passions that many of us find it difficult to indulge ourselves even when the time is right, when no harm will follow.

The dominion of work is so complete that it dampens even innocent pursuits. For example, how would your co-workers or family react if you announced that you were going to a movie over your lunch hour? So close are we— or so we imagine—to the wild abandon of our animal nature. The idea of napping, lovemaking, going for a walk, sitting idly and watching the natural world, or just playing catch with a child somehow seems unproductive. This view is needlessly shackling in twentieth-century society. In truth, simple pleasures can contribute to real productivity as well as to genuine health.

We have become slaves of the work ethic. Time for pleasure has been reduced as we work longer hours and two-income families become the norm. But what have we gained? Our "primitive" ancestors, lacking our time- and labor-saving devices and technology, had much more time for recreation and enjoyment. Today, cultures that practice early forms of agriculture or live by hunting or gathering spend relatively little time working—often less than four hours a day to provide for all necessities. A Dobe bush-woman in Australia can gather enough food in one day to feed her family for three days. She spends her free time relaxing, napping, entertaining visitors, chatting, or playing.

Our primitive ancestors may not have been rich in material goods, but they did enjoy a wealth of free time and simple pleasures. For them, time was unhurried; for us, time is money. Leisure, once a mainstay of human life, is now a luxury. We rarely have time for ourselves or for each other. The quickening pace of life may have made us more productive, efficient, and organized—but less spontaneous, less joyful, and less connected to others.

Sometimes it takes an accident to remind us that life could be otherwise. Remember the delicious days when snowfall paralyzes a city. Schools close. Work is halted. We find ourselves temporarily liberated from the tyranny of time and, perhaps, invited to enjoy unscheduled pleasures. And for a moment we sense how regulated and dedicated to work our lives have become.

The work ethic is not the only cultural barrier to pleasure. Many religious leaders and texts exhort us to view pleasure, particularly the sensual type, as morally suspect and corrupting. Banishment from paradise to a flaming hereafter awaits those who indulge the flesh. Pleasure-seekers are warned of the Seven Deadly Sins. The body is to be denied, passions reined in, and the mind disciplined.

In part, this proscription is a corruption of spiritual teachings, some of which have asked that at certain stages of our development we withdraw and detach from our ordinary world and patterns of thinking. But withdrawal from sex, food, and everything pleasurable is not the ultimate goal of religion. The goal is a mind free of the usual commanding tugs that pleasures exert. But in our society, increasing industrialization and mechanization have already removed some essential pleasures from life.

Combining an archaic religiosity with a sensory-deprived world is to place two prisons together. The result is a life lost not only to this world but to the next. Redeeming a natural and healthy sensuality requires us to buck strong historical forces. But our health, happiness, and future depend upon understanding and reversing this deep-rooted cultural denial of pleasure and leisure. Sensuality and spirituality need not conflict.

The Rise of Healthism

Today, for many people science has supplanted religion as the main source of guidance about living. The standards of good and evil are often replaced by judgments based on healthy and unhealthy. We rely increasingly on medical priests and soothsayers to advise us on how to achieve the Good Life. We are led to believe that health arises from the miracle cures of modern medicine and from the often pleasure-denying regimens of a balanced diet, "no-pain, no-gain" exercise, and all manner of recipes for clean living.

At nearly every turn, pleasure has gotten a bad name. Many of us are almost phobic about having fun. This depressing view is reinforced, in part, by an unremitting stream of medical opinion and research implying that the pursuit of pleasure leads only to ruin. Compulsion, disruption, and disease lurk if we lapse. Research and thinking in medicine and psychology reflects a pathological focus on the causes and treatment of disease, while virtually ignoring acts that build health. In researching this book we were amazed at the great amount of information about the health hazards of pleasure and the scarcity of details about its health-promoting effects.

Many more studies have been done on the disastrous repercussions of lifelong alcoholism than about the benefits of moderate alcohol consumption. There are myriad studies about noise exposure but hardly a score on the therapeutic benefits of music. Researchers dwell on sexual dysfunctions and the lethal dangers of sexually transmitted diseases, and catalogue thousands of sexual aberrations. However, they spell out little as to how a pleasurable sexual life contributes to well-being. We found thousands of articles on trauma, physical abuse, and pain, but hardly any sources on the benefits of human touch.

This strong bias against pleasure makes it difficult for many of us to see how important pleasure is to health and longevity. If you eat too many pretzels or potato chips you may develop high blood pressure, so shake the salt habit. People who indulge in food get fat; and fat people very often get sick. Watch cholesterol levels closely, so avoid eggs and malts and lay off the burgers, and certainly the ribs.

There would be no bone to pick if this anti-pleasure advice had great merit: if salt, beef, and butter were as lethal as we're led to believe. Often, these health prescriptions are premature alarms rather than solid scientific advice. They're frequently based on studies of high-risk people and gratuitously generalized to everyone. Note that the half-life of these warnings is often very short: not long ago we were advised to avoid all fats. Now the press sings the medical praises of omega-3 fatty acids, the heart-helping fat found in fish oil.

On the other hand, the public is handed thousands of goose-step, surefire programs and formulas for health promotion. Just eat this, exercise in this way, meditate, take this vitamin. The implication is often that, if we just follow this or that simple system three times a day, our health will be ensured. The information overrides our good judgment and natural instincts for a pleasurable life.

The Cholesterol Hysteria: Is Your Number Up?

Let's look at the evidence behind some of the "facts" that indicate, for instance, that cholesterol is bad for you. A recent major study, the Coronary Primary Prevention Trial, is one of the key influences on the current raging fear of fat. This study, and others like it, *did not at all prove that lowering levels of dietary cholesterol and fat decrease our chances of premature death*.

The study was supposed to involve several thousand middle-aged men with high serum cholesterol who did not have heart disease. One group would be given a cholesterol-lowering diet, while a control group would receive a regular diet. Then both groups would be checked after ten years. But the investigators didn't follow the original blueprint. Instead, they administered the drug cholesytramine to lower the first group's serum cholesterol level. The cholesytramine, not diet alone, did reduce serum cholesterol and so the intervention was successful. But was it successful in improving people's health?

Yes, but not as much as the public has been led to believe. Researchers claim that for every 1 percent decrease in serum cholesterol, risk of death from heart disease decreases by 2 percent. They advise that cutting down on saturated fats and cholesterol lowers cholesterol levels by 10 to 15 percent, reducing deaths from heart attack by 20 to 30 percent.

But a closer look at the data suggests that we exercise caution before expecting such a big payoff from a changing diet. Nearly 7 percent of the men who lowered their cholesterol levels with daily doses of cholesytramine eventually suffered a heart attack, compared to 8.6 percent of the control group, who had received a placebo. This reflects a difference of only 1.7 percent over seven to ten years. More startling: death rates in the two groups *from all causes combined* were nearly the same, largely due to an unexplained increase in violent and accidental deaths among the treated men.

Recall that this study involved a *drug treatment* to lower cholesterol; yet, somehow, on such findings, *dietary reform* is now being widely recommended. This study included only men between the ages of thirty-five and fifty-nine with initial total cholesterol levels greater than 265 milligrams per deciliter—which put them in the highest 5 percent. But the results have been generalized to everyone, even those with much lower levels of cholesterol.

The truth is, we don't really know the health benefits of a long-term, low-fat diet. One study tried to predict the effect of diet modification on longevity, with surprising results. The following question was posed: If a nonsmoker with normal blood pressure but a moderately elevated cholesterol level were to undertake a lifelong program of dietary reform eating a low-fat diet, how much would that dietary deprivation improve health? The answer was a gain in life expectancy of only *three days to three months*.

Yet many men and women, labeled as suffering from "borderline" or "moderately high" cholesterol levels, forswear all fatty treats and follow their blood test results with religious fervor. And there is even reason to view the precision and accuracy of these laboratory results with some suspicion. For example, consider what happened when a blood sample with a known cholesterol level of 262 milligrams per deciliter was sent to 5,434 different laboratories. Even after excluding about 5 percent of the results which were ridiculously far off target, the readings ranged from 229 to 312. Only half the laboratories were within 5 percent of the true value. This means that a measured cholesterol level could be off by 15 percent or more—either too high or too low. In addition, if the tourniquet is too tight, if the person has been lying down, or if the person is under stress, the cholesterol results can vary by 10 to 15 percent as well.

Think of how many people with modest or no elevations of cholesterol are terrorizing themselves. They look at a juicy burger or an ice cream cone and see some sort of lethal poison. They don't have to worry that much: Even for those people with very high cholesterol levels who are on a low-fat diet, an *occasional* fatty meal may produce little ill effect— and much pleasure. One study showed that interrupting a low-fat diet with one "splurge" (a high-butterfat milk shake and a ham and cheese sandwich) every other day does little to raise cholesterol.

There may be other surprises as the cholesterol story unfolds. One of the latest breaks in the war on fat is the recent finding that beef contains not only "bad" fats but some "good" fats as well, like stearic acid, which *lowers* blood cholesterol levels. And locust bean gum, commonly used in ice cream, has been found to lower blood cholesterol levels when taken in large doses.

The critical questions, then, are: Is your cholesterol level too high and should you try to lower it? If your serum cholesterol is high, can you lower it with a low-fat diet? And if you lower serum cholesterol levels, will you live longer for it?

Fortunately, the majority of us are blessed with a metabolism which simply doesn't produce high levels of cholesterol, no matter what we eat. And if your cholesterol level is lower than 200, given the current evidence, you fall safely within the "desirable" range and need not be too concerned about eating rich food.

If your cholesterol reading is above 200, the tests need to be repeated—several times. For those who are still high, further tests should include the breakdown of "good" HDL cholesterol and "bad" artery-clogging LDL cholesterol, so that you have a better picture of where you stand. You should also consider other heart disease risk factors such as smoking, high blood pressure, diabetes, and a family history of early heart attacks, all of which can magnify the risk of high cholesterol.

If you then choose to try to lower your blood cholesterol, you might want to begin with some simple dietary modifications. For instance, by adding generous amounts of foods rich in soluble fiber, such as oat bran, dried beans, or even a psyllium seed supplement like Metamucil, you may be able to lower your blood cholesterol levels by 10 to 20 percent—without having to necessarily avoid all fats. If you do want to cut down on fats, why not start with those that add little to taste and enjoyment. By eliminating many processed foods that contain palm or coconut oil, you may allow room for an occasional steak or ice cream cone.

Unfortunately, not all of us can lower our blood cholesterol significantly, even if we follow a low-fat diet. Some people's bodies continue to manufacture large amounts of cholesterol despite reduced intake of saturated fats and cholesterol.

Future studies may well reveal that dietary restriction of saturated fats and cholesterol do indeed significantly improve health, even for those with borderline elevations of blood cholesterol. Time will tell. But for now, most people don't need to worry all that much about the fats in their diet, and can safely indulge in an occasional rich, creamy dessert or marbled cut of meat.

And we have no quarrel with those who choose to try to lower their cholesterol levels, either because their blood levels are above 265 or because they have other risk factors for heart disease (high blood pressure, diabetes, smoking, family history of early heart attacks). We are concerned that millions of other people are beginning to worry themselves to death about their cholesterol levels and diets. Very little is known about the health effects of transforming millions of confident, healthy people into cholesterol neurotics. And there is even evidence to suggest that stress and worry about anything—including fats in the diet—can itself raise blood cholesterol levels.

Shaking the Salt Habit

We hear much, too, about the horrors of salt and high blood pressure. We look for low-sodium substitutes, give up salting foods, and even our salami says "one-third less salt" on the package. For the vast majority of us, however, salt intake has little or no effect on the development of high blood pressure. In fact, one study suggests that the number of letters in a person's last name is more highly associated with high blood pressure than the number of milligrams of salt they ingest!

Some arguments cite the deleterious effect of salt on some persons who suffer from high blood pressure. With more consumed salt, high blood pressure worsens, and salt restriction often aids blood pressure regulation. But is this true of everybody? Should all of us restrict salt intake? Approximately one out of five American adults has high blood pressure, and, of them, only about half are "salt sensitive"; their blood pressure responds unfavorably to salt and might benefit from eating less salt. Note well that 90 percent of the population doesn't have to worry.

For most of us, devouring salted pretzels, salami, and french fries is not a true health concern. It is difficult, if not impossible, to make a normal person develop high blood pressure by feeding her or him loads of salt. In one investigation fit men ate 75 grams of salt a day, fifteen times more than the average daily consumption. They didn't develop high blood pressure. The men merely excreted greater amounts of the salt into their urine. As Harriet Dustan, past president of the American Heart Association, said: "Why in the name of heaven should we restrict sodium intake of people who are not hypertensive?"

The Real and Relative Risks of Cancer

Hardly a day goes by that the headlines don't carry the dreadful news about some toxic chemical or toxic behavior causing cancer. Sometimes it gets so bad that we come away with the feeling that *everything* causes cancer: the air we breathe, water we drink, food we eat, drugs we take, love we make.

Some of the health dread comes from a nasty statistical trick. It was Mark Twain who once commented that "there are three kinds of lies: lies, damn lies, and statistics." Scientists use a particular statistic called *relative risk* to simplify and communicate health hazards. While this can be a useful shorthand, it can also be extremely misleading.

Let's take a look at a hypothetical example. A certain risk factor, say a chemical in chocolate, is found to be associated with a certain type of cancer. The relative risk of eating chocolate appears to be 10, which means that chocolate eaters are ten times more likely to have this cancer than are those who manage to avoid chocolate. And so the headlines go out, "Chocolate Increases Risk of Cancer Tenfold." Sales of chocolate plummet, and both chocolate lovers and chocolate makers suffer. But before swearing off chocolate, it's useful to take a look behind the headlines and see what the numbers really mean.

Chocolate hasn't been proven to cause the cancer; a statistical association does not prove causation. Perhaps chocolate eaters tend not to eat carrots, which may protect them from cancer. So it may be the lack of carrots, not the presence of chocolate, that accounts for the association.

Also, the hypothetical study did *not* indicate that chocolate was associated with all cancers, but only with a specific type. If this cancer is very rare, then the risk of chocolate eating may be minuscule. For example, if the *real risk* of the cancer is one in ten million in chocolate abstainers and rises tenfold to one in one million in chocolate eaters, that still means that 999,999 chocolate eaters can indulge for a lifetime without paying for it in cancer—at least not this type of cancer.

Medical Terrorism

So far, we have been very critical of medical research. We've cautioned about the risks of overgeneralization, particularly when certain pleasures are labeled as risk factors for disease. Yet, throughout the book, we highlight other studies that link pleasure and positive states of mind to better health. In many of these studies the results are, at best, preliminary and suggestive.

How, then, can we accept these positive results and, yet, be so critical of research that raises concerns about our pleasurable pursuits? First, while any individual study supporting a healthy pleasure can itself be attacked, if taken together we feel that all the pieces of evidence build a fairly strong case.

Second, and perhaps more important, healthy pleasures have no side effects and pay off twice: in good feelings and in better health. So, even if the evidence for better health is only preliminary, you can still benefit by indulging in things that make you feel good. So taking a sauna, smelling sweet scents, laughing lots, thinking optimistically, or helping other people certainly can't hurt.

However, when you are asked to give up something pleasurable—to change your diet, your exercise habits, or another major part of your life—you should demand a higher level of certainty that you'll actually benefit from the sacrifice.

Life isn't risk free. But before running scared and surrendering some of life's pleasures to medical terrorism, be sure you understand what the real risks are.

Political terrorism has such an enormous effect because small highly publicized events arouse the attention of millions. Hijackers gain worldwide notice for one murder, timed to make the television cameras for the evening news. When it comes to health, many of us fall victim to medical terrorism. We hear about the latest research findings, often based upon very limited evidence regarding a few high-risk people. We are exhorted to modify our lifestyles and asked to give up one or another of life's pleasures.

We have no quarrel with the evidence that some indulgences, such as cigarette smoking, high alcohol consumption, addictive drugs, and reckless driving, are unhealthy and should be knocked off, whether you fancy them or not. We don't recommend downing a quart of scotch a day even if you relish it a lot. We don't think you should ignore a cholesterol level of 380, or a weight of 380 either. We don't think smoking 25 of your favorite cigarettes a day is a great idea even if they give you great pleasure.

Clearly, some pleasures are injurious to health. They can become addictive compulsions, destroying lives, relationships, and pleasure itself. But whole areas of well-being and small pleasures are too often threatened by overgeneralized, overdramatized, and overstated research results, while many factors that shape our health get relatively little attention.

For example, we hear so much about the leading risk factors for heart disease: smoking, high blood pressure, and high blood cholesterol. With one risk factor, you are twice as likely to develop coronary heart disease; with two, you are more than three times as likely, and if you have all three, the risk of a heart attack increases sixfold. However, more than eight out of ten people with all three risk factors won't suffer a heart attack in the next ten years, and the vast majority who have heart attacks will not have all these risk factors.

Statistics on smoking, high blood pressure, and high cholesterol are important, but they do startlingly little to predict who stays healthy. Many of us focus on these obvious risk factors while ignoring subtle forces that may influence our resistance to disease. For example, a major study found that *the number of years of education* is a more important factor in determining risk of heart disease than all the other risk factors combined!

Most of us are in the position of the officials in the story below, who focus on entrancing embellishments rather than the entire body of knowledge.

> Mulla Nasrudin, a well-known joke figure, time and again passed from Persia to Greece on donkey-back. Each time he carried a sack full of jewels for which he always had a legal trading permit. And on each trip he would return without them.
>
> "What are you up to, Nasrudin?" the border guards would ask.
>
> "I am a smuggler," he would answer.
>
> Every time the border guards thoroughly searched for signs of contraband. They never found any. Years later, more and more prosperous in appearance, Nasrudin retired and moved to Egypt. One day one of the customs agents met him there and asked him, "Nasrudin, now that you are safely out of the jurisdiction of Greece and Persia, living here in such luxury, what was it you were smuggling when we could never catch you?"
>
> "Donkeys," Nasrudin replied.

We miss the obvious when it is in front of us. We calculate the benefits of running a dramatic marathon, yet ignore the high return of gardening and dancing, which may better promote health. Alluring studies get our attention: We read that high cholesterol cause heart disease, but we ignore the stronger, more common risks around us. Our attitude to life and our relationship with other people often counts far more than fitness or medical regimens.

As we'll describe later, going to a funny movie might help boost immunity to certain viral infections. Even the view from the hospital window can contribute more to fast recovery from surgery than can many medications. A divorce has nearly the same impact on heart disease as does smoking one or more packs of cigarettes a day. These are not minor statistical differences either; people with less than an 8th grade education shorten their lives three times faster than those who abuse both drugs and alcohol. Individuals who volunteer to help others may reduce their risk of dying by 2½ times.

We need to restore some sensibility to the pursuit of health. Many of us increasingly view ourselves as fragile and vulnerable, ready to develop cancer, heart disease, or some other dreaded disease at the slightest provocation. In the name of health we give up many of our enjoyments. The important point is that worrying too much about anything—be it calories, salt, cancer, or cholesterol—is bad for you, and that living optimistically, with pleasure, zest, and commitment, is good. Medical terrorism shouldn't attack life's pleasures.

It is time, now, to break the conspiracy against healthy pleasures and to apply the new Pleasure Principle. Feeling good pays off not only in immediate enjoyment but also in better health.

3

• • • • • • • • • • • • • •

The New Science of Mood Medicine

Pleasure, by definition, is rewarding because it feels good. When we thought both about how modern society creates barriers to enjoying pleasure and about robust people, we took a fresh look at the scientific literature to see whether stimulation of the senses, a positive outlook, and positive experiences contribute to health.

Every human being possesses an effective internal health maintenance system, one guided by pleasure. Indeed, there is good scientific evidence that we are built for pleasure. Deep brain centers respond directly to pleasure sensations.

Psychologist James Olds discovered this more than three decades ago. He gave laboratory animals levers to press that delivered small amounts of electrical stimulation to areas deep within the brain known as the limbic system. The results were astounding: the animals gave up eating, drinking, and even sex in order to continue pressing the "magic buttons" which stimulated their brains. Some animals pressed the lever until they fell to the floor exhausted, only to awaken and begin the cycle again, they seemed to want the pleasure sensations so much.

In the past decade, a surprising amount of new evidence has appeared that shows just how important pleasure is to our lives and health. Hundreds of scientific studies on thousands of people now report that individuals who expect the best, who are hopeful and optimistic, and who regularly enjoy sensual pleasures are, in general, healthier and live longer. While the results of any single study could always be debated or challenged, the collective weight of the evidence strongly points to how positive mood influences resistance to and recovery from disease. The opposite is true as well: negative moods, depression, hostility, and the lack of pleasure all seem to contribute to poor health. There appears to be a physiology of happiness which communicates to our heart, our immune system, our entire body.

Depressing Health and Immunity

The scientific understanding of the links between frame of mind, emotion, pleasure, and health comes, in part, from research on displeasures: depression, anxiety, and hostility.

Depressed people lose their *joie de vivre* and their delight in living. They give up their sense of an ongoing and meaningful life. And depression damages health. Of two thousand men at the Western Electric Company in Chicago studied over two decades, those who were depressed at the outset were twice as likely to die from cancer. Also, depressed patients with coronary heart disease are more likely to have heart attacks, undergo bypass surgery, and suffer other heart-related problems than are happier patients. Depression, in at least one study, turned out to be a *better* predictor of future heart problems than the severity of artery damage, high cholesterol levels, and cigarette smoking.

Downturns in relationships with other people also disrupt health. People tend to become ill after the loss of a loved one. A coincidence? When someone suffers the loss of a spouse or loved one, the mind floods with negative thoughts. The ensuing chemical stew may spoil immune function and health.

Single, separated, divorced, or widowed people are two or three times more likely to die prematurely than are their married peers. They also wind up in the hospital for mental disorders five to ten times as much. Heart disease, cancer, tuberculosis, arthritis, and problems during pregnancy all increase in those with weakened social connectedness.

The immune system may be the central link in the control of some of these disorders. It continually patrols the body, identifying what is foreign and what is part of the body. When invaders are recognized, the system springs into action, triggering a cellular and chemical assault on the offending viruses, bacteria, or cancer cells.

There is dramatic research that links changes in feelings to the functioning of the immune system. In a pioneering study, blood samples were taken from twenty-six surviving spouses of patients who were either fatally injured or who had died from diseases like heart attacks, strokes, or cancer. The grieving spouses' immune systems were measurably weakened by the distress and discomfort of their loss. Men married to women who died from breast cancer also have lowered immunity. This depression of immunity began immediately after the wife's death and continued for some of the bereaved spouses for over a year.

Even mild upsets and swings in daily mood can disturb the immune system. Have you ever felt that "this just isn't my day?" We all have bad days: days when nothing funny is funny, everything seems gray, and the future closes in. We're just down. Other days, everything is bright: we may get the new job, our family is thriving, and work is good. On those good days, we are healthier.

In an innovative study, researchers measured immune functions in saliva which defend the body against infections like the common cold. On days with high positive mood immune function was decidedly better than days with lower mood. So we may resist infection better when we're in a good mood! On days when our mood is up, so goes our immunity. And when we're down, immunity drops, too.

Mental Immunity

Apparently, we can boost our immunity by deliberately altering mood or through positive suggestion. In one study subjects watching a film of Richard Pryor's comic antics temporarily boosted immune function and might have improved resistance to certain viruses. This effect was short-lived, indicating that we need to laugh often.

Immune function also improves after we unload troubling memories. In a striking series of studies, immune function increased and visits to the doctor decreased in people who disclosed long-held traumatic experiences. So purging the mind of traumatic memories such as early loss, war deaths, or rapes can clear the mental deck and enhance health. Part of being robust, as we'll see later on in this book, is knowing how to shed those experiences that stand in the way of healthy pleasures.

Heart Breaks

Negative feelings can also break your heart: feelings of hostility, disgust, and contempt for others appear to be lethal. Research on heart patients revealed more heart attacks and more blockage of the coronary arteries in those who were hostile, irritable, impatient, and self-centered. They tended to hold the anger in and wall themselves off from other people.

DEPRESSION, bereavement, hostility and heart attack. Fortunately, this is not the whole picture. There is growing scientific evidence that maintaining a positive, optimistic outlook fosters health. From beliefs about medications to beliefs about the ability to remain healthy, those who expect to be well and expect to be pleased are generally healthier.

Great Expectations

For centuries men and women have suffered cutting, bleeding and shocking in the name of medical treatment, and have recovered. In most cases, it's not the remedy, but the positive expectation that heals.

Placebos (from the Latin, "I shall please") are potent medicines. Giving people a sugar pill can relieve headaches, coughs, toothaches, postoperative pain, angina, asthma, and even affect blood counts and gastric acid secretion. It appears that no symptom or system is immune to the placebo effect.

Placebos can be even more potent than drugs. Consider an experiment with a woman suffering from severe nausea and vomiting. Nothing her doctors gave her seemed to help. Objective measurements of her stomach contractions showed a disrupted pattern consistent with the severe nausea she reported. The doctors then offered her a "new and extremely powerful wonder drug," and told her it would unquestionably relieve her nausea. Within twenty minutes of taking this new drug, her nausea disappeared and the stomach contractions returned to normal.

The drug she was given was syrup of ipecac, a drug usually given to *induce* vomiting. Her expectation that the drug would relieve vomiting was powerful enough to counteract the *direct and opposite* pharmacological action of the drug itself.

Placebos stimulate the bodies' own internal pharmacy. For example, placebo pain relief appears to operate through the production of endorphins, internal opiate-like substances secreted in the brain. In studies of patients following extraction of wisdom teeth, the placebo was approximately equivalent to eight milligrams of morphine. Strong medicine, positive expectations.

When patients with warts are hypnotized and told that the warts will disappear, they often do. Blood can be clotted, to some degree, in hemophiliacs, breasts can be enlarged, and some skin diseases cured—all by positive suggestion.

Expecting Good Health and Getting It

Do you believe you're in poor or excellent health? What you believe and expect about your health may be more important than objective assessments made by your doctor. People who expect bad health get it; they die earlier and have more diseases than others who view themselves as healthy. Even sick people do better when they believe themselves to be healthy than when they believe themselves ill.

In a major study, those who reported poor health were almost three times more likely to die during the seven years of the study than were the optimists who rated their health as excellent. Even people who were reported by their physicians to be in poor health survived at a higher rate *as long as they believed their own health to be good.* Clearly, beliefs are powerful healers and killers.

Expecting Pleasure

A person who expects to be pleased is said to be optimistic. Optimism shifts the contents of the mind. So optimists and pessimists perceive, remember, and explain events differently. Optimists remember more pleasant events, look forward to pleasure, and dump difficulties. The result is more and longer experiences of positive feelings and moods, and fewer negative experiences and feelings. Positive expectations nourish the optimist through stimulating positive moods and a tendency to search out positive experiences. This seems to have beneficial effects on health.

In a series of studies (described in detail later on), people who felt that many positive things would happen to them reported fewer signs of ill health and better physical well-being. In another study of cardiac patients undergoing surgery, the optimists' lungs functioned better during the surgery, and the patients also made a speedier cardiac recovery. Pessimists, on the other hand, have measurable deficiencies in critical immune functions. An optimistic way of viewing the world can predict better health and survival twenty to thirty years later. So, Pollyanna was right: there are important reasons to believe in the best.

There's much more evidence, as we'll see, that stimulating positive moods and expectations not only makes us feel better, but also helps us live longer, healthier lives. The human organism is not a helpless, defenseless victim attacked at every turn by agents of disease, whether germs or stressors. We resist breakdown and disease through a remarkable internal health maintenance system regulated by the brain. The basic mechanisms evolved over five million years ago, giving us plenty of time to work the bugs out.

Not that we can always or easily wish away disease. But we are far more resilient and capable of managing our health than has been dreamt of in our medicine. The essential link is a pleasure-presuming frame of mind and a healthy capacity for sensual enjoyment.

The Pleasure Channels: Sensual and Mental

There are several ways to activate pleasure in the brain. Direct electrical stimulation and drugs are two artificial methods with considerable risks and unhealthy side effects. Fortunately, there are also natural channels of pleasure involving sensory stimulation such as good tastes, sounds, smells, and sights. But we also possess the capability to activate pleasure through purely mental means: we can stimulate the pathways of the limbic system with a flow of positive, optimistic messages from the higher cortical brain centers.

Understanding these two pleasure channels, sensual and mental, can help us exploit our potential for healthy pleasures.

The first channel responds to *sensual*, or felt, pleasures. These pleasures are built-in delights that everyone can enjoy: the sudden shimmer of the sun coming up in the morning, the radiant smile of your loved one or of your child, the sweet smell of a field of flowers, a warm full belly after a meal, the smell of baking apples, a blazing fire, a cold drink, warm and tender sexual feelings.

The second mental channel determines the way we judge the world and ourselves, our tendencies toward optimism or pessimism, and our interpretation of the world. While the sensual channel is filled with simple sensory delights which can momentarily improve our mood, the mental channel assesses life satisfaction.

The "programs" of the mental channel address such questions as "How's your life going?" "Are you happy with how fast you're moving up at the firm?" and "How satisfied are you with your marriage?" These questions are more intricate than those asking whether you enjoy the taste of a peach or the sound of music. So, understanding the "internal mathematics" of judgment—whether we are satisfied, optimistic, happy—is important to health.

Robust, healthy people seem to be skilled at keeping both channels operating, flooding their brains and bodies with pleasurable sensations.

Practicing Mood Medicine

Since our internal health system is guided by pleasure, improving our health may be surprisingly enjoyable. The two pleasure channels allow us two different ways of stimulating positive frames of mind, and we should take advantage of our innate biological pleasure-seeking capacities to replenish the mind with pleasurable sensations.

At a time when medicine is almost wholly drug and surgical interventions, it may seem far-fetched to suggest that health could be protected or healing promoted simply by what we hear, see, smell, taste, or feel. Yet the evidence is that everyday, minor, sensual pleasures enhance both mood and health.

As we'll discuss later, the comforting touch of a nurse seems to help stabilize heart function and blood pressure. Pleasing music piped into an operating room may be worth 2.5 milligrams of Valium. Aromas like that of spiced apple make people measurably happier, less anxious, and more relaxed. Many people find the heat of a sauna relaxing, and it also may trigger the release of endorphins, the body's own pain relievers, and bolster immunity. One study shows that when children take regular saunas, the number of days missed from school due to infections dramatically decreases.

Healthy habits don't need to be grim. Exercise doesn't need to be a painful marathon to be healthful. Puttering in the garden or taking a pleasant walk is sufficient. Relaxation doesn't need to be twenty minutes of silent meditation. Watching fish in a bowl, laughing at a funny movie, watching football on television, or even taking a quick deep breath at your desk can let you ease off. Many simple pleasures and indulgences are helpful to health.

You can also practice mood medicine by changing your mental investments. Cultivate a more optimistic outlook. Tell yourself more positive stories about yourself. You may be surprised to learn that mental illusions, such as denying others' bad opinions of you, are not always bad for you. Indeed, illusions can help you recover more quickly from surgery. Hard work is not necessarily bad for health; meaningful work may actually improve health. Getting an education may add ten years to your life. And ironically, one of the best ways to improve your health is by not concentrating on yourself at all, but by caring for other people.

Whether you turn on the sensual or mental channel, the isolated health techniques are not important. What matters is that you fashion a life filled with meaningful pleasures. And let the Pleasure Principle determine your double payoff in terms of feeling good and improving health.

The rest of the book contains suggestions on the fine-tuning of the pleasure channels. In the next section, "The Virtues of Sensuality," we look at ways to promote positive mood and health by increasing sensual enjoyment. The final section, "Mental Investment," offers counsel on how to think about yourself, your life, and your prospects, to enhance your *joie de vivre*.

TWO

The Virtues of Sensuality

4

. . . .

Coming to Your Senses

People relish nature, we don't just ingest it. Every animal scours the world for sources of pleasure. Human beings, too, originally evolved to find pleasure in sensory experiences: the sweetness of a peach, the swelling satisfactions of sex, the peaceful flow of a river, the view stretching from a mountaintop all the way to the horizon.

The human world has changed, however, and changed drastically from the one we were "fashioned" to sense. Many sensual pleasures we are primed to receive are blunted in the modern world. City dwellers often miss the glory of the sunrise and sunset as they hustle in their commutes. The synthetic foods in our markets bear little resemblance to the tasty real foods we were built to eat. Our ancestors heard the pleasant sounds of a stream and wind rustling in the trees, but for us it's the din of traffic and horns blaring. *Many of us are not getting our minimum daily requirement of sensual pleasure.*

These sensual pleasures are vital to our health. The experience of sensing provides us with reports about the world critical to our survival. The senses warn of danger. Imagine how it would be without clear-cut information: blinded, could you avoid traffic or the edge of a cliff? A loud racket may signal us to dodge a falling tree; the sulfurous stench of spoiled food may forewarn us to avoid consuming poison; a flash of pain makes us recoil and prevents a serious burn.

Our senses do more than send alarms about sporadic hazards. They shepherd us to agreeable experiences that increase survival. Smell and taste incite us to seek a wide spectrum of taste sensations, encouraging us to eat a variety of foods with a full range of essential nutrients. Pleasurable touch and sexual sensations make procreation more likely. Sensory stimulation activates brain pleasure centers, evoking a sense of well-being and positive mood.

If enhancing our moods and expectations improves health, a moderate dose of sensuality may be just what the doctor ordered.

However, we are not sanctioning senseless sensuality or heedless hedonism at the sacrifice of the rest of life. The modern world has deprived us of too many of our sensory requirements; we need to regain our balance.

Some of the pleasures are close at hand.

In and Out of Touch

You're sitting in a coffee shop watching the young couple across from you. He leans forward and gently touches her arm. She smiles. He then brushes a wisp of hair back off her forehead. They speak quietly and sip their coffee. As she excuses herself and gets up from the table, her hand rests for a second on his shoulder. He hugs her. She holds his hand tightly, then walks away. In the past hour this couple has touched each other no less than 150 times.

Where are you: England, the United States, France, or Puerto Rico? In the 1960s, psychologist Sidney Jourard roamed cafés in these countries, recording how many times people touched each other. In San Juan, Puerto Rico he tallied 180 contacts per hour. In a café in Paris, couples touched at a rate of 110. In Gainesville, Florida, twosomes touched only twice an hour. And in London, England, the men and women *never* touched.

Different cultures touch more or less often and differently. Here's a research job most readers would love: Psychologists spent time on the beaches and playgrounds of Greece, the Soviet Union, and the United States observing physical contact between young children and their adult caregivers. When the adults were chasing or punishing the children, all three countries scored equally. But when it came to soothing, holding, and playing, the American children enjoyed fewer fondles.

The lack of touching in many Western societies prompted one physician to describe "The No Touching Epidemic" in the *British Medical Journal*:

> Its symptoms include a feeling of loneliness and abstraction from one's fellows. Morbid doubts of other people's loyalty, and feelings of insecurity. A fear of unpopularity; an inhibition of feelings. Unusual reaction to others when one is inadvertently touched. Guilt feelings on touching another person. Frigidity. Loss of tenderness and ability to comfort people in distress. A hesitancy and doubt when confronting people in pain. . . . A strange, inhibited and cold attitude to strangers and foreigners. Solitary toilet habits; a tendency to keep babies in their prams and young children glued to their desks. Antagonisms to physical forms of punishment. Dislike of the involvement of relatives in boxing or wrestling sports. Horror at the sight of courting couples. An inability to communicate with people standing nearby in public places and churches. . . . An antagonism to massage as a form of therapy. Shyness and introversion. A tendency to divorce. An incomprehension of people's needs. Masturbation. Loss of interest in a tango; an exaggerated interest in no touch techniques in dancing. A preference for television rather than conversation.

The Language of Touch

Touch metaphors help us grip reality. We speak of being "in touch" or "out of touch." Some people are "touchy" or "rub us the wrong way," while nurturing is "a healing touch." We extol special attention as a "personal touch" and save "untouchable" for the lowest rung of society. Most importantly, our language links touch and emotions. Happiness and joy, sadness and melancholy are emotions yet we call them "*feel*ings" to emphasize the almost physical and palpable quality of emotions. We may be "touched by kindness," or "get in touch with our feelings." We may be "thin-skinned" or "thick-skinned," referring to our emotional sensitivity. While touch may be well embedded in language and thought, it has become somewhat disembodied in our daily life. We touch so little that we're out of it.

Out of Touch

An adequate dose of touching is vital to health. Touch alerts us to danger; a hot fire or a sharp thorn. Our sense of touch helps us locate and handle food, find a mate, and procreate. We touch to communicate. In our culture, a good indicator of the closeness of two people is how much they touch each other.

The scientific investigation of the health benefits of touching and handling began by accident. In the 1920s, anatomist Frederick Hammett removed rats' thyroid and parathyroid glands. To his surprise, some of the rats survived the operation. Most of the survivors came from a colony in which the animals were customarily "petted and gentled" by their keepers. These rats were much less timid, apprehensive, and high-strung than less-handled rats. The gentled rats were also six times more likely to survive the operation.

Animals seem to know the value of touching instinctively. Mother rats stroke their pups vigorously with their tongue. This releases growth hormone and activates a growth enzyme in the pup's brain and other vital organs. In one study, rat pups were removed from this physical contact with their mothers during their early days of life. Growth slowed and the biochemical growth factors plummeted.

However, when researchers gently stroked the separated baby rats with a wet brush (simulating the licking of the mother), the effects of maternal deprivation reversed: the animals thrived and growth factors returned to normal. Touch is the key element, since pups kept with their mother but not licked or stroked show slower growth.

The Untouchables

In the 1920s, the respected psychologist James B. Watson promoted his theory that maternal touch spoiled the child.

There is a sensible way of treating children. . . . Never hug and kiss them, never let them sit in your lap. If you must, kiss them once on the forehead when they say good night. Shake hands with them in the morning. Give them a pat on the head if they have made an extraordinary good job of a difficult task. Try it out. In a week's time you will find how easy it is to be perfectly objective with your child and at the same time kindly. You will be utterly ashamed of the mawkish, sentimental way you have been handling it. . . .

The mother knows the infant can smile and gurgle and chuckle with glee. She knows it can coo and hold out its chubby arms. What more touching and sweet, what more thrilling to a young mother! And the mother to get these thrills goes to extreme lengths. She picks the infant up, kisses and hugs it, rocks it, pets it, and calls it "mother's little lamb," until the child is unhappy and miserable whenever away from actual physical contact with the mother. Then again as we face this intolerable situation of our own creating, we say the child is "spoiled." And spoiled most children are. Rarely does one see a normal child—a child that is comfortable—a child that adults can be comfortable around—a child more than nine months of age that is constantly happy.

But being touched and cuddled is also essential for healthy human development. During the early nineteenth century, if a child was separated from its parents it was sent to a foundling institution. This was, in effect, a death sentence. A study of ten such institutions in 1915 revealed that in all but one, every single baby under the age of two died. The reasons for this tragedy were unknown. Nutrition appeared sufficient. Sanitation was adequate, if not overzealous. But the fear of germs and transmission of infectious disease led to no-touch policies. As a result, the infants were seldom touched or handled.

In the 1940s, physician Fritz Talbot visited the Children's Clinic in Dusseldorf. The wards were neat and tidy, but something peculiar caught his attention. He noticed an old, fat woman stroking and carrying around a sickly baby on her hip. He asked, "Who's that?" The medical director responded, "Oh, that is Old Anna. When we have done everything we can medically for a baby, and it is still not doing well, we turn it over to Old Anna, and she is always successful."

This observation, and others, led to a dramatic change in treatment of children in foundling institutions. Bellevue Hospital in New York instituted a new policy: every baby was to be picked up, held, touched, gentled, and mothered several times a day. The death rate for infants plummeted to less than 10 percent. A vital nutrient in the human diet had been discovered: touch.

Until recently, such findings have had little influence on the care of premature infants in the hospital. The standard policy in nurseries and intensive care units was the minimal-touch rule. This minimized exposure to germs. It also avoided arousing the infant and was thought to reduce the strain on its tiny underdeveloped lungs and heart.

However, premature infants, like other babies, require touch. Touch can comfort the infant, increase weight, and decrease medical costs. In one study, underweight premature babies received special stimulation. For ten days, the infants were given three fifteen-minute massages. Warm hands lightly stroked the babies from head to toe, and then gently exercised the arms and legs.

The massaged babies thrived, compared to other preemies left in their incubators. Even though they had the same number of feedings and consumed the same number of calories as their untouched counterparts, the massaged babies gained nearly 50 percent more weight per day, a critical factor in the survival of a premature baby. Touching seemed to improve the efficiency of the babies' metabolism, and the stimulated infants were more active and more responsive to such things as a face or a rattle.

Further, the massaged infants were sent home from the hospital six days earlier, a savings of nearly three thousand dollars per infant. This early tactile stimulation also produced lasting benefits. Eight to twelve months later, the stroked babies maintained their growth advantage and had better mental and physical abilities than the other group. All for a few minutes of gentle touch for ten days.

Though the results of touching on growth and emotional development are most striking in children, even adults respond to human touch.

Touching the Heart

We speak of something being "touching," implying a close link between touch and the emotional reactions of the heart. It's more than a metaphor—our skin does speak to our hearts. And our hearts respond.

Consider this example: The patient is 54 years old. He lies in a deep coma in the shock-trauma unit of the University of Maryland Hospital, his heartbeat rapid and irregular. A nurse enters the room, comes to his bedside, and quietly holds his hand. His heart immediately responds to the comforting touch. His heartbeat dramatically slows and becomes more stabilized.

The result of touch depends on how we are touched and how it feels to us. While the comforting touch of hand holding can slow heart rate, pulse taking by that same nurse can increase the heart rate and irregular heartbeats. Pulse-taking may remind the patient of the precarious condition of his or her damaged heart, and so produce alarm and distress.

For the most part, however, we find touching, especially light stroking of the arms, legs, back, or chest, relaxing and pleasurable. A comforting touch from another person slows the heart by reflex. One study reveals that heart rate declined when subjects were touched lightly on the wrist by a researcher, but did not slow when the researcher stood by or the subjects touched themselves on the wrist. The subjects also reported that being touched was more pleasant and relaxing than practicing a solo relaxation exercise, such as producing alpha brain waves with biofeedback.

Therapeutic Touch

From the pressure points of Oriental massage techniques to the kneading, stroking, and pummeling of Swedish massage, nearly every conceivable health benefit has been attributed to various forms of skin stimulation. Unfortunately, scientific evidence supporting most of these claims is scarce.

However, massage does seem to benefit patients with chronic anxiety. In one study, a group of patients with chronic muscle tension, body aches, and pain got massage treatment. All had previously failed to respond to anti-anxiety medications, antidepressants, and muscle relaxants, as well as standard relaxation training exercises. Researchers measured heart rate, muscle tension, and skin resistance (a measure of stress) before and after deliberately stressing the subjects with blaring loud noises.

Then came the fun part. Each patient was treated to ten sessions of deep massage, each lasting thirty to forty-five minutes. When the physiological measurements were repeated after the massage, each subject showed improvement in at least one of the measures: slower heart rate, lower muscle tension, and/or decreased arousal. Most reported a marked reduction in distressing symptoms and in their need for medication.

The treatment also apparently loosened their tongues. After the massage, the patients seemed to speak much more freely and at greater length about their problems. With the traditional focus on psychotherapy or medications for mental problems, we might do well to consider these touching alternatives.

IT'S important that you make deliberate efforts to touch more. Try watching men and women in a public place such as a café, airport, or park. How often do the people touch? Who touches whom, and who does not? What areas of the body are touched? Are there male-female or young-old differences in touch? What messages do people communicate through touch? Observation can be a great teacher.

Consider whether you are able to touch the significant people in your life enough. Our society distances us from others; we don't give each other baths, hugs, or massages much, and today's parents don't carry their young long distances as our ancestors did. But touching helps us feel close to others. We need to notice more when we're out of touch. This may be as simple as scheduling a massage instead of a coffee break (companies that provide office rubdowns are springing up), or realizing that you haven't slowly caressed your child or lover for too long.

Of course, our skin communicates much more than the pleasurable sensations of touch: we also have sensors for temperature, and when it comes to heat. . . .

Some Like It Hot

Most of us like to get hot. We seek out sunny, warm climates, saunas, steam baths, hot tubs, and solariums. Few of us show the same enthusiasm for stripping down and skinny dipping in an icy lake or for a mid-winter vacation spent sitting outside freezing in a bikini. We don't like the darkness or the cold.

Yet most research with respect to heat ignores our love of hot spots. Instead the search focuses on the damaging effects of extreme heat exposure. Titles like "Hyperthermia and Dehydration in Marathon Runners" or "The Health Risks of Hot Tubs" abound. One of the few areas in which the potential health benefits of heat have been studied is the sauna.

Exposure to high temperatures for brief periods produces profound physiological changes: stress hormones are released, heart rate accelerates, respiration increase and sweating increase, and the skin flushes as the body struggles in vain to maintain a normal temperature.

Why would people willingly subject themselves to heat stress? Many people find the experience pleasurable and relaxing, and believe that saunas are good for health. The heat helps relax tense muscles; following a sauna, electrical discharges in muscles show a more relaxed pattern.

A brief trip to the sauna decreases pain in muscles and joints. An intriguing study done in Czechoslovakia demonstrated that sitting in a sauna for thirty minutes doubled beta-endorphin levels in the blood. (Recall that endorphins are internally produced chemicals that relieve pain and may also produce a sense of well-being and euphoria.) So it may not be so far-fetched to speak of a "sauna-bather's high."

The relaxation following a sauna may also be due to other chemical changes in the brain. The heat may deplete our body stores of stress hormones. This makes us less likely to respond to stress later—a beneficial type of "burnout." Saunas also increase serotonin, a powerful hormone associated with relaxation and sleep. Following a sauna, people show more brain waves related to deeper, more restful sleep, so a sauna or hot bath may be an excellent way to relax before bedtime.

Many enthusiasts claim that a sauna helps ward off colds and other infections. They may well be right. Children who regularly take saunas have better resistance to infection. For example, forty-four kindergarteners in Germany were divided into two groups, with half the children partaking in a weekly sauna. Over the following eighteen months the number of sick days for each group due to colds, ear infections, and associated maladies was tallied. The children taking the regular sauna bath had only *half* the number of sick days, compared to the cooler control group.

Possibly, the high temperatures produced by the sauna simply cook and kill the germs. Or the elevated body temperatures may simulate the beneficial effects of a fever. There is growing evidence that a fever may actually help the body resist and fight infections. When the body is infected, pyrogens—chemicals that turn up the body's thermostat—flood the bloodstream and bolster the immune system. The invading germs are simultaneously attacked and starved of vital nutrients.

This rise in temperature appears to be healthful; when experimental animals are prevented from raising their body temperature in response to an infection, their death rate increases. A sauna may be a more pleasurable, and more functional, way to produce an artificial fever; wouldn't you rather lie back in the heat of a sauna once in a while, killing germs, than be forced to lie back for week or so in the heat of a fever?

Sauna bathing may also be a pleasant adjunct to physical exercise for burning calories and conditioning the heart. Sweating is an active physiological response to help lower body temperature. It involves the expenditure of a considerable number of calories; a person can burn up three hundred to eight hundred calories during a sauna. Like physical exercise, sauna bathing places stress on the heart, and may to some degree improve conditioning.

The healthy pleasures of sauna bathing and hot baths may go well beyond these beneficial physiological measures. A dip in the heat is a great excuse for a protected, quiet rest period from an otherwise harried lifestyle. Again, we need to return to our origins: remember that human beings evolved as tropical animals, well adapted to the warmer temperatures of the African savannah. For many northerners, separated by thousands of miles and many degrees from the tropical climes of their ancestors, a sauna or hot bath may provide a brief reminder of warm times and warm pleasures.

Lighten Up

The darkness was starting again for Paul. He felt anxious, reluctant to go to work, fearful of interacting with others. He became more and more withdrawn and self-critical, and lost all interest in pleasurable activities. Sexual desire vanished. At night, he tossed and turned fitfully. In the morning he could think of no good reason to get out of bed. Throughout the day he complained of a lack of energy, and found it difficult to think of new ideas. His world became constricted, lifeless, meaningless. Was this due to some early childhood trauma, perhaps some smoldering conflict during adolescence? An inability to love? Incompetence at work?

No. Paul's condition was due to a *lack of light*. He was, in a sense, starving for light.

Paul started experiencing unexplained depressive episodes at age thirty-five. He was a meticulous man who kept daily records of his moods and activities. After many years he began to notice a distinct annual pattern to his depressive episodes. Each year, when the days began to shorten toward the end of June, he would, as a rule, become depressed. Paul would then remain depressed until more or less the end of January, when he would switch dramatically into an energetic, upbeat mood. Suddenly he began to look forward to going to work. He said, "the wheels would begin to spin" as his mind raced and creative ideas flowed easily. He required less sleep, sometimes as little as two to three hours a night.

However, by the next fall the darkness would begin to set in again. His pessimism at this time would cause him to turn down job promotions which, unfortunately, were usually offered in the fall and winter—his low times. He had tried a variety of antidepressant medications to block the winter blues, all without success.

One dark December, in the midst of a deep depression, Paul tried a novel therapy. Since his depressive episodes seemed to correspond to the shortening daylight, he was treated with artificial light. Each morning for three hours before dawn, instead of hiding his head under the covers, he sat under very bright, full-spectrum fluorescent lights. For three hours after dusk he would also work or play under the bright lights; thus extending the winter daylight to a 13-hour spring-like day. The effect was dramatic. Within four days his depression lightened up, his mood brightened, and his activity level surged.

Almost everyone experiences some change in mood related to the presence or absence of sunlight. On bright, sunny days we tend to feel better, perhaps more energetic, and "sunny." On dull, gray days, we may feel moody, blue, and out of sorts. Most of us seem, at least to some degree, to be biologically programmed to follow the sun. For some light-sensitive people, however, changes in light exposure may produce profound mood swings.

These people suffer from Seasonal Affective Disorder (SAD). This newly identified syndrome of moderate to marked seasonal changes in mood and energy affects an estimated 20 percent of otherwise healthy people.

SAD people typically begin experiencing symptoms in their teens and twenties. Unlike most other depressive patients, they don't lose their appetites, but may even gain weight. The symptoms appear to be directly related to the amount of sunlight reaching the brain: for people in the northern hemisphere, the depressive symptoms usually start between September and October and last into March. One patient living in Chile experienced her depressive episodes between June and September, which are the winter months in the southern hemisphere.

Hundreds of patients with this disorder have now been successfully treated with bright lights. The internal clock of people with SAD appears to run a few hours behind normal—giving them insomnia at bedtime and trouble waking up. Exposure to bright lights in the morning simulates an early dawn and may help advance their body clock.

How does this work? It appears that light talks to the brain via the pineal gland. This tiny gland, buried deep within the brain, secretes a brain hormone which can induce sleep as well as depress mood. Seasonal affective disorder provides a vivid example of the sensitivity, often unrecognized or dismissed, of the brain to various types of sensory stimulation.

You don't have to be fully depressed to benefit from full-spectrum natural sunlight. Ordinary fluorescent lights are deficient in ultraviolet illumination. Such lights were replaced on a trial basis in three classrooms of a Vermont elementary school. Before the lights were changed there was no difference in the sickness rates of children in the converted classrooms compared to three control classrooms. However, after changing the light, the children in the rooms with full-spectrum lighting experienced 40 percent fewer sick days than the other students. Children tend to be ill more often during the winter and spring months; the full-spectrum lights reversed this pattern. While neither the students nor the teachers were blind to the lighting change, these findings still suggest that the amount and quality of the light we are exposed to may significantly influence our immunity to disease. Again, something as simple—and subtle—as everyday light affects our health in measurable ways.

So, if you find yourself fantasizing about a midwinter trip to a sunny vacation spot, it may not be escapism. It may be your brain writing a prescription for more light, particularly if your moods seem to follow the sun. (People who live in areas closer to the equator or spend some winter vacation time in sunnier climes are less affected by SAD.) Consider taking a winter sun break: it isn't frivolous, but might well improve your health and mood for the rest of the season. Employers might even encourage vacations that allow their staff to recharge themselves with light. Inhabitants of northern climates (where human beings settled long after our main biological evolution) and those who spend too much time indoors, with the natural world walled off, especially need to get the light they were born to receive.

If you can't take off to sunny climes, there are things you can do at home to maximize your exposure to light. Rise earlier in the morning and go outdoors, or at least sit near an open window or skylight. Replace your current lighting at home or on the job, if possible, with full-spectrum flu-

orescent light bulbs (such as Vitalite from Durotest Corporation, North Bergen, New Jersey).

If things are really bad, consider phototherapy. Though
the optimal intensity, duration, and timing of this therapy
is still being worked out, phototherapy for SAD appears to
be most effective with exposure to very bright light for two
hours between 6:00 A.M. and 8:00 A.M. Sometimes, longer
daylight hours or evening sessions of light exposure are
necessary. The light intensity should be 2,500 lux, a measure
of light intensity which is roughly equivalent to standing
by a window on a bright spring day or standing 3 feet away
from eight full-spectrum fluorescent light bulbs.

Still, sometimes it isn't just the amount of light that
brightens you up, but what you are looking at.

Looking at Life

Gazing at fish slowly wandering back and forth in a tank.
Looking out a window at a small stand of trees. Staring into
a fire as a burning log consumes itself. Watching clouds
form and reform on the canvas of a blue sky. Contemplating
the surface of a tranquil lake. Watching birds nest in a tree.

We have an appetite for such visual feasts. Given a choice
between viewing a natural scene rich in foliage or an urban
landscape devoid of vegetation or water, we nearly always
favor the nature scene. This may come as no surprise, but
there is now mounting evidence that such choices may be
more than simple aesthetic preferences. Flooding our brains
with rich natural visual stimulation helps us recover from
surgery, tolerate pain, manage stress, and attain well-being.

Most of us are aware that extreme environmental conditions like heat, cold, noise, and air pollution can be stressful.
But can minor changes in our visual world affect our response to and recovery from stress?

Look out your window. What do you see? A world of

buildings and cement, or a scene of natural beauty? When people view slides of natural scenes, they report much higher levels of positive feelings such as friendliness and elation, and reduced feelings of sadness and fear than do people looking at manmade, urban scenes. Pictures of ponds, streams, trees, and other vegetation produce lower levels of arousal and higher alpha brain waves, a brain state associated with wakeful relaxation, than pictures of treeless urban streets.

What we see also affects our recovery when we are stressed. After watching a ten-minute film on the blood and gore of disabling work accidents, viewers responded with increased anxiety, muscle tension, blood pressure, and skin conductance—measures of a stress reaction. However, if the stress-provoking film was followed by a ten-minute film of nature scenes—trees and water—the recovery from stress on all physiological measures was faster than if they watched a film of an urban scene.

And if you are really facing a stressful situation, a room with a view might help.

Room with a View

Sarah and Sally are identical twins, age forty-five. They both have gallstones and their doctor recommends surgical removal of their gallbladders. They check into the same hospital together. Sarah is escorted to her room. It is a typical, aesthetically sterile hospital room. She looks out the window and contemplates the view—a brown brick wall of another wing of the hospital. She thinks, "Oh, that's too bad, but I'll only be here a few days." Meanwhile, her sister Sally checks into her own typical hospital room but can look out her window onto a park with a small stand of trees. She thinks, "Oh, that's nice."

The next day they both have uneventful operations and are returned to their rooms. They receive identical treatment.

However, Sally, in her room with a view, recovers more quickly, requires less pain medication, is noted to be in better spirits, and is sent home from the hospital one day sooner than her sister in the room with the wall view.

A coincidence? Perhaps. Could a room with a view really influence recovery from surgery and other stresses? In a most interesting study, Roger Ulrich reviewed the hospital charts of forty-six patients who had undergone gallbladder surgery. Half the patients had hospital rooms with a window looking out onto a small stand of trees, while the others viewed a brown brick wall.

The patients with a view of the trees spent less time in the hospital after surgery (by nearly one day), were less upset, cried less often, and took fewer doses of stronger pain medications. They also had slightly fewer postoperative complications such as persistent headache and nausea. Whether similar salutary effects could be achieved by pictures or murals depicting outdoor scenes is not known but worth considering.

Unfortunately, hospitable hospital views are hard to come by. Ulrich toured thirty-six hospitals and found that poor bedside vistas were the rule, not the exception. Most windows looked out onto treeless parking lots, large expanses of rooftop, alley-like service drives, and walls of other hospital wings, or in some cases the windows of other patients. Some even had views of ambulance arrivals to the emergency room or of a cemetery. Hardly reassuring, anxiety-reducing scenes.

We seem to be designed to view natural scenes, and this is reflected in our emotional and physical well-being. We prefer certain types of landscapes, perhaps as a result of a deep-rooted evolutionary experience. Regardless of cultural background, we tend to favor parklike scenes with smooth ground cover, scattered trees, lakes, and a degree of openness and depth. It is a scene not too different from the savannahs of central Africa, where our ancestors first stepped down from the trees onto the plains.

Evolution may have given us a deep need to look at life. So, try to include some elements from the natural environment in your home and work place. Plants, pets, windows with views of natural scenes, paintings or photographs of nature, or even an aquarium can transform a lifeless man-made environment and reconnect you with nature.

Aquarium Gazing

No one who has donned mask and snorkel and watched the life of a coral reef can forget the sensation of joyous wonder at being in the midst of so much variegated, moving beauty. The effortless floating, the repetitive rush of breathing, the silent weaving of the colorful bright fish, and the undulant motion of seaweed fronds all combine to produce an envelope of sensation that can take you completely outside yourself.

You can float with almost no consciousness of self, with no thought, feeling only the intense but peace-giving movement and color of the reef. The intensity of the beauty brings a calm, almost otherworldly, serenity. Part of this rapture can be captured by gazing into an aquarium.

"Fish-staring" certainly may be pleasurable, but can such a pleasant pastime measurably enhance our health? The answer seems to be yes. Researchers asked a group of people—some with hypertension, some with normal blood pressure—to read aloud. (Reading aloud or even talking to other people almost invariably raises blood pressure.) The subjects then stared at a blank wall for twenty minutes. Next, they gazed for twenty minutes into an aquarium stocked with colorful tropical fish, living plants, and rocks.

The researchers found that fish-staring lowered blood pressure and produced a state of calm relaxation. Blood pressure during this activity dropped significantly more than during wall-watching. For those subjects with hypertension, blood pressure often fell into the normal range. However, the relaxation effect was canceled if subjects were asked to stare into an *empty* fish tank. They quickly became bored, and their blood pressure rose.

The calm induced by contemplating fish also reduced the subjects' response to stress. When they were again asked to read aloud after aquarium-gazing, their blood pressure rose by less than half as much as it had at the start of the experiments.

Aquarium-gazing might well be enough for minor stresses, but could it help people relax while facing a major threat like dental surgery? The prospect of having a wisdom tooth extracted is decidedly anxiety-provoking. The injections, drilling, and extraction of the tooth are enough to stress anyone.

A group of patients facing such a tooth extraction were asked to gaze into an aquarium for forty minutes before the surgery. They were told that during the operation they could relax by recalling the peaceful image of the fish tank. Indeed, fish watchers reported less discomfort and anxiety during the operation. The pain and anxiety were reduced as much by aquarium-gazing as by hypnosis, and fish-watching may be a lot easier and much more pleasurable.

Natural Reverie

How does looking at fish relax us? Focusing attention on pleasurable sights and sounds seems to have a relaxing effect. When we start to think about something, no matter the subject, the body initially becomes activated and tenses. Blood pressure increases, heart rate speeds up, and palms become sweaty. But when we focus our attention on events outside of ourselves, on external sights and sounds, our heart rate and blood pressure fall and our palms become drier, signaling relaxation.

Of course, not all sights and sounds reduce arousal and anxiety. Predictably, watching a horror film increases blood pressure and heart rate. Exciting external events cause internal excitement. There might seem to be little difference between gazing at fish in a tank or people on a television screen, but the effect can be quite different due to the content of the images. Television programs excite us in order to keep our attention—hence the rapidly changing images, confrontation, violence, sex, and humor—all designed to prevent us from slipping off into a relaxed reverie and ignoring the commercials.

But try watching television with the sound off. Because you are unable to understand the meaning or follow the action, the images become transformed into mere visual patterns more closely approximating the continual random motion of fish in a tank.

Better yet, try looking at life. Gazing at fish, watching a fire, contemplating the waves at the seashore, bird watching, looking out a window into an arboreal scene—all natural scenes—evoke a pleasurable, relaxing calm. They return us to the natural world we evolved to live within. These visions also attract attention outside ourselves, arresting the internal monologue of worry and concern.

A peaceful reverie, decreased blood pressure, and stress reduction may be no farther away than an aquarium, the smoldering embers of a fire, or a picture of a waterfall. Spend some time each day deliberately noticing and gazing at some aspect of the natural world around you. You may not have the Grand Canyon or a view of majestic mountains at your doorstep, but no matter where you live you can find some small aspect of nature to contemplate. Perhaps it's the veins of a leaf from a tree, an anthill, a bird nesting, or the kinetic sculpture created by rain pounding the pavement.

You may not need an esoteric mantra or meditation technique, a long course in biofeedback training, or weeks of instruction in stress management to be able to relax. You may need only to direct more attention to the everyday, ordinary beauty of the natural world around you. People once lived surrounded by fields, trees and animals. Natural scenes were hard, if not impossible, to avoid. Today we may need, for the pleasure and health of it, to make a special effort to look at life.

And listen to its sounds.

Musical Medicine

You are sitting in a darkened room. At moments you feel intense, spine-tingling thrills which seem to begin at your neck and radiate over your head and all the way down to your toes. You actually shiver with pleasure and get goose bumps and may even weep. What could possibly be the source of such delicious sensations—fabulous sex? A well-wrought movie? A glorious painting? The birth of a great idea?

Had you participated in this study at Stanford University, you would have been responding to music. Music can be an intense as well as healthy pleasure; indeed, one survey showed that some of us find music more thrilling than anything else—including sex (which tied with nostalgic moments for sixth place on the all-time thrill scale).

And at least part of the thrill of music may come from the release of endorphins, the powerful opiate-like chemicals produced in the brain that relieve pain and induce euphoria. When a drug is administered that blocks these pleasure-releasing chemicals, some of the thrills of listening to music are significantly blunted.

Good Vibrations

You don't have to be musically inclined to be influenced by music. By choice or by chance, music is a part of your life—

beginning, in a way, before you were born, with the rhythm of your mother's beating heart. Her voice is the beginning of a lullaby. Perhaps Muzak is an ersatz lullaby for adults— soothing us unawares in elevators, at the dentist, in banks— persuading us to joyfully hand over our credit cards in shopping centers and department stores.

Almost everyone has a musical preference, playing "radio roulette," tapping feet in time to music, singing along with a favorite tune at the top of our lungs. We don't have to splurge for a subscription to the symphony, retreat under headphones, or go to church to tune in to how music affects us. Be it Bach, jazz, rock, gospel, or pop, music is a mood mover. The right music at the right time brings us joy and serenity and soothes frazzled nerves. It lifts us up when we're down, and calms us when we're too excited; it can move us to tears, or get us in the mood to eat, study, work, or make love.

We seem to have a built-in response to certain tones: people uniformly describe high-pitched music as happy and playful, low-pitched music as sad and serious. On the other hand, tempo may be the most important factor for our hearts and our heads. Our hearts normally beat between seventy and eighty times per minute. Most Western music is set (coincidentally?) to this tempo. Some studies have shown that heart rate will synchronize with music, speeding up or slowing down accordingly. Music also alters the brain's electrical rhythms.

Music influences respiratory rate, blood pressure, stomach contractions, and the level of stress hormones in the blood. Though people react differently, slow, quiet, nonvocal music generally lowers bodily reactions to stress, while the faster variety heightens alertness and arousal. Perhaps some of music's allure stems simply from its ability to distract us from less pleasant thoughts and feelings, albeit temporarily.

Distraction may partly explain why exercise feels better

to music—because it helps us gain with less pain. One study
showed that moving to an even rhythm made muscles flex
and extend more smoothly. And music may get you in tune
with your body, increasing endurance, regulating breathing,
and getting you in the mood to exercise. With upbeat rock
music, exercisers tend to *feel* as if they haven't worked as
hard.

Brahms Valium

If the thought of surgery, hospitalization, or the dentist's
drill sends chills up and down your spine, you can tran-
scend-dental medication with sound. When music is played
for patients before, during, or after surgery, it has been
found to reduce anxiety, lessen pain, reduce need for pre-
and post-operative medication, and speed recovery. In one
study, when soothing music was piped into an operating
room throughout surgery, the amount of sedative required
by patients was cut in half. The patients were generally
enthusiastic about the experience, remarking "It was very
enjoyable indeed," "I heard Pachelbel Canon when I awoke,
and it was a nice, underlying thing." Not exactly a typical
postoperative reaction. In another study, the investigator
estimated that music had an effect comparable to that of an
intravenous dose of 2.5 milligrams of Valium.

"Musical Valium" has worked for male and female, young
and old, and in patients undergoing a wide variety of surgical procedures, from tubal ligation to spinal fusion. Two
studies conducted on surgical patients in Japan indicate that
listening to music before and during surgery reduces the
level of stress hormones in the blood. Since the surrounding
noises and voices in the operating room are a common
source of anxiety for patients—even those who receive general anesthesia may be able to hear them—part of the beneficial effect may be due to the music blocking out these
distressing sounds.

Now you know why you're subjected to "dentist music." When played during a variety of dental treatments, including drilling and tooth extraction, an earful of music enhances the effect of the anesthetic. Music can even make childbirth a more pleasant experience. When combined with Lamaze exercises, music reduces the pain and duration of labor by as much as two hours, while enhancing the euphoria of birth.

So, the next time you or someone you know is scheduled for a dental or medical procedure, consider bringing or requesting music.

Take Two Arias and Call Me in the Morning

Music as medical therapy began in ancient times. The oldest known medical document is a papyrus that refers to incantations used to heal the sick. To the ancient Greeks, Apollo was the god of both medicine *and* music. Early physicians used music to regulate heartbeat and music and singing were traditionally used to cure many ailments, including "melancholia." Healing with sound, rhythm, and chanting is widely accepted in many cultures throughout the world.

Our culture's version of music therapy helps people cope with the emotional and physical effects of many types of illness. Helen Bonny has used music to facilitate psychotherapy, but when she developed heart disease, she turned to music to help heal herself. She knew firsthand how important music could be to vulnerable hospital patients trapped in a cold, sterile, often boring environment. She began her pilot project by piping quiet music into the intensive coronary care units of two hospitals. The music reduced heart rates, lowered blood pressure, increased pain tolerance, and lessened anxiety and depression.

Music therapy is a useful adjunct in the treatment of many illnesses including cancer, respiratory problems, stroke, arthritis, and diabetes. It's used to ease the administration and counteract the side effects of such potentially unpleasant treatments as chemotherapy, radiation, and kidney dialysis. It works to ease the pain, calm the anxiety, and lift the spirits of the terminally or chronically ill.

Music is used extensively for treatment of diseases like headaches, digestive problems, and depression, which have a strong emotional component. It has also been successful in breaking through to autistic children.

Music is also used to reduce depression, anxiety, and isolation in burn victims, organ transplant patients, and people with contagious diseases, who spend long periods of time in otherwise sterile environments. A particularly bittersweet application is reaching comatose or brain-damaged patients.

One thirteen-year-old auto accident victim appeared comatose and wasn't responding to anyone or anything. He gradually responded to a variety of music. His therapy began with the simple act of turning his head towards the music. Eventually, he sang and played musical instruments. Before he was discharged from the hospital four and a half months after the accident, he said to his music therapist, "Music makes me happy."

Music may also be nourishing for premature infants. When Brahms's "Lullaby" was prescribed for these babies, the results were striking. The infants gained weight faster and were able to leave the hospital an average of one week sooner than the babies who didn't hear the music, at a savings of $4,800 per infant.

Musical Immunity

If music can make such a difference in the outcome of medical procedures, illness, and treatment, what are its benefits in supporting good health and preventing illness in people who are basically healthy?

An answer may lie in the effect of music on immune

function. High levels of stress hormones appear to suppress our immune systems, but music may help control these hormones. Music therapist and researcher Mark Rider studied night- and rotating-shift hospital nurses who suffered health problems due to the stress produced from working at odd hours. The nurses listened to a twenty-minute tape of relaxation exercises, guided imagery, and mellow music. During the days of musical relaxation, the nurses' stress hormone levels rose less steeply and their biological rhythms were more in sync. Interestingly, two of the subjects remarked that although at one point during the study they felt as though they were getting sick, they felt better after playing the music/relaxation tape.

WE can make the effort to put more music in our lives, in either a structured or informal way.

Experiment with music and mood. Play a new or familiar recording and do nothing but listen, perhaps lying down in a darkened room. Does it relax you? Stimulate you? Does it evoke a certain mood, feeling, memory, or image? Try measuring your pulse before, during, and after listening.

You might want to try some music which takes advantage of your mood—start with tense music to match your mood, and then use a piece that gradually makes the transition to more soothing sounds. This has been effective in reducing chronic pain. If you are in pain or a particularly anxious mood, listening to soft, quiet music may at first clash with your feelings. However, if the music first matches your mood and resonates with your physiological state, it can lead you to a more relaxed state as you get in sync with it. A few soothing suggestions: Bach's "Air on the G String," Pachelbel's Canon in D, Haydn's Cello Concerto in C, and Debussy's "Claire de Lune." But personal reactions and preferences differ, so experiment.

Over twenty-five hundred years ago, the Greek philosopher Pythagoras may have been on to something. He advocated daily singing and playing of an instrument as a cathartic to cleanse the emotions of worry, sorrow, fear, and anger. Learning to play a musical instrument can increase the pleasure you get from music, and give you a sense of mastery and pride in your accomplishment. And while a sonata a day may not keep the doctor away, it will probably feel good regardless. Enjoying music is one of the best examples of human-made sensual pleasures, and is an easy way to reclaim some of the sensuality lost in our lives.

5

. . . .

Good Scents and Good Sex

Without the sense of smell, we would be in great danger. We might die of poisoning—unable to identify the warning odor of a noxious gas or smoke, oblivious to the stench of rancid foods, and much more vulnerable to toxic chemicals. Smell helps us judge distance, location, and danger: as a rule, we smell smoke before we see a fire. And without a sense of smell, others might react strangely to you. Would it be as a result of your body reeking? Hard to tell. You might try to correct it and splash on some perfume. Did you overdo it?

You'd miss a universe of scentual pleasures: the aromas of freshly baked bread or newly brewed coffee. Your food would be virtually tasteless: 80 percent of flavor comes from the volatile fragrances piped up the back of the nose. (Try to taste the difference between an apple, an onion, and a potato when you block your nose.) And who would dare to eat the food you prepared, seasoned without olfactory guidance? The briny air at the seashore would be indistinguishable from the pungent aromas of a pine forest. And without a lover's fragrant bouquet to arouse our interest, sexual desire might wane.

Smell is perhaps the most ignored and underappreciated of the human senses. Ever since our remote ancestors stood

upright and headed for the trees, the two "distance senses"—sight and sound—became our predominant means of
gathering information with respect to the threats and opportunities in our environment. Nevertheless, smell, because
of its connection with the emotion-generating areas in the
brain, has a great, though often subconscious, influence on
our mood and memories.

Let's track an odor from volatile molecule to pleasurable
cognition. The nose reacts to gaseous molecules carried on
currents of air. It is strategically located over the mouth,
where it can survey all food entering the body. The chemicals we inhale stimulate two pea-sized membranes secluded
deep within the nose. Spirited sniffing supplements the
amount of odor-laden air reaching these olfactory antennae.

Once inhaled, the gaseous molecules stimulate the olfactory receptors and trigger an electrical signal which speeds
directly to an ancient part of the brain, the rhinencephalon
(literally, "nose-brain") in the limbic system. Basic life processes are regulated from here: heart rate, respiration, temperature, and blood sugar levels all depend on messages
from the limbic system.

The rhinencephalon is also involved in the experience of
pleasure and fear. This primitive network of neurons gov-
erns basic emotional reactions related to survival, such as
sexual desire and the "fight or flight" response. It is also
here that memories are activated. Since scents speak directly
to this part of the brain, it is no wonder smells can so
powerfully affect our moods, behaviors, and memories.

Aromatic Memories

Smells, perhaps more than sights or sounds, command our
mind. Once a smell has been presented, it is rarely forgotten.
Memories triggered by smell can rush into awareness, drag-

ging along a vivid multisensory recall. Boyd Gibbons in *The National Geographic* recalls:

> On the wall outside my bedroom hangs a photograph of my grandfather, in his brown hat and windbreaker, standing with my father and me. My grandfather died years ago, and his image in the frame, caught in a moment of posed reunion, often reminds me of my boyhood, when he doted on me as his hunting and fishing companion. Yet the recollections are vague and distant.
>
> Recently, however, I took his old deerskin hunting vest out of the closet and on an impulse pressed it to my face and sniffed. Abruptly there came over me a rush of emotion and memory as intimate as it was compelling. No longer was I an adult squinting across a chasm of years at dim events: Suddenly I was a boy again, and there in all but the flesh was my grandfather, methodically reloading his shotgun as the flushed quail sailed beyond the mesquite.
>
> This was no hazy reverie. I could feel his whiskered cheek against mine and smell his particular fragrance of age, wool, dust, and a touch of Old Grand-Dad. Momentarily I was once more on the floor of my grandparents' breakfast room, the linoleum cool against my belly as I sketched B-17s, then sneaking down the hall into my great-uncle's gloomy bedroom hung with mounted pheasants and deer head—musky and mysterious. The epoch slowly faded as I lay curled up in the back seat of my grandfather's Ford, returning from a long hunt in Mexico, half-listening to the men up front and Fred Allen on the radio, drifting into a sweet exhausted sleep.
>
> All this from the whiff of a vest. I was not consciously trying to recall my boyhood. Such is the involuntary power of the sense of smell, my boyhood was recalling me.

Though olfactory experiences may be fleeting and evanescent, their effect on us is sustained and unforgettable. Because odors converse directly with the part of our brain that controls memories and emotional states, scent can mold our moods. It is well known, at least to real estate agents and used car salespeople, that the smell of freshly baked bread helps sell houses, and that a "new-car" odor can move even an old jalopy. Why not take advantage of this yourself? Sell your house to yourself anew by filling it with good smells that call forth good feelings.

The perfume of a lover, the smell of fallen leaves, or the reek of rancid food forcefully evokes feelings ranging from elation to depression. Consider what happened when a group of students took a simple written test, one that they expected to complete easily with high marks. Following the test, the experimenters released an odor at the same time they gave the bad news to the students—they failed miserably on the test. This particular scent became subconsciously linked with failure. Later, when the students smelled the same odor, it evoked pronounced feelings of depression. In this case the not-so-sweet smell of failure continued to produce strong effects on mood.

If past associations with odors can evoke depression, can it also lift moods? Can specific scents be used to influence mental and physiological functioning?

Aromatherapy: The Science of Scent

Ancient papyrus fragments suggest that in the time of the pharaohs, the Egyptians regarded the aroma of spices such as cinnamon as medicinal. In the traditional herbal medicines of ancient Greece, Rome, India, and the Far East, medications and perfumes were not distinguished—both were thought to have medicinal properties. In traditional Chinese medicine, brewed tea was inhaled as well as ingested. Fragrant medicinal baths are still widely used in Japan. In Germany, "forest therapy" involves inhaling eucalyptus and other arboreal vapors. Yet, modern medicine has looked down its nose at these practices of so-called aromatherapy.

However, recently the scientific eye has been focused on the therapeutic potential of fragrance. In one experiment, subjects in a laboratory were wired to physiological monitoring equipment, and interrogated with stress-provoking questions, like "What kind of person makes you angry?" Then they rated mood, while changes in blood pressure, heart rate, respiration, and brain waves were measured.

Sometimes, before the stressful questioning, a subject sniffed a fragrance. A whiff of spiced apple seems to modify the stress response: lower blood pressure, slower breathing, more relaxed muscles, and slower heart rate. The fragrance-inspired subjects also reported feeling happier, less anxious, and more relaxed. In other studies the spiced apple fragrance was more effective than eucalyptus or lavender in increasing a brain wave pattern associated with a relaxed but alert state.

Fragrances inspire us. While savoring a pleasant fragrance we take slow deep breaths and become relaxed. A strong aroma focuses awareness, distracting us from less pleasant thoughts. Pleasant smells may also evoke positive memories or emotions with their associated beneficial physiological effects.

Patients with insomnia, anxiety, panic attacks, back pain, migraine, and food cravings are now being treated with modern aromatherapy. For example, some patients with chronic pain are instructed in deep muscle relaxation while inhaling peach fragrance. Later, the patients simply take a whiff of peach, and the relaxed state is quickly induced. One company now offers a strawberry scented surgical mask to help calm patients under anesthesia. Another corporation has applied for a new patent for fragrances designed to reduce reactivity to stress. Meanwhile, Japanese researchers are studying the effects of aromatherapy on dizziness, nausea, anxiety, and other disorders. And at least one psychoanalyst in France uses the evocative power of vanilla to help patients recall early childhood memories.

Research may eventually discover that particular scents, like specific drugs, have specific effects on mood and physiology. Meanwhile, we do know that conditioning of specific reactions is a major influence of smell. People tend to have very different associations with odors, and therefore different responses to them. A whiff of vanilla may remind some of a fine wine, others of grandma's kitchen, the scent of an old lover, or a favorite piece of music, while still others may associate it with a terrible tasting medicine foisted upon a sick child. It could well be helpful to understand and perhaps begin to organize our olfactory capabilities. We might be able to control our moods, concentration, and memories, all by smell.

Test out various odors (perfumes, colognes, spices, foods) and observe their effect, if any, on your moods or memories. Use them at a later time to evoke an agreeable state of mind. Or practice a relaxation exercise while sniffing a particular pleasant scent. The scent will gradually become associated with a sense of relaxation and well-being. Later, see if taking a whiff of the fragrance helps you recall the pleasurable feeling.

Expand your olfactory vocabulary. When presented with a "blind" odor such as toothpaste, bubble gum, lemon, or coffee, the average person can usually identify it correctly 70 percent of the time. Many notable noses, from Helen Keller to great perfumers and wine connoisseurs, have developed highly acute and sensitive olfactory talents. However, nearly everyone can, with practice, increase his or her odor vocabulary and powers of discrimination. You can test your own smell acuity with a Pocket Smell Test (available from Sensonics, Inc., 15 South Haddon Avenue, Haddonfield, NJ 08033), or test yourself by identifying various spices or household products.

Subliminal Scents

Most often we move through the world oblivious to scentual information. But watch a dog enter a backyard. Nostrils flared, nose to the ground, racing from one fence to the other, he explores a mysterious universe of olfactory delights and distastes. "Ah, here are signs of a dog in heat. Oh, no! A recent visit from a neighborhood bully." We stand by as curious onlookers to the dogs' conversation.

Animals produce odors to communicate. Many creatures pick out kith and kin by scent alone. Within moments of birth, a mother wildebeest and her newborn form a permanent bond, based on their odors. Even during long migrations surrounded by thousands of other similar looking herd members, mother and baby can sense each other by smell.

Compared to those of a bloodhound, human olfactory abilities may seem paltry, but let's not be so quick to dismiss our scentary talent. There is evidence that human beings can identify familial scents with great precision. Each of us is born with our own personal smellprint. Mothers, even after spending as little as two hours with their newborn, can accurately pick out by smell a garment worn by their baby. Young children can sniff out clothing worn by a brother or sister, and spouses can usually identify T-shirts after they have been worn and spiced up by their mates. Perhaps this is an heirloom of our evolution. Animal families stick together, attracted to each other by familiar scents. In a dark cave or at night, prehistoric mothers may have been able to quickly locate wandering babies, or perhaps detect the absent scent of a wandering lover.

Animals use scent for survival—to communicate danger and prepare for stress. When experimental rats are shocked, they release a "stress odor." If normal rats are exposed to odors produced by other, stressed rats, they react as if they, too, had been exposed directly to stress. Just one whiff of the "stress odor" sends the unstressed rats scurrying: ready to fight or flee.

The same scent also triggers the release of endorphins, the brain's natural painkillers, making the rats less sensitive to pain and able to ignore physical injury long enough to either fight or flee the immediate threat.

Do human beings have a similar capacity? We don't know yet, but humans and rats share similar endorphin-mediated mechanisms for pain relief. When stressed, we also prepare for flight or fight: our nostrils flare, we suck in more air as our breathing becomes more rapid, and the sensitivity of our olfactory nerve endings increases. Are we searching for chemical signals? Perhaps the expressions "a nose for danger" or "the scent of fear" are more than metaphors. Maybe someday pain relievers will come in the form of a scent rather than a pill.

Many animals communicate by relying on odors produced by body glands, feces, and urine. Your cat is claiming you as home territory when it rubs your leg, as it is depositing a scent from its facial and rump glands. Dogs mark the boundaries of their space with urine.

There is some evidence that human beings, too, are sensitive to such olfactory markings. An unusual set of experiments tested the effect of androstenol, a musky compound excreted in sweat and urine and chemically related to male sex hormones. On alternate weeks the researchers sprayed androstenol or an inert compound on a rest-room stall. Then they watched and waited. During the weeks when the androstenol was used, men avoided the treated stalls and chose to use unmarked ones. *The men were completely unaware that their behavior was being influenced by subtle scent messages.*

In another experiment, androstenol was sprayed onto a chair in a waiting room. Women tended to sit in the scented seat more often, while men avoided this seat. Again, the subjects remained completely unaware that they were being led by their noses.

How often is our behavior, mood, and well-being being influenced by subliminal scents? We may have greatly underestimated the hidden influence of odor. We live in a world of scent, and whether we are conscious of it or not, odors strongly influence our moods, behavior and physiology. Even the phrase "take time to smell the roses" reminds us of the wealth of good scents that await our enjoyment. By becoming more aware of our noses, we can begin to deliberately use this sensory capability for our pleasure and better health.

The Scent of Love

Sex is strongly linked with smell. A male moth may travel miles in hot pursuit of chemical molecules released by a female. Lewis Thomas, in his delightful essay "Fear of Pheromones," takes us into the mind of such a moth.

The messages are urgent, but they may arrive, for all we know, in a fragrance of ambiguity. "At home, 4 P.M. today," says the female moth, and releases a brief explosion of bombykol, a single molecule of which will tremble the hairs of any male within miles and send him driving upwind in a confusion of ardor. But it is doubtful if he has an awareness of being caught in an aerosol of chemical attractant. On the contrary, he probably finds suddenly that it has become an excellent day, the weather remarkably bracing, the time appropriate for a bit of exercise of the old wings, a brisk turn upwind. En route, traveling the gradient of bombykol, he notes the presence of other males, heading in the same direction, all in a good mood, inclined to race for the sheer sport of it. Then, when he reaches his destination, it may seem to him the most extraordinary, the greatest piece of luck: "Bless my soul, what have we here!"

From moths to monkeys, animals use scents as sexual attractants. Pheromones, special aromatic chemicals secreted by one party to affect the sexual physiology of another, kick off sexual interchange and intercourse. Around ovulation, the female monkey secretes copulins, which signal male monkeys that she is available. It is a combination of the scent, the feminine amorous calls, and inviting postures, that attracts the males. However, if experimenters block the male monkey's nostrils, the unsmelling males show more interest in bananas than in receptive females.

Human beings probably release and respond to sexual scents as well: we speak of a chemical attraction between people, yet little is known with respect to how much of this is actually chemistry. Somerset Maugham once inquired of one of H.G. Wells' mistresses why such a paunchy, homely writer had such success with women. "He smells of honey," she replied. When we meet someone we are attracted to, how much of this is due to olfactory signals?

Recent scientific research offers some tantalizing clues. In one experiment, women wearing masks containing the musky pheromone androstenol responded favorably to the more assertive of two male "job applicants." In another experiment, women felt more attracted to men whose clothing had been treated with the substance. And women's reactions to photographs of male strangers improved when small amounts of androstenol was secretly sprayed into the air or when they wore masks containing it.

There is new evidence that we not only respond to such

chemicals, but also seem to produce and release our own pheromones—scentual body talk. The human pheromones investigated thus far are not, strictly speaking, sex attractants or aphrodisiacs. Some human pheromones, however, can act as olfactory signals which modify, over months, women's reproductive cycles. For example, women living together in college dormitories synchronize menstrual cycles. At the beginning of the school year each woman arrives with a unique cycle. However, by the end of the year, the women tend to start their menstrual periods at the same time.

Some type of odor signal was suspected as the cue to reset the women's biological clocks. In an intriguing experiment, several women were identified who could "drive" their roommates menstrual cycles. Samples of perspiration were collected from these donor women from cotton pads placed under their arms. These pads were then wiped across the upper lips of other women three times a week. Throughout, the "driver" women and their recipients never came in contact. Still, within five months, most of the recipients shifted their menstrual cycles in synchrony with the "drivers'."

Men also have a strong effect on menstrual cycles. Researchers have recently found that women who have sex with men at least once a week are more likely to have regular menstrual cycles, and a more benign menopause than celibate women or those who have infrequent intercourse.

The crucial element, aside from sexual intercourse itself, appears to be exposure to aromatic chemicals secreted in a man's normal body odors. When a woman receives these chemicals, by smell or skin absorption, even though she may not consciously notice them, they automatically improve her physiology.

The male chemicals, which are discharged from special sweat glands in the armpits and around the nipples and genitals, cross from man to woman in intimate sex contact.

Researchers hope some day to develop nasal sprays to correct certain forms of infertility, make the menstrual cycle regular, make the rhythm method of birth control more reliable, and alleviate some of the difficulties in menopause.

Researchers can also duplicate male pheromones' effects. In one study, women who had no current sexual relationship were exposed to male pheromones. This "male essence" contained substances from pads that males wore under their arms. When women with irregular menstrual cycles had their upper lips swabbed three times a week with the pads (hardly as satisfying as the natural method of delivery), their periods tended to become more regular.

While both male and female pheromones can signal changes in reproductive cycles, their mode of transmission appears to differ. The female pheromone can diffuse through a room and still be strong enough to synchronize menstrual cycles. However, the male pheromone requires intimate contact. Women do need men for something, anyway. It's the pits.

Sexual Harmony

Ancient Greek texts warned that sex—because it could create another life—depleted the body of "precious" elements that are vital to our existence. According to the old wives' tale, masturbation causes blindness, hairy palms, and warts. Although we don't believe these anymore, it is ironic that the simple act of sex—a body function as natural as eating—remains a moral issue, a guilty taboo. And now we have rampaging sexually transmitted diseases to worry about. With each sexual encounter we run some risk of exposure to such earthly scourges as gonorrhea, syphilis, chlamydia, herpes, crabs—and deadly AIDS. These days, it may again seem out of step to even suggest that sex may be a healthy pleasure.

But most personal experience attests to the fact that we feel better after good sex: it puts a spring in your step, a sparkle in your eye, a glow in your skin. Like a full belly, when your sexual appetite is satisfied, the world seems like a more wonderful place. Some people claim sex helps them relax; others swear it helps them sleep better, or eases menstrual cramps and other aches and pains, or cures the common cold. We were most surprised to find little in the scientific literature on the effect of a healthy sex life on happiness and well-being. In fact, when questioned about why sex is good for you most sex researchers responded, "That's an interesting idea, but no one has worked on it." But there is growing evidence that singer Marvin Gaye was right—there is such a thing as sexual healing.

The most obvious benefit of sex is survival of our species. In spite of artificial insemination and in vitro fertilization, the old-fashioned method of sexual intercourse remains the most popular way to reproduce human beings. And you probably have noticed that people have sex rather more often than is strictly required for procreation.

Testosterone is the hormone primarily responsible for the sex drive in both males and females. Female testosterone levels are highest around the middle of a woman's menstrual cycle, when ovulation takes place. It is this peak in testosterone that causes women to be more sexually aroused at this time, when they are most likely to conceive. Some women produce up to ten times more testosterone than others, and these women tend to make love more often throughout their cycles and enjoy it more. They also tend to have cheerful dispositions and form relationships more easily.

Testosterone also may help men and women bond together as a couple. In long-term couples, testosterone levels tend to eventually synchronize, and so does their desire for each other. This may lead to a more contented, harmonious relationship. Human beings have a unique style of sex: We use it not just for biological procreation but to form lasting bonds that keep a couple together. We're the only primates to engage in sex throughout the menstrual cycle, even when conception is not likely. And human fathers are the only primates to form a family and participate in the ongoing care and feeding of children.

And a good sexual appetite seems to help marriage: one survey indicated that young, newly married women with high testosterone levels had the best marriages. Young or old, mutually supportive couples said they had more active sex lives than those in conflict-prone marriages. But we don't know which comes first—does good sex lead to a good marriage, or is it the other way around?

Cynics might argue that married couples have less frequent sex than unmarried people. But a number of surveys suggest that married men and women have more frequent and satisfying sex than do their unmarried couterparts.

Loving Touch

Sex is largely an experience of touching, as is the bond between mother and infant. So much can be expressed with touch: acceptance, love, disapproval, and desire. Certainly we touch because it is pleasurable. The comforting touch of a mother's hand, the warmth of a child's hug, the relaxing strokes of a skilled masseur, the tactile feast of sexual intercourse—all send messages via our skin to the pleasure centers of the brain.

Sexual, or even close, affectionate, touching may also be an effective way to express many feelings that we find hard to put into words. A gentle caress, a firm embrace, a comforting stroke—these can, at times, say far more than words alone. You can't touch without being touched. And perhaps, if we included liberal doses of loving touch in our daily diet—hugs, mini-backrubs, massages, and snuggles—we would need less therapy in the first place.

As we have seen, a loving touch is crucial for human health. Sex encompasses all the senses, but it is especially a touching experience—emotionally and physically. More than any other interaction, sex can be the primary or sole source of physical and emotional intimacy with another human being. It provides the foundation for sharing confidences and for social support, both vital for health.

Healthy Sex

Sexual fulfillment may help reduce the impact of certain stresses in a marriage. In one fascinating study, married couples monitored sexual intercourse and arguments on a daily basis. The result could be dubbed the "F Index": *the frequency of fornication minus the frequency of fights*. The higher the F index, the happier the marriage. For example, if a couple fights ten times per month but engages in sex twelve times per month, their F index is +2, which points towards happiness. Conversely, a couple that fights only four times monthly but has sex only twice, has an F index of −2 and is probably less happily married. It does not necessarily follow that we can increase the marital happiness of people who argue a lot by encouraging them to have intercourse more often—but it would be interesting to try.

Remaining sexually active might help stave off at least one distressing change that women undergo during menopause: vaginal atrophy. As hormone levels drop, the tissue lining the vaginal canal becomes thinner, less elastic, and less able to produce lubrication, causing discomfort during intercourse. In their classic study *Human Sexual Response*, Masters and Johnson reported that three female subjects who remained sexually active during and after menopause responded to sexual stimulation with considerable vaginal lubrication.

More recently, other researchers studied fifty-two post-menopausal women to see if the "use it or lose it" principle really applied. They discovered that women who had intercourse three or more times per month experienced significantly less vaginal atrophy than those who were inactive, that is, who had intercourse less than ten times a year.

Some people get headaches from sex, while others use this affliction as an excuse not to indulge. You know the classic plea, "Not tonight, dear, I have a headache." While headaches can be a turnoff, getting turned on may actually relieve some types of migraine headache. In a survey of migraine sufferers, one-quarter reported that orgasm helped soothe the pain, and the stronger the orgasm the greater the relief. Even though sex may be the last thing on your mind when you have a splitting headache, you might consider sexual healing as an alternative to aspirin.

Why Sex Should Be Taken Seriously

Some of us seem to be able to do perfectly well without sex. In others, nature has implanted a powerful drive that appears to be as necessary to health as food, air, sleep, exercise, love, and laughter. Remember that sex combines many needs: being touched, being caressed, and feeling close to others. When sex is not available, make sure you can substitute other forms of closeness. Get a massage. Give one. Talk to people in trouble and try to help them. These and other recourses can never completely replace sex, but they will help you more than you think, as well as helping others. This will put you in a better mood, make you feel better about yourself, and make you less lonely. And, maybe, you'll meet someone, too.

Unfortunately, many erroneous beliefs, resulting from upbringing, cultural traditions, and media images, can interfere with sexual pleasures. Work and other interests or demands compete for our time and energy. Sex may be the first thing to go during times of physical and mental stress, illness, pregnancy, parenting, and aging. You may take it for granted that you can always return to it later on. Don't.

While we're not offering a sex manual, we do suggest you make time for sex, touching, and loving. Don't let other events interfere. It may cost you some points at work to take a long weekend off with your lover, but after all, what are you working for?

Think about the qualities that make a sexual experience satisfying for you. Is it the setting? What you did before and afterward? The degree of emotional commitment? Make sure you can arrange the scene so it works.

If your sex life isn't working, give it the attention that you would to problems in other areas of life. Communicate your sexual likes and dislikes with your partner, even if it's difficult. Where do you like to be touched, and how? Your partner is not a mind reader, and neither are you. Many lawyers now say that sexual incompatibility is the primary but often hidden issue in divorce. It isn't mentioned in the complaints, which focus on cruelty or lack of commitment or broken promises, but often the real problem is sex. Don't be prudish about it: people have very different sexual appetites. If your sexual relationship is a problem for you, even a small one, heed it, and give this essential pleasure the attention it needs to make it nourishing.

6

· · · · · · · · · · · · ·

Consuming Passions

The Evolution of Good Taste

Fortunately, food is not one of the sensory pleasures that has disappeared from the world we've inherited from our ancestors. All animals feed, but only human beings savor food with such passion. We eat to nourish, to celebrate, to commemorate, but most of all we eat for pleasure. We are rewarded not only in enjoyment but in health.

While the modern world offers different fare than that available to our ancestors, our natural good taste for gustatory pleasures is still with us. And we don't need to worry as much about being a little plump or about the minutiae of our diet as we've been lead to believe.

In 1825, Jean-Anthelme Brillat-Savarin, perhaps the greatest culinary philosopher, asserted that "the discovery of a new dish does more for human happiness than the discovery of a new star." Closer to our gist, Aldous Huxley observed that "a man may be a pessimistic determinist before lunch and an optimistic believer in the will's freedom after it."

But taste is more than a matter of enjoyment and pleasure. It can be a matter of survival. Taste and smell evolved to help us avoid poisons and seek nutrition. Our "sweet tooth" evolved to guide our ancestors toward ripe fruits, ready sources of energy and certain vitamins. Our taste for fatty foods rich in calories once served our forebears well, tiding them over through times of famine.

Nonetheless, we no longer live in the innocence of a nutritional Garden of Eden. We are now confronted with a cornucopia of processed and synthetic foods that taste, smell, and look like what they're not. We can consume gallons of sweet liquids which contain not a single nutrient. We have regular access to mountains of food for which we have not been evolutionarily prepared.

One day driving home we counted the places where we could get fast fat foods. On our one hour commute we found thirty-four rib and chicken places, twelve pizza parlors, fifty-five burger joints, and more than thirty ice cream shops. This survey didn't count grocery stores (each of which has more food inside than a tribe might need for a year) or candy or convenience stores. Modern life may stint on sunlight and exercise, but it certainly doesn't deprive us of fat. And our natural love of fat can get confused.

While our ancestors survived on grains and vegetables, today we have the choice of feasting solely on fats or sugars. The challenge for us is to make peace with our inborn appetites for pleasure in a land of phenomenal food temptations. Our taste alone can no longer guide us through the maze of edible choices. While we can still enjoy eating, we now need to know a bit more about what's in our food and its effect on mood and health.

Guess What's Coming from Dinner

At every meal we can eat foods that either enliven or depress us, and if we choose correctly we may be better able to sleep, work, and think. Consider, for example, this dinner for four. Sophia, on a continuous diet, longingly looks at

the bread basket and the pasta offerings, but spartanly declines these "fattening" carbohydrates in favor of a large
salad with cottage cheese. She finds it even more difficult
to just say no to the tempting dessert tray. Throughout the
meal she bemoans the ten pounds she is trying to lose.

Meanwhile, Alicia chooses a shrimp cocktail followed by
a fillet of broiled fish served with carrots, and a bowlful of
fresh berries for dessert. She enjoys the lively conversation
throughout the meal and afterwards returns to the office
clear-headed for a few hours' work before retiring.

Alex hits the bread basket, downs a large plateful of pasta,
and tops off his meal with a fruit tart. He comments repeatedly how tasty and satisfying the food is. Even before he
finishes eating he begins to slip into a mellow mood. His
eyes become slightly glazed and the tensions of a hard day
at work fade. He returns home, satisfied, for a good night's
sleep.

When Bret takes the first bite of his main entree, his
mouth explodes, his eyes bulge, and his breathing halts.
Tears stream from his eyes, the flood gates of his nose bolt
open, and each sweat gland of his brow weeps uncontroll-
ably. For a brief moment he becomes oblivious of the restaurant, the other guests, and the rest of the world as his
attention is consumed by the fiery assault on his throat and
sinuses. Then, slowly, a warm smile spreads over his face
and he sighs, "Boy, that was good." He has just eaten a dish
laced with hot chili peppers.

Sophia, Alicia, Alex, and Bret all consumed different
foods, and experienced different degrees of pleasure during
and after the meal. Why should Alicia, after a protein-rich
meal, feel alert and full of pep while Alex, feasting on carbohydrates, feels relaxed and drowsy? Should Sophia really
deny herself the pleasures of the table for fear of fatness? Is
there a way to maximize enjoyment without maximizing
weight gain? And how it is that Bret has come to love the

burn of hot chili—a burn that may bring pleasure and, as we'll see, perhaps a healthier heart?

Pleasantly Plump

Sophia is worried sick about her weight. She's constantly checking herself against the "desirable" weight tables. She also watches gloomily the media parade of "ideal women"— winners of Miss America pageants, Playboy centerfolds, and Barbie dolls. Even they are losing weight.

But our beauty ideals change rapidly. Thinness has only recently become becoming—throughout history, a plump figure has been the ideal of feminine beauty. Consider Lillie Langtry, a beauty who entranced many suitors, including the Prince of Wales, around the turn of the century. She was portrayed on television recently as an attractive woman, about five feet seven inches weighing about 130 pounds. Imagine our shock, however, when we saw a photo of her. She actually weighed 220 pounds!

Losing weight has also taken on a moral tone. Overweight and obese individuals are seen as slothful gluttons without the will power and resolve to deal with a simple problem— eating too much and not exercising enough.

And for many millions, prandial pleasures are cut short by an overwhelming fear of fatness. Dieting is a national obsession. Sixty million adult Americans are trying to lose weight. *More than half of these people are not overweight.*

Is being fat all that bad for us? Is fat itself harmful, or is it the emotional stress from the social prejudice against fat people or the physiological stress of "yo-yo" dieting that causes the damage? More important, is being thin worth the daily torture of deprivation, calorie counting, and rigid exercise regimens that it takes for most of us to maintain our "ideal weight?"

Probably not. In fact, being pleasingly plump is healthier

than subjecting ourselves to the ups and downs of constant dieting. And while there is no question that what and how we eat is related to our health, "dieting" is not a healthy way to eat.

How Bad Is Fat?

We usually think of thin people as healthy people—and for years, actuarial tables have been built around this assumption. But the truth is that people who are of *average weight or slightly overweight* by these standards are actually the healthiest. The people at greatest risk are the very lean and the very obese. According to a major study, a gain of about a pound per year from age twenty-five to sixty-five keeps us at our healthiest weight. And most people in western societies naturally seem to gain a little less than a pound a year.

For example, Sophia, a five foot four inch woman, weighed a healthy 130 pounds at age thirty. Now, at sixty, she's at a healthy weight of 160 pounds. Her body seems to know what a healthy pleasure is, even though she deprives herself through continuous dieting, driven by the false belief that she is dangerously overweight.

In the past few decades, Americans have been getting fatter and fatter, yet *life expectancy has continued to increase.* If fat were as lethal as many believe, we should see a more striking effect on mortality rates. There is less we can do to lose weight than we think—because we're supposed to be gaining.

So, when should you worry about fat? If you have diabetes, high blood pressure, high cholesterol, heart disease, or back pain, you should try to maintain your weight near the desirable range in the weight tables (see notes page 265). If you are 40 percent above your desirable weight (some would argue 20 percent), weight reduction *may* be beneficial in protecting your future health. However, if you tend to "yo-yo" diet, losing weight and then gaining it back, you would probably be better off staying where you are, fat or not.

Where you are fat may also make a difference. Fat around the waistline—the "spare tire" or "middle-age spread"—is linked with diabetes and heart disease. Fat carried in the hips and thighs carries lower risk. Apparently, we are better off with thunder thighs than with beer bellies. Luckily, a fat belly seems to be easier to shed.

There's more good news. If you do have a good medical reason to lose weight, you may not need to lose as much as you think or as much as the weight tables suggest. Small reductions in weight in significantly overweight people (at least 60 percent above ideal weight) can pay huge health dividends. In one study, results showed that after losing as little as 10 percent of their weight, one-third of those with diabetes were able to be weaned off insulin, and 40 percent of those with high blood pressure discontinued their medications.

In spite of social discrimination and the tyranny of dieting, fat people do not seem to have any greater psychological problems than do slim people. There may even be some advantage in being pleasingly plump. Some studies support a "jolly-fat connection," in which overweight people show significantly *less anxiety and depression* than do their slimmer peers.

So, our fear of fat, except for the very obese, is really about appearance, not health. Getting fatter really signifies growing (and looking) older, since almost everybody gains as they age. Most of us want to lose weight to look good; for the same reason, we dye our hair or smooth our wrinkles. But even though there is undoubtedly a correlation between the number of wrinkles and life expectancy (the more wrinkles, the fewer years remain), no one presumes that losing wrinkles will increase our life span. Wrinkles aren't a health issue, but a cosmetic one; and so, for the most part, are small weight gains.

The Losing Battle

Still, millions continually struggle to lose weight on pleasure-denying diets that are not only ineffective, but cause us to *gain weight*. Most diets are nutritionally unbalanced and programmed to failure. Losing weight is usually the easiest part; but less than 5 percent of dieters can keep it off.

It seems simple: we gain weight when we eat more calories than we burn. However, losing and gaining weight is *not* that simple, because the body manages weight around a "set point." It is this set point, not what we want to weigh, that keeps our weight around a predetermined level.

Some people, then, are born to be fat; their set point is higher. Fatness begins in childhood: it is related to the number and size of the body's fat cells, which are established in the first two years. Obese people have three times the number of fat cells as do individuals of normal weight. For them, this makes losing weight to a desired ideal difficult, if not impossible.

Still, you begin yet another diet with great hopes. In the first days of a low-calorie diet, you may quickly and easily lose five or more pounds. At first glance, you're encouraged. Hey, this diet really works. Unfortunately, most of the weight lost in the first few days and weeks of a diet is water and muscle, not fat. It takes several weeks of dieting for the body to really start losing fat.

If this isn't bad enough, when you diet your body plays a nasty trick on you: metabolism slows down by as much as 20 percent. Your body can't really tell the difference between a diet and a famine. In times of famine, reducing the number of calories burned makes good sense for survival. But for the dieter, the slowed metabolism undermines weight loss. This is one reason why so many dieters hit a plateau several weeks into a diet, finding that their weight won't budge on a low calorie diet that melted away pounds in the beginning.

Finally, when you do go off the diet and start eating again, your metabolism doesn't rev back up very quickly. You gain weight more easily now, even if you are eating fewer calories than before you started the diet. Dieting or fasting makes our bodies more efficient at storing fat, which makes it even easier to gain weight later.

Dieting is a losing battle for many of us who are born to be fat. People with too many fat cells have a high set point, and continue to be hungry even after they manage to get their weight to a desirable point. They face constant hunger or ridicule for being overweight. So these people lose and gain weight constantly. Their diets do not work.

Cycling up and down in weight—yo-yo dieting—increases the percentage of body fat and redistributes it to the abdomen, where it is more of a health risk. Many habitual dieters develop an even greater taste for fatty foods, which are high in calories and are more readily converted into body fat.

Yo-yo dieting also increases the risk of developing heart disease. In the Framingham Heart Study, people who lost 10 percent of their body weight showed a 20 percent reduction in the risk of coronary heart disease. However, those who gained 10 percent increased their risk of heart disease by 30 percent. This suggests that if you *lose weight and then regain it you may be at higher risk than before*. Most of us are, therefore, better off not dieting at all than bouncing up and down in weight.

Perhaps you're still concerned about your weight and shape on the one hand, and the dangerous effects of dieting on the other. You enjoy eating, and don't particularly want to give up that pleasurable sensation of fullness and satisfaction that follows a wonderful meal. Understanding how different foods affect your appetite, satiety, and weight can guide you to a lighter, healthier, and even more satisfying diet. Here are some tips on how to maximize pleasure while minimizing excessive weight gain.

Fat Stuff

Until recently, most experts believed that a calorie was a calorie: it didn't matter much if it came from a thick milk shake, a cream pie, a carrot stick, or an orange slice. But not all calories are treated equally by our bodies. Calories from fatty foods are more readily converted to fat in the body, while those from carbohydrates such as breads and pastas are much less fattening. While ounce for ounce fats have more than twice as many calories as do carbohydrates and protein, their effect in the body may be more comparable to five or six times as many calories.

Part of this is due to the different ways we burn calories as we digest food and use it in the body. To convert dietary fat to body fat requires a short metabolic trip, consuming only 3 percent of the fat calories consumed. In contrast, nearly 25 percent of carbohydrates are burned during their conversion into body fat. Carbohydrates turn on the body and stoke the internal furnace more than fats.

So you can get fatter by eating *fewer* calories on a *high-fat* diet than *more* calories on a *high-carbohydrate* diet. It is difficult, if not impossible, to get fat without a lot of fat in the diet. The problem is that we love the taste of fat—that "mouth feel" of creamy, dense foods. In the past, this preference for fat saved many of our ancestors from starvation—when refrigerators weren't in nearly every house and supermarkets weren't on nearly every corner, and you didn't know where your next meal was coming from.

Fats slow the emptying of the stomach, making us feel full, and stimulate the liver to send pleasurable messages of satiety to the brain. So eating a small amount of fat at the beginning of a meal may bring on the satisfying sensation of fullness sooner; and eating creamy, low-calorie foods, like nonfat yogurt or fruit purees may fool your body into thinking you are eating rich, satisfying foods.

Many dieters, like Sophia, carefully avoid potatoes, breads, and pasta, thinking that carbohydrates are particularly fattening. It's not the carbohydrates, but the "company they keep" that makes them fattening: the oil in fried potatoes, the butter on bread, and the cream sauce on pasta.

Carbohydrates can be comforting, relaxing, and very satisfying. Complex carbohydrates, like whole grains and vegetables, can therefore be excellent diet foods. The bulk provided by fiber-rich carbohydrates stimulates a satisfying sensation of fullness. Dieters given unlimited quantities of high-carbohydrate foods eat fewer calories than those feasting on more calorie-dense dishes. And the feelings of satiety among high-carbohydrate diners may last hours longer.

Even carbohydrates such as sugar, long regarded as the nemesis of the calorie conscious, can play a useful role in satisfying the appetite. Mother was right: eating sweets before dinner can spoil your appetite. So consuming a piece of fruit or a glass of fruit juice, both rich in fructose, before a meal can quickly satisfy hunger sensations and decrease calorie intake.

The Pleasure Diet

We love variety and crave different taste sensations. This has led some experts to recommend that the road to weight loss is paved with monotony: eat only one type of food at a meal and consume blander, less tasty fare. At least in the short run, facing a limited plate of food is less likely to result in an orgy of calories than choosing from a limitless smorgasbord. Yet, there may be ways to indulge our craving for taste without overdoing it in the calorie department.

Diets weak in flavor and variety of texture tend to fail in the long run because they're not pleasurable. They do not satisfy our basic needs for taste. Obese people in particular seem to have an increased flavor set-point. They crave more intense stimulation and down bite after bite in search of satisfaction. Unfortunately, much of the taste of food lies in its odor, and many of the most satisfying aromas are volatile compounds carried in fatty foods. One solution to this problem is to improve the flavor of foods with noncaloric flavor enhancers.

One researcher has increased the satisfaction and weight loss of dieters by boosting the flavor, but not the calories, in their food. One group of dieters ate standard, low-calorie fare. A second group ate similar meals but with the taste amplified with noncaloric flavorings. A third group treated themselves to a burst of chocolate or vanilla spray on their tongues before meals and whenever they had a craving for food. Enhancing the flavor boosted weight loss and made for happier, more satisfied dieters. And on the horizon, the fruits of food technology promise even better-tasting low-calorie substitutes for fats and sweets.

Another approach is to liberally sprinkle your diet with tasty, low-calorie foods. For example, spices can be helpful for dieters or for those who want to up their taste sensation. Meals laced with hot chili pepper and mustard help boost the body's metabolic rate and actually burn calories. In one study, twelve people ate identical 766-calorie meals. Some of the test meals contained 3 grams of chili and 3 grams of mustard sauce, while the other meals were spiceless. After the meal, the subjects' metabolic rate was tracked for three hours. The spicy meals boosted the metabolism by 25 percent—burning an average of 45 additional calories. If this increased caloric flare up persists with repeated spicy meals, a person might lose nearly five pounds per year due to the internal combustion sparked by foods liberally dosed with chili. (This is not true for all hot spices, however; ginger, for example, does not kindle the metabolic rate.)

It is intriguing to consider hot chilies joining cottage cheese and celery sticks as a preferred diet food.

The way we eat also affects how much pleasure we derive per calorie. Our senses of taste and smell tend to become fatigued and unresponsive when flooded continuously with the same flavor or texture bite after bite. So try switching from food to food with each bite and avoid homogeneous foods, like sandwiches, in which all the flavors blend together. A wide variety of foods in the diet also helps ensure that we're getting all the nutrients we need. (An all-grapefruit diet may be low in calories, but it is also low in most essential nutrients.)

Whether you're fat or thin, *slow down* and enjoy your food while you're eating it. How often have you finished wolfing down some tasty treat only to discover that you hardly tasted it? It's gone, and you've lost the fun and gained the weight. No pleasure, lots of gain. Next time savor every bite. Pay special attention to the initial burst of flavor as well as the lingering aftertaste. Chewing your food thoroughly not only breaks it down, releasing more tasty molecules, but also creates air currents to carry volatile odor molecules up the back of the throat to the waiting olfactory receptors of the nose. Avoid cold foods, which can put a chill on the senses and reduce satisfying aromas.

Eating slowly also allows time for the satiety signals to go into effect. If you gulp down your food you may have rushed past the optimal level of satisfaction and into that postprandial stuffed feeling. If you slowly sip a bowl of soup at the start of a meal, you'll probably feel full and satisfied earlier. And for every calorie in the soup, you will consume about two less during the main meal.

You don't always have to eat when you crave food. We often crave pleasurable sensation and since eating is such an easily available pleasure, we reach for food. A piece of delicious chocolate just sits there, waiting to be consumed at any time, day or night. Many other pleasures, from the touch of a loved one to a visit to the theatre, are not as easily or quickly accessible.

The next time you automatically reach for food, consider whether you're truly hungry. Perhaps another type of sensual pleasure will satisfy you even more. Sometimes you don't really want to eat, but you want to have fun. Try going for a walk or to a movie, playing ball, or cuddling. You may find more satisfaction—and fewer calories.

Run to Eat

If you walk into a room and spot the *thinnest* people, they're likely to be the ones who eat the *most*. They're also the ones most likely to exercise regularly. We have a friend who runs, primarily so that he can sit down one or more times a day and eat enormous quantities of food.

Physical activity appears to be the key to successful weight loss and maintenance. It is not merely calories burned up during exercise. Reading the calorie charts can be depressing when you add up how many miles you need to run to burn up one ice cream cone. Fortunately, our bodies don't read those charts.

Following exercise, metabolic rate stays up for as long as twenty-four hours, so you may continue to burn up extra calories while relaxing after a workout. This boost in body metabolism is critical, since it helps offset the decline in metabolism that occurs when you diet. In addition, exercise seems to readjust the body's set point for fat. Signals are sent to the brain to reduce the amount of fat stored in adipose tissue, so fat levels drop naturally, albeit slowly.

Food for Thought

Food is pleasurable not only because of its taste, smell, texture, and ability to fill hungry bellies. Recent research suggests that foods may act like weak drugs, affecting our moods, thoughts, motivation, and performance—even hours after we've eaten. Certain foods trigger the release of brain chemicals which we experience as pleasure.

But how do foods get inside our mind? The brain is specially protected from the world. Our skulls obviously protect us from outside physical blows. We also have a "blood-brain barrier," a special network of cells that guard the brain from toxins in the bloodstream. Until recently, it was assumed that our brains were completely isolated from the food we eat. But new studies are beginning to unlock some surprising secrets: neurotransmitters, the chemical messengers of the brain, affect our appetite for certain foods—and certain foods affect production of brain neuro-transmitters.

Since these chemical messengers carry signals between nerve cells in the brain, they can influence our moods and behaviors in many ways, acting like natural drugs. Dopamine and norepinephrine, "alertness chemicals," make us think and react more quickly, and feel more attentive, motivated, and mentally energetic. Serotonin, "the calming chemical," relaxes us, eases tension, and causes drowsiness. It also helps decrease sensitivity to pain and encourages us to fall asleep.

Our brain produces neurotransmitters that influence appetite. We're naturally more alert and mentally energetic during the first part of the day, when noradrenaline is at its highest (perhaps causing a preference for carbohydrate food like Cocoa Puffs). At our next meal, we may gravitate toward protein. As we gradually slow down to prepare for sleep, other neurochemicals make carbohydrates and fat more alluring. It may be instinctive, then, when we eat certain foods to bolster production of these neurotransmitters to help us get through stressful situations or to satisfy a hunger for a specific nutrient. So, the next time you "feel like a steak" or "need a cookie" it could be your brain—and not your stomach—talking.

It's fun to go all-out during a business lunch once in a while, especially if someone else is footing the bill. But you may have noticed that you're not as sharp afterwards. As many studies suggest, the real "power lunch" is not the lush extravaganza usually associated with expense accounts.

Research by Judith and Richard Wurtman and others has shown that people feel much better—are more alert, communicate more clearly, and perform to their best potential —after lighter fare. School children had more trouble learning after being fed heavy meals, and pilots' visual perception and reaction were affected.

So, power lunching is more like power munching— mostly on protein, less on carbohydrates, and as little as possible on fats. Like Alicia, who feasted on protein-rich shrimp and fish, to stay more alert, you might begin with a small protein appetizer, progress to a low-fat protein main course, then a vegetable or salad, perhaps some pasta or potato, and fruit—or nothing—for dessert. If your alertness chemicals are being used up, the protein helps replenish them. Beginning with protein helps shift you more quickly into an energetic state of mind, or will at least block the relaxing effects of carbohydrates (see below). A low-fat meal digests faster than one that's heavy and fatty, which diverts too much blood to the digestive system from other organs, including the brain.

Power munching your way through lunch may also help you stay more alert later in the day—a boon if you have professional or social obligations. Overeating at lunch often leads to a lethargic feeling because your circadian rhythm is already winding down.

The Edible Tranquilizer

Carbohydrates appear to have the opposite effect of protein by raising brain levels of tryptophan, a building block of the calming chemical serotonin. This may explain why, when anxiety strikes, your hand instinctively reaches for a comforting high-carbohydrate food, like pasta, toast, or cookies, or why Alex felt so relaxed and drowsy after his carbohydrate-rich meal. As little as one ounce of a sweet or starchy food allows enough tryptophan into the brain to stimulate production of serotonin. That's only half a candy bar, a couple of cookies or crackers, a handful of dry ready-to-eat cereal, or a plain white potato. A small carbohydrate snack can be just the thing to help you feel calm, focused, and patient during a trying afternoon. Raising the level of serotonin, which regulates appetite, could also help you stick to a diet.

But too many carbohydrates, when eaten alone, and especially when your daily rhythm is on the downswing, can make you sleepy and too relaxed to be productive. People over forty, especially women, seem to be especially sensitive to carbohydrate overload, while men under forty tend to feel more relaxed.

Sweet Dreams

Carbohydrates, which stimulate serotonin production, may be most useful at the end of the day, especially if you normally have trouble unwinding. It appears that serotonin is one of several brain chemicals needed to induce and sustain sleep.

A high carbohydrate, low-protein dinner—for example, pasta or cereal—can help set the stage for relaxing, replenishing sleep. A light bedtime snack of a sweet or starchy food may even be as effective as a sleeping pill, especially when it's part of a bedtime ritual that cues the body for sleep. So have milk and cookies—but forget the milk (it contains too much protein, which might block tryptophan entry into the brain).

Preliminary evidence from animal research also suggests that eating sweets may trigger the release of endorphins, the brain's own opiates, blocking pain and producing a sense of euphoria. This may help explain why some people seem to have an insatiable "sweet tooth."

Although the research on food and mood is incomplete, you can experiment in your own internal laboratory. Try a low-fat, high-protein power lunch to see how it affects your alertness in the afternoon. Or have a midafternoon carbohydrate snack. Does it make you feel calmer, better able to concentrate, or more drowsy? If you have trouble sleeping, you might switch to a high-carbohydrate dinner and a bedtime carbohydrate snack.

In addition to indulging in the pleasurable tastes of foods, knowing how you react to the various nutrients may help you control your mood, boost your energy level when you're low, and calm you when you're uptight.

The Life of Spice

Recall our friend Bret at the dinner described in the opening of this chapter. He burned his mouth with hot chili peppers in the pursuit of pleasure. He's not alone. Since its humble beginnings in the New World, the vitamin-rich chili pepper (Capsicum) has spread to ignite the cuisines of Szechuan, India, Thailand, Mexico, and the American Southwest.

Why do people all over the world enjoy burning their mouth out, something that's initially rejected by almost everybody? Chili eaters don't adapt to the burn; except for extreme cases, the burn threshold for the spice is the same for American chili novices as for experienced Mexican chili lovers. Aficionados savor that burning sensation, and feel that chilies improve the appetite and spark up otherwise bland food.

One interesting theory holds that human beings come to like chilies *as a result of the pain they cause.* The pain, though essentially harmless, sparks an exciting defensive reaction.

Like other sought-out dangers, such as riding a roller coaster, watching a horror film, or jumping into a cold lake, eating a hot pepper is "benignly masochistic." It triggers an alarm reaction, but because the situation is not genuinely dangerous, we can enjoy the intense arousal. Eating chili peppers is a controlled risk that can be indulged without fear of harm.

Since so many of us crave that mouth flare-up, it is encouraging to find that modern science recognizes the hidden health benefits of chili peppers. Recent discoveries suggest that chilies may loosen congestion from a cold, burn up excess calories, thin the blood to prevent heart attacks, prevent some types of cancer, supply essential vitamins, and literally keep heads cool. The painful bite of a chili pepper may trigger the release of endorphins, which might explain the euphoria we feel after a fiery meal.

Ironically, the highest consumption of hot chilies is in hot climates. At first glance it may seem strange that people could think of eating hot chilies when the mercury climbs into the hundreds. Yet, chili-spiced foods can actually help us stay cooler. The hot foods trigger massive amounts of sweating—especially of the head and face. As the sweat evaporates it draws away heat from the body, producing the sensation of a cooler head.

Dr. Peppers

Chili peppers may also help prevent blood clots, which can threaten the circulation of the heart and lungs. A group of Thai researchers wondered if something in their cuisine might account for the very low incidence of life-threatening blood clots among their people.

A group of Thai volunteers devoured a plate of tangy noodles spiced with two teaspoons of freshly ground chili pepper, while other subjects consumed plain, spiceless noodles. Immediately after the meal the hot-noodle eaters showed a significant, though brief, increase in clot-dissolving activity in the blood.

One brave woman volunteered to swish a hot pepper solution in her mouth for five minutes without swallowing. She lasted only four minutes and twenty seconds, but showed a similar increase in clot-dissolving activity. This implies that the burning sensation in the mouth may itself trigger blood thinning. The Thai habit of eating hot peppers at nearly every meal may regularly clear the bloodstream of clots.

Chili peppers may also benefit your heart by lowering cholesterol levels. Experiments performed on rabbits showed that doses of capsaicin, the active ingredient in chili, suppressed the liver's production of cholesterol and lowered blood cholesterol levels—even when the rabbits consumed cholesterol-rich foods.

Why Garlic Lovers Can Also Take Heart

There are good reasons to praise the medicinal qualities of another spice, garlic, respectfully known as the "Stinking Rose." Studies of laboratory animals and humans show that generous daily doses of garlic can reduce dangerous LDL cholesterol levels from 10 to 20 percent, while at the same time increasing the heart-saving levels of good HDL cholesterol. Garlic also prevents blood clots and stimulates clot-dissolving activity in the bloodstream; both actions may help avert lethal heart attacks. Other studies support the use of garlic to significantly lower blood pressure by about 20 percent—reductions in the range expected of antihypertensive medications that have side effects well beyond that of bad breath.

A diet rich in garlic may also protect against cancer. Laboratory animals treated with compounds derived from garlic seem to be more resistant to cancer when exposed to chemicals known to cause cancer or injected with tumor cells.

Investigations in the provinces of China also indicate that eating garlic protects us from cancer. Residents in Quixia are ten times more likely to develop stomach cancer than their neighbors in nearby Gangshan County. Garlic may be the critical ingredient: the people of Quixia rarely touch the stuff, but the Gangshanites consume *seven cloves per day*. Garlic reduces nitrites and cancer-causing nitrosamines in the stomaches of the garlic-lovers of Gangshan.

Garlic may also boost immune function. The Japanese garlic extract Kyolic appears to affect the performance of natural killer cells, which comprise one of the first lines of defense against cancer and infection. Consuming the equivalent of twelve to fifteen cloves of garlic per day was found to increase the cancer-destroying capacity of natural killer cells by 140 to 160 percent. Lower doses may also be effective.

So whether you choose the hot stuff like Jalapeno, Serrano, or cayenne, or the milder burn of paprika or even the unique zest of garlic, you can be assured that the pleasures of spicing it up may be good for your health.

ALICIA, Alex, Sophia, and Bret all ate a meal. Alicia became more alert, Alex more relaxed, Sophia more worried, and Bret got pleasantly hot. By understanding a bit more about what we eat, when we eat, and how eating affects our health, the potential of food as a healthy pleasure can be enhanced. As the author of a cookbook written in 1821 proclaimed: "Cookery is the soul of every pleasure, at all times and to all ages. How many marriages have been the consequence of a meeting at dinner, how much good fortune has been the result of a good supper, at what moment of our existence are we happier than at table? There hatred and animosity are lulled to sleep, and pleasure alone reigns."

7

· · · · · · · · · · · · · ·

Why Kill Yourself to Save Your Life?

It's 7:00 A.M. Our neighbor George is just leaving his house to start his daily commute. Although he lives only three miles from work, it takes him a half-hour to get there in bumper-to-bumper morning traffic. Then the real trouble starts. He circles block after block looking for just the right parking spot. He passes up a couple of spaces because they seem a bit far away. Finally, with great satisfaction, George sees someone pull out in front of his office, and he zips right in. He enters the building and stands, waiting, for several minutes for the elevator to arrive. He ascends to the fourth floor, walks across the hall, and sits down in the executive chair behind his desk. Still sitting behind the desk, at lunch he eats a sandwich delivered from the corner deli.

After work George jumps into his car and fights the rush-hour traffic once more. This time it's the crosstown crush on the way to his health club. Again he circles, looking for the closest parking space. He enters the club, dons his sweats and athletic shoes, and chooses his weapon. Today it will be the "Exercist" bicycle—easier on his shins and knees, which he injured running two weeks ago. As he pedals and pants, he repeats "No pain, no gain," and he checks his heart rate periodically to make sure it's in the "optimal target zone" of 125 to 140 beats per minute. He thinks about an upcoming ten-kilometer "Fun Run": will his sore heels and knees be able to make it? He looks forward someday to running a twenty-six-mile marathon or competing in a triathlon.

After exactly thirty minutes of huffing and puffing, sweating and straining, George grunts, dismounts, and hits the showers. It's now 8:00 P. M., and George heads home. Today he has to pay the young boy who is mowing the lawn and talk to the gardener digging up last year's tomatoes.

Now, what's wrong with this picture? George spends almost his entire day abstaining from any meaningful physical activity. Then, four times a week, he faithfully follows his exercise prescription of thirty-plus minutes of aerobic exercise at 70 percent of maximum intensity four times per week. But it has cost him more than he thinks: in injuries, pain, car expenses, parking fees, health club dues, gardener and lawn maintenance fees, and his time commuting to and fro.

But George, like many of us, has confused exercise and physical activity. Exercise is usually a deliberate, sometimes odious, sweat-soaked endeavor that can take time away from life, whereas physical activity can be any daily undertaking, work or play, that involves movement.

Instead of following his exercise prescription, George might have bicycled or walked to work in less time than it took him to drive and park. He could have walked up four flights of stairs instead of waiting for the elevator. He could have skipped the health club altogether and spent the thirty minutes mowing the lawn or working in the garden.

And George could have had fun. He could have used the time it took to drive across town to the club, pedal, shower, and drive home to chase a football with his children, play golf with his friends, or dance with his wife. In forty-five minutes of any of these enjoyable activities, as many calories are burned as in thirty minutes of more intense bicycling, jogging, or swimming. Even a half-hour of spirited love-making has fitness benefits equivalent to swimming the crawl, hiking with a twenty-pound pack, or doing calisthenics. In short, George could have received the *same or greater* health benefits from simple pleasurable activities. But George had joined the Fitness Revolution.

"No pain, no gain"—the battle cry gasped by grim marathon runners as they hastened toward the Holy Grail of Cardiovascular Fitness. Even many armchair athletes agree that we have to suffer for cardiovascular health. But "no pain, no gain" may be on its way to the graveyard, to join other outdated health slogans. Human beings did not evolve to run twenty-six miles at a time, but to walk; we didn't evolve to bench press two hundred pounds, but to carry twenty or thirty pounds long distances.

So ease off: you don't need pain to achieve health. The aches, pains and injuries that accompany most of us who "go for the burn"—for the kind of maximum cardiovascular fitness that wins marathons—are simply an unnecessary price to pay. Cardiovascular fitness is not the fitness you really need to promote health. You really don't have to kill yourself to save your life.

The natural exercise necessary to be healthy is much less than most of us think, and doesn't have to involve burdensome regimes. Ideally, it should be a part of life. For example, gardening—hoeing, digging, pulling weeds, and pushing a lawn mower—can increase heart rates by 20 to 25 percent; for a sedentary person, this may be enough of a boost to improve health. A mile and a half of walking is equivalent to jogging a mile, and for many walking is safer and more enjoyable.

Measurable, pleasurable benefits of exercise for mind and body may be close, easy, and even fun. A flight of stairs here. A brisk walk there, an occasional wild dance, bowling, tennis, squash, football catch, or a swim now and then.

"No pain, no gain" is simply and completely wrong: the *biggest* gain comes with the *least* pain. Every little bit counts and can pay off in better health, particularly at the beginning.

How Much Exercise Do You Really Need?

Fitness should be a healthy pleasure. Popular health advice hypes vigorous aerobic exercise and most often ignores less intense, more enjoyable forms of physical activity. Because of the hype, many people feel discouraged; they can't achieve the ideal prescription of vigorous exercise sessions, and the sleek look of the sinewy models glowing out of magazines covers somehow evades them. So they do nothing.

Human beings, of course, *do* need some daily activity to be healthy, but it need not be a grim regimen. It is true that the life of a modern couch potato is more inert than the life of our ancestors. Our physiology evolved over millions of years to prepare us for physical exertion. Our hunter-gatherer forebears were, from what we can gather, fairly active. The hunt itself required long treks with short bursts of intense exertion. Then the spoils of the hunt had to be carried off many miles to base camp. Gathering food, digging up roots, cutting firewood, and, most important, trekking to the next campsite kept our ancestors active. Even carrying children was physically demanding. (Remember, this was thousands of years before strollers).

Until recent times, survival depended on at least a minimal amount of exercise. Daily living ensured a degree of physical fitness through tilling the soil, lifting wood, and carrying water. We evolved to walk, haul, and bear loads, so we need activity. And it is certainly true that modern society has gone a bit too sedentary. However, our ancestors didn't ever run a twenty-six-mile marathon or pound the pavement for miles each day, but had more continuous, gentler demands, especially long walking.

As an (over)reaction to our sedentary ways, the American College of Sports Medicine issued a formula for fitness which became the credo of the Fitness Revolution of the 1970s.

> Fitness requires 15 to 60 minutes of continuous exercise three to five times per week. Exercise strenuously enough to raise the heart rate to 60 to 90 percent of maximum. (Maximum heart rate is calculated as 220 minus your age.)

So, millions took to the roads, tracks, slopes, exercise bikes, rowing machines, ski simulators, and Nautilus machines while breathlessly repeating this formula to themselves. Many millions more stood on the sidelines, intimidated by this prescription. They were all misled.

It takes very little physical activity to achieve many health benefits. Even the most dedicated sloth can make great gains in health and well-being merely by increasing activity from none to some. Beyond that, there may be diminishing returns.

In a long-term study of nearly seventeen thousand Harvard alumni, it was found that the health benefits began for those who burned up as few as five hundred calories a week. That could be achieved by a fifteen-minute walk each day, two hours of bowling, or a one-hour squash game per week! Even with this modest level of activity, death rates declined by 20 percent. Granted, you might get even more benefit by burning up two thousand or more calories a week (death rates dropped another 10 to 20 percent). However, *the bulk of the benefit accrued to those who went from complete couch potatoes to modest movers*.

According to another study of twelve thousand middle-aged men, those who used about sixteen hundred calories a week in leisure activities had nearly 40 percent fewer fatal heart attacks than those who burned less than five hundred calories a week. That's only a half-hour a day of walking, gardening, dancing, doing chores, fishing, golf, or bowling. However, logging in over two hours a day of more intense activity and consuming a hefty forty-five hundred calories a week in hard exercise *did not further decrease cardiac fatalities.*

Evidence from over forty studies indicates that people who are physically *in*active have roughly twice the rate of heart disease and heart attacks as do more active people. That makes complete physical *in*activity approximately as risky as cigarette smoking, high blood pressure, and high cholesterol. Stepping up daily physical activity even a little can markedly reduce the risk of heart disease.

The benefits of moderate physical activity go well beyond the heart. Lung capacity goes up, cancer rates go down. Regular exercise not only helps burn calories but adjusts the body's metabolic rate to offset the metabolic slowdown that occurs with dieting. And there are more promising findings for those interested in preventing osteoporosis: Even a low level of exercise—say three hours of walking each week—helps build bone density in people below age thirty, and slows bone loss in older people. And physical activity may also help boost immunity to infection.

Another reason to consider easier, more agreeable physical activity is that strenuous exercise can hurt. Every year, 20 percent of all joggers who run ten miles per week are injured severely enough to have to cut back on their exercise. The injury rate rises to 40 percent for those logging thirty miles of pounding the pavement. Injury rates also skyrocket for those who exercise vigorously *every day*, those who spend longer than thirty to forty-five minutes per session in strenuous exercise, or those who go at it with a vengeance at 90 percent of capacity. The tortoise who keeps a steady pace is more likely to pass the running rabbits nursing their injured feet, knees, and backs on the side of the road.

Extremely high levels of exercise can also wreak havoc on women's reproductive systems. Some women may not ovulate, or they might miss their menstrual periods. Hormone levels may drop, increasing the risk of osteoporosis. Also, early research in laboratory animals suggests that the benefits of moderate exercise on reducing cancer rates may disappear at higher levels of exercise. If a little is good, a lot may not be better.

For the Fun of It

Gentle exercise can make you feel terrific. When you begin an exercise program you improve mood, happiness, confidence, and body image, and achieve a sense of self-mastery. *It doesn't take much exercise to make a difference*: walking a mile or two substantially reduces your anxiety level. And it doesn't seem to matter whether you walk slowly or fast.

Exercise can dramatically boost your energy level. For as long as two hours after taking a brisk ten-minute walk, people feel increases in energy and decreases in fatigue and tension. Even short daily walks can make personal problems seem less serious and boost optimism.

Exercise can also work wonders for depression. A group of mildly to moderately depressed patients were randomly assigned either to run or to receive psychotherapy. Within a week most of the runners reported feeling better; within three weeks they were "virtually well," with the beneficial results lasting at least a year. The runners did as well as patients receiving short-term psychotherapy, and did *better* than patients undergoing unlimited long-term therapy.

But how does exercise work its mental wonders? Endorphins, the body's own opiates, are released during the stress and pain of extremely vigorous exercise. The euphoria, or "runner's high," that energizes some long-distance runners may be due to a spurt of these chemicals. On the other hand, when exercisers are injected with a drug that blocks the action of endorphins, they still report reduced anxiety, tension, depression, anger, and hostility. So endorphins aren't the only actors: other chemicals may contribute to the benefits of exercise. For example, norepinephrine levels, low in some depressed people, may rise with exercise and help stabilize mood.

There are social and psychological benefits, too, from satisfying physical activity. Getting together with others for exercise or sport may improve your mood as a result of the social activity. Exercise may provide a channel for the body's excess energy, a healthy way to release anger and anxiety, and an outlet for the physical tensions associated with the "fight-or-flight syndrome."

Taking the time to focus on a sport, or a game, or the view while taking a walk can distract you from your troubles and provide a "time-out" from work and personal problems. This may be one reason why even though housework such as mopping and scrubbing the floors may burn calories, it doesn't seem to provide the same mental refreshment that comes from purely recreational pursuits. You need to decide for yourself what kind of action can give you pleasure, and set aside some time for it.

Whether you go for physical activity that burns five hundred calories or a more ambitious two thousand calories a week, there are many safe, pleasurable ways to get more physical and improve your health. (For more details, see pages 111–115).

Look for opportunities to include more physical activity in the everyday things you do. You may not have time to "exercise," but if you build pleasant physical activities into your life you won't need to set aside additional time. Park your car at some distance from your destination and walk. Take stairs instead of elevators. Climb a hill. Walk through the park. Talk vigorously and wave your arms; "aerobic talking" burns a lot of calories! Instead of driving to the store all the time, walk and carry a bag of groceries home.

Take seriously dancing, bowling, playing with your children, or golfing. These moderate activities may be frowned on by fitness fanatics, but they can make significant, pleasurable contributions to your health. And don't underestimate the boost from aerobic gardening. You can usefully, and often pleasurably, burn up nearly three-hundred calories an hour raking leaves, pushing a lawn mower, using a hoe, or pulling weeds. Gardening gets you outside and, instead of running nowhere, you end up growing something new, something alive. And you can burn up almost as much in sex, too.

We're not saying that people who wish to push their bodies to the limits shouldn't do so, but that this isn't necessary for better health. So if you do enjoy the feeling of strenuous workouts, fine. But remember that if you are active in your everyday life you won't have to exert yourself as much. And you won't hurt yourself. Don't obsess over the numbers. Relax and enjoy the activity. People who think pleasant thoughts ("go slow and smell the roses") while they exercise are more likely to continue with it than if they concentrate on bodily sensations (i.e., pain) or challenging goals.

Above all, pick activities that you enjoy and, remember, this is supposed to be fun. As we'll see, the pleasurable feeling of moving may be more relaxing for many than lying quietly trying to "relax."

The following chart shows the approximate number of calories per minute burned during various activities. Multiply the number of minutes you do an activity by the number of calories burned per minute to estimate the total calories expended. The actual number of calories varies depending upon how vigorously and constantly you do the activity as well as how much you weigh. Values are given for a person weighing 120 pounds and 180 pounds, so you may need to adjust the number of calories burned up or down depending upon your weight.

CALORIE BURNERS: Activities That Add Up

ACTIVITY	CALORIES EXPENDED (per minute)	
	120 lbs.	180 lbs.
Aerobic dance	6.2	8.2
Backpacking (40 lb. pack)	5.8	7.9
Badminton	4.8	6.5
Basketball (halfcourt)	4.3	5.6
Bicycling (13 mph)	9.0	14.0
Bowling	2.9	4.0
Canoeing (4 mph)	5.7	8.4
Climbing stairs	6.3	8.4
Dancing (ballroom)	4.0	5.4
Dancing (rock 'n' roll)	6.0	8.0
Dancing (square)	5.8	7.7
Football (touch)	4.3	5.8
Gardening (weeding, digging)	5.4	7.2
Golf (carrying clubs)	3.5	4.8
Gymnastics	4.4	6.0
Handball	8.5	11.5
Hiking	4.3	5.8
Horseback riding	3.4	4.6
Jogging (5.5 mph)	9.2	12.5
Judo	4.4	6.0

CALORIE BURNERS: Activities That Add Up (*cont'd.*)

ACTIVITY	CALORIES EXPENDED (per minute)	
	120 lbs.	180 lbs.
Making beds	3.0	4.5
Mopping	3.5	4.2
Mowing lawn (handmower)	4.2	5.3
Ping Pong	3.4	4.6
Playing with children	4.0	5.3
Pool; billiards	1.8	2.5
Racquetball	8.5	11.5
Raking leaves and dirt	3.1	4.0
Rope jumping	9.9	13.4
Rowing (crew)	11.6	15.7
Running (6.5 mph)	9.6	12.6
Sailing	2.6	3.5
Scrubbing (walls, tub)	4.0	5.0
Sexual intercourse (active partner)	4.2	5.5
Shopping	3.6	5.4
Shoveling snow	8.0	10.0
Skating (ice)	5.0	6.7
Skating (roller)	5.0	6.7
Skiing (cross country)	9.9	13.4
Skiing (downhill)	8.5	11.5
Soccer	7.7	10.4
Softball (fast pitch)	4.0	5.4
Squash	8.5	11.5
Surfing	7.8	10.6

CALORIE BURNERS: Activities That Add Up (*cont'd.*)

ACTIVITY	CALORIES EXPENDED (per minute)	
	120 lbs.	180 lbs.
Swimming (50 yd. per min.)	8.8	12.6
Tennis (doubles)	4.0	6.0
Tennis (singles)	6.0	8.0
Volleyball	5.0	6.7
Walking (2 mph)	3.0	4.8
Walking (4.5 mph)	5.5	9.0
Washing dishes by hand	1.8	2.6
Waterskiing	6.8	9.2
Weight training	6.7	9.0
Wood (chopping or sawing)	5.8	7.5

Exercise Lite: Pleasurable Ways to Burn 500+ Calories*

There are many enjoyable ways to get the health benefits from burning a *minimum* of 500 calories per week in pleasurable physical activity. Of course, you may find that you'll want to go for 1,000 or 2,000 calories of fun.

SUNDAY	MONDAY	TUESDAY	WEDNESDAY	THURSDAY	FRIDAY	SATURDAY
15 minutes of walking (72 calories)	20 minutes of sex (110 calories)	15 minutes of walking (72 calories)		15 minutes of walking (72 calories)	20 minutes of sex (110 calories)	20 minutes of sex (110 calories)
1 hour of shopping (324 calories)		20 minutes of playing with children (106 calories)				20 minutes of mowing lawn (106 calories)

30 minutes of gardening (216 calories)					45 minutes of ballroom dancing (324 calories)	
			45 minutes of bowling (180 calories)			1 hour of hiking (348 calories)
20 minutes of raking leaves (80 calories)	1 minute of climbing stairs (8 calories)	30 minutes of pool/ billiards (70 calories)				45 minutes of roller skating (301 calories)

* The estimated calories burned in the examples are for a 180-pound person.

8

. . . .

The Rest

Why Relaxation Isn't Always Relaxing

When you think of relaxing, what images come to mind? Sitting quietly, meditating, contemplating a sunset? Not everybody thinks so. For some people this type of relaxation can provoke anxiety. On the other hand, you would hardly think that driving a race car at over a hundred and fifty miles an hour or plummeting thousands of feet out of an airplane, only to arrest your fall at the very last second by pulling a parachute cord, could be very relaxing. Yet many people find that thrilling stimulation relaxes them much more than sitting quietly contemplating their navel.

Not everyone finds "relaxing" relaxing. In one study of anxious patients, nearly half reported feeling more anxious when they started to meditate. When they attempted deep muscle relaxation, nearly a third suffered increased restlessness, sweating, heart-pounding, and rapid breathing.

One cause of relaxation-induced anxiety may be a reaction to the new sensations—heaviness, floating, tingling, or muscle twitches—that sometimes accompany states of relaxation. Another may be fear of losing control or an aversion to self-observation.

One reason for so many different ways to relax is because

there are different types of tension, anxiety, fear, and fatigue. Some people tend to experience stress more in their bodies. For instance, do you often feel tight muscles, aches and pains, nervous stomach, racing heartbeat, or jittery? If so, you're probably more of a "body reactor." On the other hand, do you suffer more from excessive worrying, difficulty concentrating because of distracting thoughts, anxiety-provoking images intruding into your mind, or problems with your "mind racing?" In this case, you may be experiencing stress more as a "mind reactor."

Of course, each of us reacts to stress in body and mind. After hours of writing or number-crunching you may feel mentally fatigued or bored. However, switching to another activity, even if it is physically strenuous, can revive you. Understanding your symptoms can help you better select the type of relaxation that may work best.

By matching the type of relaxation strategy you use to the type of tension (body or mind) you are experiencing, you may be able to relax more readily. If you are feeling more body tension, you might try muscle relaxation, deep breathing, walking, or a hot bath or sauna. If mental distraction and worrying is your problem, you might try a mind-absorbing approach. This includes meditation, visualization and imagery, watching television, going to the movies, listening to music, reading, or losing yourself (and your tension) in a hobby or game. Vigorous exercise and competitive sports tend to be good for relaxing both physical and mental tension.

If a certain relaxation method makes you more tense, try another one (see page 271). Or shift back and forth between techniques. Sometimes a mental relaxer will work better for body tension, and vice versa, so don't hesitate to experiment. Remember, true relaxation is more than a matter of sitting down and practicing a relaxation technique for twenty minutes a day. It's not like popping a pill. As much as you can, allow everyday activities and involvement in work, play, and hobbies be your relaxers.

Getting in Sync

People differ greatly in their optimal set point for stimulation. You may feel that you hunger for a different level of excitement at different moments. We all teeter on the brink of overload and boredom. Shifting gears and changing speed to find the optimal level of stimulation seems to be the key, rather than being locked into one technique or exercise, whether it be twenty minutes of sitting silently or twenty minutes of running.

How can we recognize when we are getting the right amount of stimulation? There is an intuitive sense of being in balance. Some people refer to it as "being in sync" or experiencing a sensation of "flowing." It has a timeless or, at least, out-of-time quality. You focus attention fully on the activity, and self-consciousness fades into the background. A sense of control and engagement pervades your participation.

This comes from total immersion and involvement in a work or leisure activity, particularly one in which there is a balance between the demands of the situation and your skills and capabilities. It could be an intense game of tennis against an equally matched opponent. (If you are much better than your partner or vice versa, the game is more likely to result in frustration or demoralization than in an enlivening sense of absorption.)

Many healthy pleasures can provide opportunities to experience this sensation of optimal stimulation: involvement with work, sports, or games, talking to a pet, shopping, or joking with friends; listening to music or playing an instrument, walking, running, eating, reading, watching television, or daydreaming.

"Now I Lay Me Down To Sleep . . ."

What would you be willing to give up good food or hot sex for, or even risk your life for? Many people would say "nothing" but they'd be wrong. We give up a lot of our life for sleep. Most of us, if sleepy enough, would forgo almost any pleasure. We might even forfeit life itself by falling asleep at the wheel to capture a few moments of delicious, compelling sleep—our essential rest.

The Pleasures of Napping

Winston Churchill, a confirmed napper, wrote, "Nature had not intended man to work from eight in the morning until midnight without the refreshment of blessed oblivion, which, even if it lasts only twenty minutes, is sufficient to renew all vital forces." Nevertheless, modern work life seldom allows time for midday naps. Most people imagine that the natural sleep pattern is a single long period at night followed by extended alertness during daylight. But what nature already knows, science may now be confirming: the value of napping.

When people in a laboratory were allowed to sleep without restrictions, an interesting pattern developed: in addition to normal hours of night sleep, they began to prefer a midday nap. This afternoon snooze tends to be restful, "slow wave," sleep. Outside the laboratory, napping is quite common among college students and elderly people, two groups often liberated from conventional demands of work and time.

The napless day we usually experience is probably an unnatural, fairly recent innovation. Our early ancestors possibly slept through the darkness of the night, hunted in the early morning, then escaped the midday heat by napping in a shady spot. Our biological rhythms appear programmed for a midday rest, accounting for the afternoon slump—that listless, dreamy mental state most of us experience.

A catnap can be very refreshing—relaxing your body, improving your mood, clearing the mind, and offering a break from the stressful pace of daily life. With an afternoon liedown, you probably don't even have to sleep to get the rejuvenation you need. In one study, a group of students were invited to either nap, rest quietly in a darkened room, or watch a nature video for one hour. After *either* napping or resting, they reported being more alert and clear-headed, and less anxious, confused, and fatigued.

Life-Saving Siestas

An afternoon nap may also help us by-pass heart disease. In general, people living in the tropics and in Mediterranean countries have much lower rates of coronary heart disease than those in Northern Europe or North America. Though there are many important contrasts between these countries, one intriguing difference is the virtual absence of the afternoon siesta in heart attack country.

In a hospital in Greece, a team of researchers compared the sleep habits of ninety-seven male heart-attack victims with the habits of ninety comparable patients without heart problems. Those who routinely took a thirty-minute afternoon nap were 30 percent less likely to suffer a heart attack. For those taking a double doze, that is, an hour or more of siesta time, the chance of a heart attack was cut almost in half.

There is further evidence that sufficient sleep protects health. In a study of over five thousand adults over nine years, those subjects who slept seven to eight hours a night had the lowest death rates for heart disease, cancer, and stroke—in fact, for all causes of death. The short sleepers (six or fewer hours per night) and the long sleepers (nine or more hours) were 30 percent more likely to die prematurely.

In another study, people who slept for extremely brief or

extended periods had 50 to 280 percent higher death rates from heart disease, stroke, cancer, and suicide. Neither study distinguished between those for whom short or long sleep was natural or forced by circumstances or stress. So, while excessively short or long sleep may not be the actual cause of death, these findings may still be something to make you gain or lose sleep over.

Wake Up Your Immune System

The advice to get a good night's rest to prevent disease may be more than just folklore: a biochemical link has been found between deep sleep and the function of the cells of our immune systems.

A variety of chemicals, including muramyl peptides, interleukin-1, and interferon, trigger slow-wave sleep—the deepest, most restful kind—as well as rouse the immune system into action. A study of six healthy volunteers revealed that the onset of slow-wave sleep correlated with a surge in blood levels of one of these chemical messengers in our immune system. In addition to giving us the sleepies, this messenger appears to stimulate lymphocytes and natural killer cells that defend the body against viral and bacterial infections, and, possibly, cancer.

This biochemical language common to the sleeping brain and the waking immune system may help us understand why people feel sleepy when they are ill. Is it due to the illness itself, or to an intelligent recuperative response of the organism which arouses the immune system while resting the rest of the body? The answers are not known, but a good night's rest may be protective.

Why Sleep, Anyway?

Despite thousands of years of speculation and over fifty years of scientific investigation, the reasons we sleep away nearly one-third of our lives remain a mystery. Did sleep evolve to help keep us out of harm's way? Sleeping animals would be less likely to stumble onto a predator. Sleep immobilizes us and may help conserve energy by reducing needless movement during the dark hours. Or perhaps sleep—what Macbeth called "balm of hurt minds, great nature's second course; chief nourisher in life's feast"—provides an opportunity for restoring vital bodily processes. Though the body may appear quiet, sleep is a time of great activity and tissue repair. Still, it may not be sleep itself that restores the body. Rather, sleep may simply force us to keep still, to get rest and relaxation.

We do know that the brain requires sleep for restoration. Unlike most other organs, it can't relax outside of sleep. But even during sleep the cerebral cortex reshuffles and reorganizes the waking day's events. We experience that reorganization as a dream, an often incoherent and bizarre combination of events. When we are deprived of sleep, it is the brain which suffers most. Thoughts become disorganized; memory lapses, irritability, and confusion reign. "The madman is a waking dreamer," wrote Immanuel Kant.

The reward of sleep is often recognized by its absence. Millions of people spend night after night tossing and turning in a sleepless living hell. They stumble about day after day, weary and bleary-eyed, the "waking wounded." Irritable, listless, robbed of the pleasures of sleep, they also lose a vital mental sharpness and the zest for living. They are victims of a growing "national sleep debt." And this deficit may have a profound effect on the health of our society.

If you have trouble sleeping, you may be suffering from a sleep disorder, or maybe you simply aren't sleepy enough. *To sleep better, make sure you get tired.* There are two kinds of tiredness, mental and physical, and each seems to have different effects on sleep. Healthy doses of regular physical activity and/or taking a hot bath seems to produce deeper, more restful slow-wave sleep. However, if you do exercise, many people find the late afternoon the best time. Vigorous exercise after six in the evening can be stimulating, possibly making it more difficult to fall asleep.

In contrast to being physically tired, the mental fatigue that generally follows intense intellectual activity or emotional distress usually produces an unpleasant feeling of having been "drained." This type of mental exhaustion may interfere with sleep and may benefit from some of the mind-absorbing techniques we discussed earlier.

Our World and the World We've Lost

So far, we've described ways to reintroduce some missing sensuality into your life, from ways of resting to ways of touching. We've done so because our society is the first to have lost touch with the natural human world. It is a world we long for—in our bones, in our cells, in our hearts. We are transforming the world that made us into a world we make. And we have made that world increasingly one that deprives us of vital sensory pleasure.

Until the end of the last century, most people lived surrounded by or close to lands which contained plants and animals, so gazing at nature was unavoidable. These lands are now being destroyed to grow silicone chips, or sprout supermarkets. Our birthright demands closeness and human contact, yet many people are now starving to be touched. We can't rely anymore on the natural match between life, work, activity, and health. Instead we need to seize more sensuality from the world when and where we can.

Doing so, we can fracture bad moods and expand pleasures. Some of these, like saunas and exercises, have immediate and direct health rewards; others, such as looking outside ourselves, over the horizon, or even at fish, influence us strongly, but not as directly. There's more to looking outside ourselves and being part of the larger life around, and more to learn about the mental barriers to pleasure.

We turn, now, to ways of shifting the mind to experience more pleasure, optimism, intimacy, and health.

THREE

Mental Investment

9

. . . .

". . . And the Pursuit
of Happiness"

I've been riding the carousel in Central Park since I was
five years old. Back then there were silver and gold rings.
You had to get five silver rings or one gold ring to get a
free ride. I spent my childhood in Central park because I
went to school on Central Park West. If I'm very depressed
or if something's bothering me today, my husband, Larry,
and I go back to the park. We get on the carousel horse
and we start riding, and I start singing at the top of my
lungs. It is pure and absolute joy and happiness.

—*Eda LeShan*

Being happy should be easy—we have our pick of sweet
smells, sunlight, massages, natural views, and uplifting music. However, even if we accept such invitations to sensual
pleasure, we might still find a good mood elusive. Many
people have their fill of sensuality and the "good things" in
life—a lovely home with a swimming pool, trips around the
world, a large income—and still don't seem very happy or
healthy.

The problem lies in the human mind, which filters,
screens, censors, and ultimately passes final judgment on
our overall happiness. The surge from good experiences to

good feelings can easily be blocked by the negative internal stories we tell ourselves. As Abraham Lincoln said, "A man is as happy as his mind allows him to be." So how can we change our minds to allow ourselves real happiness?

We carry within us very different ideas about what should make us happy. And in each of us, these ideas form stories about growing up, marriage, work, morality, and pleasure. These stories come to reside within us like a political ideology. Sometime while growing up—no one really knows exactly how or when—we establish our life story, a set of beliefs, assumptions, and expectations about ourselves and the world we live in.

One person's story about happiness might be, "I can't be happy until I am married and have two healthy children." Another's might be, "I can't be happy unless I am an officer of the company I work for." Yet a different version might be, "I can't be happy until all people on Earth have an adequate amount of food."

These expectations are basic to the way the mind works, and determine a lot more of our life than we might think. For we base most of our judgments upon a shifting scale of standards, and not on facts. For example, a political candidate does well or badly "compared to expectations." Someone doing "better than expected" in the polls is judged to do well, while another, who might be getting more votes but doing worse than expected, is seen to do poorly.

Similarly, a person might have a comfortable income, but because she is not doing as well as her colleagues in business, she takes little pleasure in her life. Another person might have a perfectly wonderful home, but because he doesn't live in exactly the right neighborhood, in a residence that might have pleased his parents, he may be miserable. Still others base their happiness on the amount of social injustice in the world, often discounting any improvements made or how much their own life is pleasurable.

It is crucial to know that our judgments, even about something as "obvious" as the color of an object, are based on comparisons, not on absolute reality. These comparisons are important to the pleasure principle. If you can control your comparisons, you might be able to shift your judgment toward increased optimism and happiness. *For happiness lies in narrowing the distance between where you see yourself and where you expect to be.*

A more robust experience of life—reclaiming the sensuality lost in the modern world—should be a first step toward a richer existence. However, if the benefits are discounted in our minds, they don't endow us with real pleasure. If we set ourselves up, even unconsciously, to think pessimistically, sensual experiences and life achievements contribute little to our happiness and health.

We need to invest in our mental life in the same way we invest our money or our time. Our minds can shift to allow us greater health and happiness if we learn the tricks of sound mental investing. For this reason, we shall now turn our attention from the sensual to the mental. There are two aims here: first, to become aware of how people tell themselves what the world is like; and second, to learn how some people, with fewer advantages than others, arrange their lives to be healthy and happy.

THE mind can enhance enjoyment, or squelch it. Taking a sauna can be dismissed as a frivolity, owning a pet as a waste of food, receiving a massage as narcissistic self-indulgence. A plant in a hospital room could be considered a contaminant or going to a silly comedy a waste of time. No time to play, no time to smell the roses.

But we can influence our wheeling, dealing, changing, churning mind. The human mind is built to play tricks on us, so that our situation seems much more constant, self-centered, and unchanging than it really is. If we understand this, we can learn to play the game too.

This chapter focuses on how our thought processes, judgments, and ideas about the sources of happiness can interfere with that happiness. We will examine ways in which we can change our minds and moods to maintain our health when we are well, and restore it when we are ill.

Knowing Happiness

There is no good reason why most of us can't make ourselves happy. However, it takes some searching to spot the right opportunities. If more of us know *about happiness*, and about what determines happiness, many more might *know happiness* itself.

The pursuit of happiness may be an inalienable right guaranteed by the Declaration of Independence, but social attitudes block a pleasurable and happy life. Some of the stumbling blocks arise from misconceptions about the nature and sources of well-being.

Those healthy and happy men and women we wrote about at the beginning of the book haven't made a formal study of happiness. They seem, somehow, to live in a way that attracts health and joy. But the option for the rest of us isn't "Born to be happy or else"—condemned to desolation row for life. Happiness *can* be taught. One problem is the mystique around being happy and a kind of embargo connected with approaching it. "I know that [some admired person] is really happy, but nothing I do ever makes me happy. I'm successful, have a good marriage, a good income, but . . ."

Since it is so central to our lives, it's surprising that the majority of women and men don't target *happiness* as a primary goal. Most of us lower our sights and aim for halfway rewards. Many of us believe that well-being depends almost solely upon success on the job, so we separate work from life and aim for wealth, status, power, and property.

All this striving *has* paid off for society as a whole: our affluence is unprecedented. The wealth of many ordinary citizens now greatly exceeds that of all but the richest in any other culture. In personal affairs we lust after great loves, unflagging adulation from our families, and hope for countless other things all great and memorable.

Unfortunately, for many, the actuality doesn't match their lofty aspirations: they don't move up in business, or link up to a successful family life, or rack up prominent social status and so they wind up unhappy. Others "make it" in their career and family life and still find they're not satisfied. Then they wonder why all these great experiences don't make them as joyful as they hoped.

The problem for those of us who aren't born happy is how to get there, or, more accurately, where to go: *which* events, *which* states of mind, *which* decisions really produce happiness, and, in turn, promote health.

There is a surprise here: many people search for happiness in the extreme highs of emotion, money and status. And they are misled to do so. It is not those unforgettable and sought-after "great" events or memorable successes or excesses of power that bring happiness. Instead *many small and often overlooked daily events*, even trite and obvious experiences, add up in the long run.

Let's examine how you rate your own happiness. To begin, please mark the place on the scale below which indicates how happy you are at the present time. On this scale, 9 is the happiest you could be, and 1 the most unhappy.

not at all   1   2   3   4   5   6   7   8   9   very

Where do you think most people in our society would judge themselves? The average rating turns out to be approximately 6.5 on the scale.

Now let's see how some major events, positive and negative, affect your sense of well-being. First, contemplate the
best and the worst experiences that happen to you: say,
winning first prize in a large lottery or becoming incurably
paraplegic.

Suppose you won a lottery and got a tax-free windfall of
ten million dollars. How happy do you think you would be
a year after winning this lottery? Again, on a scale of 1 to
9, choose a number that best reflects this.

Now, suppose the worst has happened—you were in a
terrible accident which left you alive, but barely, and you
lost the use of your legs and became paraplegic. A year later,
how happy do you think you would be? Again, pick a
number between 1 and 9.

If you are like most people, you would assume that winning the lottery would move you right up the scale toward
the top—a 9—and that becoming a paraplegic would stretch
you downwards and more or less zero you out.

However, in reality the results turn out to be quite different. When lottery winners were surveyed immediately after
winning, they were much happier. But one year after winning, their happiness rating virtually dropped back to where
it was before the lottery, increasing only slightly from 6.5 to
6.8. And when paraplegics were surveyed, the happiness
rating after one year dropped only about one-half point,
from about 6.5 to 6.

These scores are approximated below. The paraplegics' is
marked **P**, the average is **A**, and lottery winners' is **L**.

not at all   1   2   3   4   5   6   7   8   9   very
                                    ^ ^ ^
                                    PAL

You are probably a bit surprised with respect to how little
happiness changes even after delightful or devastating life
changes. The majority of people guess that they would be
devastated forever if they lost the use of their limbs. Getting

around town would be a major difficulty, even getting something from the refrigerator would be hard. What if I lost my key on the floor? Could I ever enjoy sports? And, of course, what about romance?

But the happiness of actual paraplegics doesn't match our expectations. Of course, there is an initial period of shock and dismay after the trauma. But even after this extreme damage, the sufferers' lives aren't as dismal as most people would imagine.

The same kind of surprisingly small alteration in happiness occurs in lottery winners a year after they win. Imagine how thrilled you'd be winning first prize in a lottery. No more worry about work. You might finally move up to a big new house with a pool, quit work and travel around the world. Maybe you'd buy a grand home in the South of France or a chalet in Aspen, or a beach house in Maui, or get a new Mercedes roadster and a big limo. Maybe you'd do all of these. Fine art, fine dinners, and a fine life would be yours. You might even make an appearance on *Lifestyles of the Rich and Famous*. It seems obvious that, over the long term, people who win a lottery are much happier than those who do not.

Nonetheless, lottery winners are almost no happier one year after winning than before they won. Interestingly, the winners found *considerably less pleasure in daily life activities*—their relationships, working around the house, their job if they did not leave it, taking care of the garden—than did those who had not won. Why? The winners adapted to their new fortune; as a result, their expectations, and what is called their "comparison level," probably shifted upwards.

To understand this, we need to consider how our mental yardsticks are constructed and how they change with new experience. If our minds accurately represented reality, there would be no problem; more money, status, power, or privilege would increase our happiness. But they don't. Why?

The mind tries to make an inconstant world seem constant, so our judgment is not truly objective. How we view any event or experience depends upon *what we are comparing it with at that moment*. Suppose your boss hands you $100 at the end of the year. You are delighted, because you weren't expecting anything. But suppose she tells you that she was originally going to give you $1,000, then changed her mind. In either case you receive the same amount, but by comparing the $100 to the "lost" $1,000, your happiness is discounted.

We apply incongruous comparisons at different times. A friend of ours, who usually complains about paying more than $250 for a suit or $195 for a sport jacket, recently bought a jacket for more than $450. He luxuriated in the dapper blue linen blazer, a style no one else was wearing at the time. But the high price? How could he justify it? Easy. He told us, "It isn't one of [famous designer's] top-of-the-line signature models. Do you know how expensive *those* jackets are? Why, some of them cost more than $800!" So, the $450 purchase can rest securely in his mind as a bargain, *compared with what he might have spent*.

As most people become more and more prosperous, it takes more and more to satisfy them. Remember buying your first car? Even if you bought an old clunker, it was probably a memorable event. Buying your second car, a good, standard, economy sedan, wasn't as spectacular an adventure, but you might have found it a real improvement. Having a fortune and buying a Rolls Royce, however, may prove to be unexpectedly disappointing. Why? These disenchantments come about as a result of the shifting level of our comparisons.

At the beginning, being able to drive anywhere at will may seem miraculous, especially compared to waiting for the bus. Your first car, then, is a fantastic change upwards from your comparison level. (And there is going out late on dates.) Later on, a car that simply doesn't break down when you need it may also feel wonderful in comparison to that old clunker you just got rid of.

But when you finally hit the jackpot and buy the Rolls, you expect much more from it. You are hardly amazed when the Rolls starts every time in the morning. It is obvious that you can count on it to keep you drier than standing outside in the rain waiting for the bus. And, it damn well better get you around town any time. When you nab the Rolls, however, you expect much more from it—prestige, comfort, speed, which you never imagined could come from the first car or from the adequate sedan that pleased you before the lottery.

Then you begin to dwell upon the shortcomings of the Rolls Royce, not its virtues: the Rolls doesn't look as good as a BMW. It isn't as comfortable as a Cadillac. It isn't as safe as a Volvo. It isn't as reliable as a Mercedes Benz. Besides there is now a newer model just released with improvements you just can't live without. These "it isn'ts" are the tipoff: they're the hallmark of your suddenly inflated expectations. Your mind is now filled with what you *don't* have rather than what you *do* have. The Rolls is half empty, but the clunker was half full. And you were elated with your first clunker, but now you're quite disappointed in the Rolls.

The negative comparisons have served to depreciate your happiness. Your mind, trying to keep things uniform, adjusted your comparison level. When you got rich, your comparison level changed: it takes more to keep you happy now. It changes, too, in other areas of life: in education, friendship, marriage, and health.

We should experience happiness as a result of what happens to us. Instead, we gauge it by comparing what has gone before and what is yet to come with a flexible mental yardstick. However, knowledge of our shifting basis of judgment can allow us to increase happiness, in part, by changing our frame of reference. We'll discuss how later on.

Is the Road to Happiness Really Paved with Gold?

Though many people stake their happiness (and lives) on the accumulation of wealth, vast amounts of wealth don't increase happiness very much, perhaps as an end result of shifted comparison levels. What, then, happens when an entire society, such as ours, increases prosperity year after year? Surveys conducted in the United States indicate that happiness goes up and down, and up and down again, from era to era. In 1946, 39 percent of those surveyed said they were very happy (7–9 on our scale). In the late '50s, the figure was 53 percent. Between 1971 and 1974, it was 27 percent; and in the late 1970s, 35 percent. During this 30-year period, the average income in this country increased dramatically, by more than 50 percent.

Given this increase in wealth, why such a small rise in happiness? Our conceptions of happiness may include some vestigial beliefs inherited from the late nineteenth and early twentieth centuries, when increasing material progress did bring many people happiness. For many, if not most, people in the western world, life in the nineteenth century was as a rule an existence where the primary aspiration was escaping poverty, establishing a skill or a profession, finding good schooling, and trying to get adequate or good housing.

And they succeeded: the increased wealth paid off, and happiness increased. And this relationship is still true today in societies where the average income is low, and necessities like shelter and good food are not plentiful. For example, in India and Malaysia increases in wealth still bring increased happiness, as is true of those below the poverty line in Western societies.

However, in our culture, once a person has attained a

minimal standard of wealth—owning a car (even if it is not the best) and an adequate, if not palatial, place to live, when you can get education (even in state schools) and adequate, if not gourmet, food—increases in wealth don't seem to matter as much as we think and certainly don't merit planning our whole lives around them. The bottom line: If you want money to make you happy, you'll have to be poor.

Is Happiness Hopeless?

Most of us are heirs to pervasive cultural assumptions, such as the work ethic, which direct thought away from pleasure. One important concept is that human beings cling to familiar, pleasurable routines, but our innovative nature disrupts our lives, stability, and pleasures. This conflict is expressed poignantly by the Czech author Milan Kundera in his novel *The Unbearable Lightness of Being*.

He offers a tiny vignette on the nature of happiness. The heroine, Tereza, has developed a daily routine: each morning she gives her beloved dog, Karenin, a roll. Day after day he takes the offered roll in his mouth and joyfully parades around the house again and again before devouring his prize in front of Tereza and her lover, Tomas.

> The love between dog and man is idyllic. It knows no conflicts, no hair-raising scenes; it knows no development. Karenin surrounded Tereza and Tomas with a life based on repetition, and he expected the same from them.
>
> If Karenin had been a person instead of a dog, he would surely have long since said to Tereza, "Look, I'm sick and tired of carrying that roll in my mouth every day. Can't you come up with something different?" And therein lies the whole of man's plight. Human time does not turn in a circle; it runs ahead in a straight line. That is why man cannot be happy; happiness is the longing for repetition.

Yes, happiness is the longing for repetition, Tereza said to herself.

Kundera observes that the longing for repeat performances is a retreat. Human beings, in this "progressive" view, cannot rest in the comfort of past experiences, since we are continually driven to progress. It is the human urge, then, to reconstruct ourselves constantly and move on and move forward.

Happiness is the orphan of progress. Unlike other animals, human beings transform the world, and in that alchemy we lose the comforting routines and stability that support happiness.

While dogs and children may relish the security of familiar routines—games played again and again, stories told and retold—adults are urged to leave such pleasures behind. In the modern world, men and women, equipped with a brain and biology better suited to an older, simpler, and more comforting one, now face new challenges.

We are victims of the new world we've created. Harassments of all sorts, from loss of car keys to loss of a loved one, attack us. The flight-or-fight response which evolved to allow the body to cope with physical threats is now repeatedly mobilized. Financial difficulties, unsympathetic bosses, traffic jams, and unemployment are met with adrenaline, rapid heart rate, increased respiration, moist palms, and tense muscles.

This constant reaction to change often results in disease, much as germs cause infections. The answer for many is to calm out, don't get excited, and try to shun anything that might upset your equilibrium. Avoid stress through avoiding change and challenge. We should sidestep conflict and even progress, if necessary, because human adaptation can be overwhelmed by too much progress, a problem animals such as our dog and his roll do not have to face.

For a dog like Karenin the world of the twentieth century is the same as that of the middle ages. He scratches in dirt, buries and digs up bones, deposits his waste, and chases cats. For human beings the fabric of society doesn't remain so stable: elements in the earth's crust that could sit at the bottom of a sandbox instead become the central chip in a desktop computer, dirt from the ground can become metal and metamorphose into steel buildings, the bones can become dinnerware, and dung fuel. More and more people live in new cities and create new challenges. So we can't be happy because happiness relies, in part, on comforting repetition.

This view brilliantly ties what is most transcendent in human nature to the unique quality of ongoing despair. Our civilization has made unprecedented moves away from the familiar and comfortable into the new and strange. Our ancestors began it all when they first left the comfort of the East African savannah and began to stand erect, walk, and to change the course of their anatomy.

Think of that first moment when our ancestors moved away from their comforting environment and into a world filled with new circumstances and challenges. In a way, we are all still doing so. Sometimes we meet new challenges well, and at other times not so well. The great many changes we encounter in modern life take their toll on us, causing us distress, not pleasure.

But human happiness springs as much from novel challenges as it does from the solaces of familiar routines. In truth, no one has a life involved all the time in this relentless "moving on, moving up" and the avoidance of repetition. Only a few moments within a life or even in an era are radically creative. Only a few developments actually cause humanity to move forward.

Nevertheless, and most important, the creative impulses within us and the need for solace do not really conflict, except to some intellectuals. Happiness lies in a balance between seeking novelty and cultivating our continuous and familiar comforts.

Small solaces, even repetitive and commonplace releases, like playing with the dog or watching soap operas, lead to healthy pleasures. They don't detract from the rest of life, but can add. They might even provide the secure platform for some to leap out from. Expecting to be pleased by recurring experiences might even increase a long-lived ability to work and create. And move further forward. Play, leisure, simple pleasures should not be pitted against progress. Within the lives of our most creative thinkers, there are countless moments of small, repetitive pleasures. Even Einstein played with his dog.

All Pleasures: Great and Especially Small

One of the sources of my happiness is small things. I get great joy from absolute nonsense. I'm very weather reactive. A sunny day can just start things wonderfully. I also love encounters with strangers that bespeak a kind of human warmth. It makes me happy.

I'm a great reader. I get pleasure from reading something that I think is just wonderfully done. I care how the words get together. I can feel on top of the world sitting around with a good newspaper and a cup of coffee and killing three hours.

—*Margo Howard*

Which experiences and frames of mind really make us happy? Is it necessary to have intense moments of pleasure, or are little pleasures more important? Is happiness built up over many small occurrences or is it somehow organized around a few fantastic events, such as a first love, a long-awaited job promotion, or a once-in-a-lifetime trip to Europe? The answers may surprise you.

Psychologist Ed Deiner asked men and women to observe their mood over six weeks. Each person carried a beeper which recorded how he or she felt at any moment and also rated their levels of happiness. Was it *how positive* people felt or *how often people felt positive* that mattered most? Results were clear: happiness springs from *how much of the time* a person spends feeling good, not from the momentary peaks of ecstasy. Simple pleasures—hours spent walking on a sunny day, gardening, running with the dog, chopping wood, or working on a new craft—are more allied with happiness than are strong, momentary feelings.

A life filled with *many small moments* of happiness—even simple ones such as playing hide and seek with one's child, strapping on a portable cassette player and blotting out the delay of your plane's departure with your favorite Mozart, playing the harmonica (even badly), trying to paint a landscape, or doing meaningful work—seems to deliver happiness. These small pleasures, whether they're sensual or mental, reading or roller skating, can absorb some of the shocks and difficulties of life and contribute to ongoing happiness.

Why, then, do most of us plan our lives around, and remember, special, dramatic events such as a promotion or a marriage day? Why are we more likely to recall news of one airplane crashing than to notice the four thousand planes taking off from and landing at a major airport every day of the year? The news never begins with "One hundred fifty million pleasant dinners served in U.S. tonight. Two hundred million good nights of sleep. One hundred million interesting discussions today." Not very exciting, not very interesting. It won't sell newspapers. It won't even get noticed.

As the media are primed to highlight the new and spectacular, so our own minds skew in that direction. We remember a single earthquake rather than the countless hours spent walking in undisturbed hills. We tend to notice and recall only things that are out of the ordinary events and filter out the commonplace ones. We tend to remember only very important episodes in our life, and those tend to be either extremely positive or negative. So, when we tell ourselves our own life story, we wrongly believe that happiness depends on dramatic events that blot out the small daily events in the background of our life.

So don't bet your whole life on the big events, winning the lottery, becoming president of the company, or doubling your income. Instead, make sure you have enough of the small daily things of life, and attend to the pleasures of smells, tastes and sounds, rewarding relationships, and meaningful work.

Mood Swings

You're walking through a shopping center. Suddenly you notice a dollar bill lying on the ground. You scoop it up, thinking, "This must be my lucky day." You probably wouldn't believe that finding a dollar would change your opinion about the possibility of nuclear war or economic depression. But it does. Our moods are extremely changeable, and shift on the basis of small occurrences.

A group of researchers planted dollar bills in a shopping center and watched as unsuspecting passersby stumbled upon their lucky find. A half-hour later the researchers interviewed the people, asking such questions as "How happy are you with your marriage," "How frequently does your car need major repairs," and "Do you plan to buy the same make of refrigerator again." Compared with people who did not find the dollar, those who did reported better marriages, had fewer problems with their cars, and were more likely to get the same fridge again!

When we are in a given mood, such as sadness, anger, or joy, we are more likely to recall other times when we were in a similar mood. This is probably why seemingly minor uplifts, such as receiving flowers, can "make your day" or why you might worry about asking for a promotion if your boss "got up on the wrong side of the bed." You have a feeling that, although it had nothing to do with you, your boss's ill humor will cause him or her to remember upsetting things about your job performance.

Mood dampens on rainy days and brightens in sun. It is affected by the pleasantness or unpleasantness of the room you're sitting in, and by whether or not your favorite team just won or lost a match. Further, if people are hypnotized and asked to assume a mood such as sadness, they remember more sadness, they expect more in the future. Their estimate of the chances of war go up, their estimate of their own future potential for joy goes down and their general outlook appears bleak.

When we are thinking about something that is happening to us at the moment, we take on the mood of the moment. We can hook right into the up feelings, we can anticipate doing more kayaking, more times out with that favorite person, more great theatre, more great meals, more work satisfaction.

Here the built-in tendency of our mind to overgeneralize helps a lot. Maybe this is why so many business deals are made in good restaurants or pleasant country clubs! In the same way, we can also anticipate less future satisfaction when we are asked to dwell upon negative events. Again, small changes in our current contents of mind have great future consequences. When the stock market drops, the future closes in; when we have a fight with our spouse, suddenly frustrating feelings and events long gone resurface. We can get flooded one way or the other.

Since the mind automatically projects into the future, simplifies the present, and makes everything seem constant, how can we turn the tables and take advantage of this? The key is to direct attention to those parts of our mental operating system that control our feelings. Since the mind is so biased towards short-term events, we can see that the effect of recent happy events make a very big difference to us.

The Benefits of an Unhappy Past

Our present mood and happiness is also strongly, and sometimes surprisingly, shaped by our recent and distant past. You might assume that thinking about an unhappy childhood is a one-way ticket to depression, while savoring the memory of a former lover would brighten your day. However, the results of these mental gymnastics can sometimes be paradoxical.

Try this:

First, think about an unpleasant event that took place ten or fifteen years ago, perhaps something related to school, work, or family that you were unhappy about.

Second, think about something exceedingly pleasant that happened to you ten or fifteen years ago.

Third, think about the *most negative current experiences* that you are having.

Finally, think about your *most positive current experiences*.

Which condition do you think would make you feel the happiest or saddest?

Studies of men and women performing similar exercises revealed that dwelling on present negative events produced the most unhappiness. No surprise. However, unhappiness also followed thinking about *positive past* events. Savoring *present positive* happenings improved mood, but the greatest boost came from contemplating *negative past* events! Tricky, this mind of ours.

But why does thinking about a negative event in the past

produce increased happiness in the present? This is probably a result of changing the level of comparison in the mind. Remember the car discussion: a Rolls Royce might not seem so good compared with other possibilities, but an average car might seem great compared with a poor or nonexistent one. Similarly, an adequate present experience (the kids are healthy, you have sufficient money, not enough to travel but enough to go to the movies a few times a week and get good clothes) may seem pretty good compared with childhood poverty or the first few years of marriage, when you lived in a shabby house and you didn't know where your next rent check income was coming from. People who were brought up in poverty during the Depression were more likely to rate times of relative prosperity as being very positive than people who were brought up prosperous.

John Naisbitt, author of *Megatrends*, writes,

> I grew up in real poverty. We didn't have any money. My father, bless his heart, refused to join the WPA (Work Projects Administration). I have images of all the WPA guys building the curbs and the streets in Salt Lake. My father had too much pride for that. He would go around and knock on doors to see if he could shovel snow or do odd jobs. I remember as a kid we lived for quite a number of days on just flour and water, to have something stick to our stomachs. I remember being teased by my schoolmates for the shabbiness of my clothes. I decided somewhere along the line I had to get through. I vowed at the time that I would never be that poor.

So, a remembrance of bad things past has a contrast effect: our present seems brighter. For example, you might feel a sense of joy and vitality when you finally recover from a persistent cold. Often one of the best things about being sick is how good you feel later (by comparison) when you recover. However, a well remembered cheery moment makes the work-a-day world of the present seem very dull, if not disagreeable. On the other hand, recalling one's past poverty, past difficulties, past long hours at work, or perhaps a past failed marriage, may make us evaluate more highly a present marriage, a present work situation, a present family life.

Evidence on how we make decisions, on the effects of current and past events, and on the nature of the comparative processes of mind leads us to ways in which we can manipulate our thought processes to render our moods more positive and our lives happier. It is a matter of directing our mental investments.

Remember, then, to think about what is going on in your life now that makes you happy: a winning team, a good meal, a craft project, or the joys of parenting. It's important to dwell on your present happiness, because this concentration can act as a buffer against sad times and can directly influence your current well-being. Keep what is pleasing you higher in your mind. Count your blessings.

Don't mull over your shortcomings. Remember happiness lies in narrowing the distance between your expectations and your perceived assets. So either temper your expectations or, more enjoyably, appreciate your assets.

Consider the essence of saying grace before a meal. It's a time to be thankful for what you are about to receive. You might try saying your own grateful graces once or twice each day. You could think about the good things happening in your family, work, what you are reading, your plans, your joys. You've got time for it; try to pick something different to be thankful for at odd moments—on the train, waiting for planes, raking leaves.

Try to think as much as possible about how you've progressed in life. Focus on those ways in which your life is better off than before, but be aware of the effect on your present mood of savoring past loves, triumphs, and achievements. Dwelling on past loves can sabotage your current happiness.

Of course, the benefits of reflecting upon an unhappy past has its limits. If your past is troubled by severe traumatic experiences, these unresolved feelings can overwhelm your present capacities for happiness. Other techniques, which we discuss later, can help you clear the mind and open the way to happier thoughts.

It's important to direct your thoughts to increase happiness. Make it a weekly goal to think about positive current events and daily experiences as much as possible. Focus on what you have, not on what you lack. The good feelings are likely to spill over into a healthy, optimistic view of your future.

10

. . . .

The Optimism Antidote

Why the Unexamined Life May Be
Well Worth Living

You try to know yourself. Almost all the advice you encounter, in philosophy or pop psychology, preaches that knowing the full truth about yourself will guide you to mental, physical and even spiritual health. The aim of most psychotherapies, too, is to help us perceive ourselves more clearly. Psychologist Abraham Maslow, among others, considered people who know the truth about their frailties, weaknesses, and evils to be healthy individuals.

So you want to recognize these blemishes, and understand what others really think of you. You keep your guard up against unwarranted self-confidence. You laugh cynically when you read that 80 percent of the population consider themselves to be "better than average," a statistical impossibility. You assess your accomplishments with no holds barred.

You are well along on the road to depression.

Socrates' venerable declaration that "the unexamined life is not worth living" may well be true in certain very important respects. Through relentless self-examination, an individual's strengths and weaknesses can be exposed, supposedly leading to a sound perception of reality and ultimate happiness. Nevertheless, complete and merciless self-knowledge, contrary to the pronouncements of many respected authorities, is not beneficial for health.

Psychologist Sidney Jourard wrote: "The ability to perceive reality as it 'really is' is fundamental to effective functioning. It is considered one of the two preconditions to the development of [health]." However, modern psychological and clinical research contradicts this view. We may think that healthy people should be accurate perceivers of reality, but in reality they're not. Expecting to be pleased, healthy people cultivate a *set of positive illusions*. They inflate their own importance and have an exaggerated belief in their ability to control their destiny.

They believe that other people hold them in high regard, even when some of their friends don't esteem them nearly so highly. When bad things happen to these people, they perceive the calamity in a decidedly biased way. They concentrate on the positive while denying the negative. They have a generalized and, at times, surprisingly baseless optimism with respect to their future.

Singing the praises of Pollyanna, however, is often met with the criticism that incorrigible optimists are unrealistic. Better to be a realist. But it's not so.

Why Realism Is an Unrealistic Way to Live

For health and happiness, there are two things to remember concerning the nature of the mind: *human beings never directly perceive the outside world*; like all animals, we select a tiny part of it to live within. Second, most judgments are comparative: we sense, judge, and remember only the *difference* between one moment and the next. This begins at the very first synapse of our senses. We evolved to detect sudden noises, sudden darkness, and sudden touch; noticing threats kept our ancestors out of danger.

We'd never get through the world if we knew it as it is: enormous and chaotic. We'd need a brain so large that we couldn't keep our heads off the ground. The brain's simplification of reality means that anything that gets into the mind is immediately overemphasized, whether it is an emotional slight, a change in the weather, or a matter of statecraft. So we give the most recent news the greatest weight in decision making. This can shift the mind from positive thoughts to negative and back again. This fragility of mind is one reason why small changes in our mood can effect such large changes in our happiness, in our health, and in our life.

No one faces reality.

We all react to a simplified, filtered model of the world, a personal story we tell ourselves with respect to the world and our place in it. And for some, the fictions created are happier ones.

Healthy Illusions

Most people see themselves as happier and more competent than most others. Most people think they are better-than-average drivers, better workers, and better spouses. Look back at the happiness scales at the beginning of the previous chapter. Didn't you rate yourself higher than average? How can *most* people be above average?

Try another exercise. On the scale below, mark what you think your spouse, boss, children, and co-workers think of you. How would they rate you on a scale of 1 to 9 for each of the following qualities?

not at all   1   2   3   4   5   6   7   8   9   not at all

_____ happy	_____ trustworthy	_____ warm
_____ considerate	_____ aggressive	_____ cheap
_____ conscientious	_____ generous	_____ intelligent
_____ cold	_____ loving	_____ inept
_____ competent	_____ charming	_____ kind

Next, ask your friends and family to fill out the same scale, but to describe what *they* think of you. Then have someone compare the results. Most healthy people see themselves with a sort of rosy glow. They typically believe that others feel they're more valued, more important, more loving, more generous, more sincere than is actually the case.

You might feel that your boss values your work highly, while she considers you to be an average worker. You may feel worshipped by your children, while they laugh at your foibles. But this *overvaluation of oneself is normal and healthful.* Most well-adjusted people do so: they believe that others like them more than they usually do.

Some people maintain a more accurate view of themselves. They will often openly admit such things as "My boss doesn't trust me," "My husband believes I am lazy," "My wife thinks I am stingy." For this select community, negative statements regarding themselves correspond well to others' judgments. These men and women are quite realistic. They *know* they're not respected and that others don't like them, and they're right. As you may guess by now, these are the people who are either mildly depressed or are on their way to a depression.

Mildly depressed people are, therefore, the closest we human beings come to true realists. Severely depressed people, of course, greatly distort their perception to confirm their negative outlook: "Nothing I have ever done has ever worked out well"; "For my entire life everyone has hated me." On the other side, the rose-colored glasses of optimists skew their reality toward the positive. So take your choice.

If some illusions and zooms of attention seem to lock people into a depressed state, others are more useful. Someone tells you what they think of you: you are mean, aggressive, charming, domineering, brilliant. The healthy person will remember "charming," and "brilliant," and maybe "aggressive." There is a built-in process toward selecting the positive and screening out the negative. This partiality maximizes positive emotions and staves off depression.

Healthy people remember success better than failure. They see their own shortcomings—say, an inability to communicate well or to think clearly—as common to everyone. They think their positive abilities are distinct and exceptional. If you can paint well but can't speak well, you might think that painting well is unusual, while speaking poorly is usual. So, there is built-in rosy illusion: positive attributes are remembered, cherished, and projected more than negative ones.

Healthy people also assume their ability to influence events is much greater than it is. If they are throwing dice (where the outcome is random) they believe they have greater control if they are throwing the dice than if someone else is. If they are working on a project, they believe that the positive aspects of the project stem from them, and the negative aspects from their collaborators.

Healthy people also view the future differently. How likely do you think you are to have an automobile accident, become a crime victim, have difficulty finding a job, or get sick or depressed? Healthy people estimate a much lower probability of having these misfortunes befall them than do average or depressed people.

Again, the only group that seems to be less susceptible to this sort of unrealistic illusion are mildly depressed individuals. They and those with low self-esteem have a more balanced and accurate view of reality. They are much more likely to realistically assess their chances of getting mugged, hit by a car, or raped. On the other hand, most healthy men and women look slightly on the bright side. They anticipate that "the future is going to be okay by me, it's the other guy who is going to get hurt."

But what about knowing yourself and understanding yourself quite accurately? Is this not important to happiness and mental health? No. People who are "always trying to figure themselves out" and who have a high degree of self-consciousness are also much more likely to be depressed. Even psychotherapies aimed at insight through self-examination are not as successful as treatments which shift beliefs towards optimistic illusions.

Why, then, do some people thrive and others not? Crucial is the talent to control thoughts and moods, so that they can go forward, undistracted, with a whole heart. And sometimes this takes a strong dose of unreality.

Healthy and Unhealthy Denial

Some events cannot be avoided or changed by confronting them directly, and the mind may become flooded with anxious thoughts. Memories or anticipations of threatening situations intrude into consciousness. Fortunately, the brain evolved with mechanisms to deal with anxiety and psychic discomfort, mechanisms that clear the deck and make possible other, more hopeful thoughts and actions.

One such mechanism is denial, the mental operation by which thoughts, feelings, acts, threats, or demands are reduced. Unfortunately, denial has received a bad press. It is often viewed as a negative defense mechanism which leads to pathology, since we are supposed to face reality, "get in touch with our feelings," and be honest regarding them. The traditional view holds that illusion, self-deception, and denial are unhealthy and must be rooted out. This view, however, is not consistent with recent information revealing how the brain works, and implying that sometimes we need our illusions.

The mind makes up its own story about reality from a narrow trickle of information received, reduced, and filtered through our senses. These constructed beliefs, many based on denial and illusion, have adaptive value.

The brain's elaborate pain relief system evolved to block transmission of painful stimuli. This system appears to be turned on during acutely stressful situations when the organism must prepare to flee or fight. Numbing the pain of attack by a charging wild animal allows the organism to ignore physical trauma and handle the immediate threat— to flee or to fight.

Analogously, the brain developed adaptive mechanisms, such as denial, to block awareness of threatening information that arouses unnecessary anxiety and contributes little to changing the situation. Therefore, whether denial is healthy or not depends on circumstances and outcome.

Denial *can* interfere with necessary actions and thereby undermine health. The diabetic who needs to regulate insulin dosages or the woman who discovers a breast lump need to attend to details about their health to take actions to preserve it. Denying a breast lump can lead to delays in treatment for breast cancer. The patient with chest pain who does push-up or runs up and down stairs to prove he is not having a heart attack clearly illustrates the danger of unhealthy denial.

But denial can be helpful. When patients about to undergo surgery for hernia and gallbladder disease were asked how much they wanted to know about their disease, the operation, and the risks, two basic coping strategies emerged: vigilance and avoidance. The avoiders denied the threatening aspects of the surgery. They were not interested in listening to anything related to their illness or surgery. They would say things like: "All I know is that I have a hernia. I just took it for granted. It doesn't disturb me one bit. I have not thought at all about it."

The vigilant patients were ever alert to the emotional and threatening aspects of the upcoming medical event. They attempted to cope by trying to control every detail of the situation and were aroused to every danger. One vigilant patient commented after a detailed description of the operation: "I have all the facts, my will is prepared. It is major surgery. It's a body opening. I'm put out, I could be put out too deep, my heart could quit, I can go into shock. I do not go in lightly."

Which group fared better? As you might guess, the avoiders were discharged from the hospital sooner, had fewer minor complications (nausea, headache, fever, and infection), required less pain medication, and showed less distress than the vigilant patients.

Denial may also be healthy immediately following an acute crisis or catastrophic illness, such as a spinal cord injury or severe burn. The victim may be able to buy some time by denying the implications of the trauma. A temporary disavowal of reality helps the person get through the devastating early period of loss and threat, when there is in truth little to be done. Later, the patient can face the facts at a gradual, more manageable pace and mobilize other means of coping. Illusion can allow space for hope.

Flexibility is crucial to successful denial. Consider a person suffering a heart attack. At different stages in the illness, different means of coping might be adaptive. At the onset of chest pain, denial is dangerous—getting immediate medical assistance is imperative. However, once in the hospital or under medical care, some denial and avoidance may help. Patients in intensive care following a heart attack survive better if they downplay the seriousness of their illnesses.

Following discharge from the hospital, a different balance of denial and vigilance is most useful. Patients who practice excessive denial of their disease are less likely to take their medications or follow an appropriate diet or exercise program.

Those who remain vigilant, however, may be more prone to develop "cardiac neurosis," in which patients fear a return to normal life lest it provoke a recurrent heart attack. Hence, they may be slower to go back to work, resume sexual activity, and otherwise function normally.

Arousal, fear, and vigilance are useful only if they alert us to take corrective action to alleviate a threat. When there is nothing that can be done over the long term, denying or ignoring the threat protects our health and leaves room for optimism and hope.

Physicians describe some patients as having lost the will to live or given up hope. Hope represents a special type of positive expectation. Unlike denial, which involves blocking out reality, hope selectively focuses attention on the positive. No matter how grim a situation may appear, certain people seem to be able to extract its positive aspects and concentrate on them. They fill their minds with hopeful scenarios and stories with happy endings.

People can also learn to be hopeful when they are helpless. Even if you can't control the outcome, as with many serious accidents or illnesses, you can still hope that somehow, from somewhere, help will come and the situation will change for the better.

But does the belief that things will get better actually make a difference in recovery? What determines whether someone mobilizes hope or despair? Not much is known scientifically about the effects of hope, but there are hints that it may be a powerful force in recovery. New research is beginning to elucidate the physiology of hope and positive expectation.

In one series of studies, patients entering the hospital for open heart surgery or surgical repair of a detached retina were evaluated before and after the operation. Those who expressed greater optimism regarding the results, confidence in their ability to cope with the outcome, and trust in their surgeon recovered more quickly. Among patients undergoing open heart surgery there were lower death rates.

Hopeful expectations may also help predict who has cancer of the cervix. A group of women were interviewed before undergoing cervical biopsies to determine if they had cervical cancer. The interviewers evaluated the degree of hopefulness or hopelessness of the women. More than three-quarters of the time they were able to correctly predict which women would be cancer-free. The more optimistic the woman, the less likely she was to have cervical cancer.

The Confidence Game

The optimistic beliefs we have about our own health can sometimes be more important than the reality of our situation. For example, we seem to have a deep-rooted need for control. If you are in a stressful situation and have the illusion you can control it, *even if you can't,* your stress reaction will be reduced. Researchers asked people to perform difficult math problems while distracting them with random bursts of loud, nerve-jangling noise. Half the people were told that they could stop the noise by pressing a button (a button which actually had no effect on the noise). The other subjects were given no such illusion of control. Even though no one pressed the button, the people who thought they could control the stressor experienced fewer stress symptoms (sweaty hands, racing hearts, ringing ears, and headaches).

The sense of control even affects our immune function. Some laboratory rats learned to shut off a mild electric shock by turning a wheel in their cages. Other rats got shocked every time the first group did, but could do nothing to control the shocks. The immune function dropped in the helpless rats, but not in the rats who could control the shocks. Uncontrollable stress also appears to promote the growth of cancer in experimental animals.

The most difficult times are the ones we think we can't control. But even in the most seemingly helpless situation, things can be done to help people feel more in control.

Consider surgery. Each year over twenty million Americans go under the knife. Whether or not the patient is unconscious, surgery is a stressful experience. And in preparing for surgery doctors often spend more time washing their hands than preparing the patient psychologically. But patients, if instructed, can reduce anxiety and the risk of blood loss. They experience anxiety not only before surgery but also during the operation. If you observe patients during surgery, even though they're asleep or anesthetized, their bodies still react to this stressful experience.

Patients facing spinal surgery usually suffer hours on the operating table and sustain considerable blood loss. The bleeding is a direct risk to the patient and makes the procedure much more difficult for the surgeon.

How can this situation be improved? One group of patients received instruction on how to relax before and during surgery. Another group was told that they could successfully shunt the blood away from their spine to reduce bleeding and return the blood back into the area to help improve healing. A third control group received no special preparation.

The results were remarkable. The group with no special preparation and those given general relaxation instructions lost 900 cc of blood. The patients who were advised that they could control their blood flow lost only half as much blood—about 500 cc. This is an important difference since a loss of 900 cc is much more likely to require a blood transfusion than a loss of 500 cc.

There's a very real risk of a transfusion reaction or of contracting an infectious disease from contaminated blood. So anything that can reduce the need for transfusion would be in the best interests of the patient. The surgeons were so impressed with the results that it has become a little difficult to continue the research, since they now want their patients to learn how to control their blood flow.

The optimistic belief that we are in control, capable and competent to make changes, is critical to health. Consider a series of experiments conducted at the Stanford Arthritis Center. The project began innocently enough. A self-management course was designed to help arthritis patients cope better with the pain, disability, fear, and depression often associated with this condition. The program consisted of six weekly two-hour sessions attended by patients and their families and led by instructors, many of whom had arthritis themselves. The patients learned a lot of detailed information about the physiology and treatment of arthritis, strengthening and endurance exercises, relaxation techniques, joint protection, nutrition, and the interrelationship of stress, pain, and depression.

Impressively, participants demonstrated significantly greater knowledge, self-management behavior, and less pain. But why? The people who improved were not those who knew more about arthritis or did the therapeutic exercise. Those who improved had a *positive outlook and felt a sense of control* regarding their arthritis. Those who failed to improve, even if they exercised, felt there was nothing they could do about arthritis.

The key difference appeared to be in the patients' perception of their ability to control or change their arthritis symptoms. The critical feature here is *belief* in this ability, not what skills or capacities the patient actually had.

There is a biology of self-confidence. When it comes to health promotion, a confident attitude may contribute more to health than specific health behaviors. Think about all your good intentions—the plans for new diets, exercise regimens, stress reduction techniques. If asked, most people can recount a litany of failures. What are the consequences of failing at a health behavior change? So much emphasis has been placed on changing lifestyles, adopting the good life, that what is often missed is that the *feelings of success or failure* may be more important to health than the actual behaviors. Success, even in small things, supports a feeling of self-confidence and competence.

One mistake many of us make is trying to change everything at once. Part of the problem is that most of us can't attain our ultimate, often unrealistic, goals immediately; we then don't take the small steps that could move us forward. Recall a previous experience in which you successfully changed. Why did you change? What were the keys to your success?

If feeling confident and successful is perhaps more important than the specific changed behavior, then the focus should be on developing a series of successful experiences in changing something, no matter how small. Set yourself up for success. Choose something that *you* want to change and take a small step that you are confident you can achieve. Make sure that at regular intervals in your life you take up something new—maybe playing a musical instrument, learning to cook a new dish, studying a new language— something you can learn, something that makes you grow, something you like and is yours. It will pay off more than twice. It may be exercising, losing weight, managing stress more effectively, developing a new hobby—anything you really want to do. It all bolsters hope and optimism.

That sense of confidence not only makes it more likely that you will succeed in changing a behavior—from pain control to quitting smoking—but itself may foster health. Successful change in any part of your life, in hobbies or work, can reinforce this vital sense of confidence.

The health benefits associated with confidence are striking. For example, confidence in our own health turns out to be one of the best predictors of future health—even better than the results of extensive laboratory testing or a physician's examination.

People who rate their health poorly die earlier and have more disease than their counterparts who view themselves as healthy. Even people suffering from illness seem to do better when they believe themselves to be healthy than when they believe themselves weak.

In Canada, more than thirty-five hundred senior citizens were asked, at the outset of a seven-year study, "For your age would you say, in general, your health is excellent, good, fair, poor, or bad?" Those who rated their health as poor were almost three times more likely to die during the seven years of the study than those who perceived their health as excellent. The rating system proved more accurate in predicting who would die than the objective health measures of physicians.

Nearly 15 percent of the people rated their health as fair or poor, even though according to the objective health measures it was excellent or good. These "health pessimists" had a slightly greater risk of dying than the "health optimists," who viewed themselves as healthy in spite of negative reports from their doctors. The predictive power of self-rated health was the same regardless of sex, age, environment, or health. Only increasing age appears to have a more powerful influence on death rates than self-rated health.

How can this be? Perhaps we have a very sensitive internal mechanism that detects subtle changes in health before symptoms appear and before a doctor can detect any problem. Or our attitude with respect to our health may influence future health—pessimistic attitudes translating into physiological malfunctioning and optimism into bolstered immunity.

Finding ways to increase the confidence of a "health pessimist" may pay rich dividends. With all the emphasis on medical technology and diagnostic evaluation, let's not forget the most sophisticated diagnostic machine, the human brain. Quickly assessing a person's overall perception of his or her health may help us identify individuals at greater risk. Perhaps by encouraging more positive self-perceptions we may be able to effect physiological processes and improve health.

What you expect is what you get. Or so it seems. Try this: Write down as many as you can of the wonderful experiences you anticipate in the future. Then describe all the difficult and trying things you expect to happen. How many positive experiences did you write down? How many negative?

The way we respond to this surprisingly simple test seems to predict future health and well-being. In one study, a group of elderly subjects considered their future. They listed all the positive things they had to look forward to. Two years later the optimists reported fewer physical symptoms of ill-health and more positive physical and psychological well-being than did the pessimists. They felt less tension, reported fewer colds, took fewer days off from work, and had more energy.

Another way to assess optimism is by the Life Orientation Test (LOT) developed by psychologists Michael Scheier and Charles Carver.

You might want to try filling it out yourself. Mark how much you agree with each of the items, using the following scale: 4 = strongly agree, 3 = agree, 2 = neutral, 1 = disagree, and 0 = strongly disagree.

_____ 1. In uncertain times, I usually expect the best.
_____ 2. If something can go wrong for me, it will.*
_____ 3. I always look on the bright side of things.
_____ 4. I'm always optimistic about my future.
_____ 5. I hardly ever expect things to go my way.*
_____ 6. Things never work out the way I want them to.*
_____ 7. I'm a believer in the idea that "every cloud has a silver lining."
_____ 8. I rarely count on good things happening to me.*

In scoring, you'll need to reverse the numbers for the items marked with an asterisk (*). That is, if you strongly agree with the statement "If something can go wrong for me, it will," give yourself a score of 0 instead of 4. Do this for items 2, 5, 6, and 8. Then total up your score.

When college students completed this test four weeks before final exams, the higher-scoring optimists (with 20 points and over) reported many fewer health problems. The pessimists complained of more dizziness, fatigue, sore muscles, and coughs.

The effects of a bright outlook on the future are perhaps even more striking for people facing major trauma, such as open-heart surgery. In one study, the attitudes of patients about to undergo a coronary bypass were assessed just before the operation. Those with a more hopeful, positive outlook showed fewer complications during surgery: their electrocardiograms and blood tests revealed less evidence of heart muscle damage. Those patients with a sunny disposition also recovered more quickly. Their lung function returned speedily, they sat up in bed sooner, and they were able to walk around the room earlier than their gloomier counterparts. Six months later, those who expected an improved quality of life—a quick return to work, hobbies, and exercise—tended to get just what they expected.

Again, Pollyanna may have really been onto something.

When Negative Things Happen to Positive People

Loved ones die. Businesses fail. Jobs change. Marriages hit the skids. Families quarrel. Shoelaces break. Cars break down. Keys are misplaced. In short, things change, and not always for the better.

The fashionable view is that the major events in a life, such as losing or getting a job or moving, all cause stress. Stress wears us down and makes us ill, causing headaches, stomach aches, insomnia, and other maladies. It makes us susceptible to all sorts of disorders and diseases, such as cancer, infections, ulcers. So the message goes out: Watch out for stressors and try to avoid them at all costs.

However, there is no pleasure in ducking change and challenge. It's the reverse: human beings have a genuine and healthy need for novelty and stimulation. The pessimistic view that we are passive victims of stress is wrong. We are resilient, and stressors don't act on a defenseless, mindless organism.

Stress to illness to disease is not an inevitable double play. Some people cope with change without getting anxious and aroused; they learn to tame it. A charging lion may spark a different reaction in you than in an experienced animal trainer.

Some men and women keep confident and optimistic with a hardy attitude toward life. Suzanne Kobasa and her colleagues studied business executives in a division of AT & T. At the time, the company underwent the largest corporate reorganization in history. In this period of great stress and uncertainty, some executives remained healthy, experiencing less than half the number of illnesses suffered by others. They had the kind of attitude, or the kind of healthy illusions, described earlier: self-perceptions that produced optimism. Specifically, they had a strong *commitment* to work and families, expected that they could *control* their life, and viewed changes as *challenges* rather than threats. In contrast, the executives who became ill felt powerless, were threatened by change, and suffered in the face of uncertainty.

Hardy people tell themselves positive, optimistic stories about their lives. When pessimists lose their job, they are more likely to view this as a catastrophe which confirms their own sense of worthlessness. Hardy sorts might view the job loss as a chance to get a new job better suited to their capabilities.

What is important is not "reducing the horrible frightful stressors" but viewing the world as a changing, challenging place. Optimists transform problems into opportunities and avoid a stress response in the first place. What is vital is to find the right amount of change in your life.

What makes a person more stress resistant? Certain childhood experiences seem to foster hardiness. Commitment appears to emerge from strong parental encouragement and acceptance. Control is cultivated in children who successfully encounter a variety of tasks which are neither too simple nor too difficult. An orientation to challenge blooms when children are faced with a changing environment in which variety is construed as richness rather than chaos. Optimism and hardiness can continue to develop throughout life. A work environment which encourages self-mastery of a variety of tasks and is accompanied by strong encouragement of peers and superiors is more likely to assist in the development of good healthy attitudes.

A Healthy Dose of Optimism

So life has its turns. Your company is bought up by a conglomerate and you're out of work; your great idea for frozen chicken drinks flops in the marketplace; your husband unexpectedly decides to leave you and goes to live permanently on a small island near Mauritius; the painting you've been working on for months is flayed to death by the critics. What does it mean to you? What do you tell yourself?

We regularly try to tell ourselves a story to explain what is happening to us, to explain the events, bad and good, that take place. Everyone has disappointments—presentations fail, relationships break up, we have bad luck at the races—but the way we narrate the reasons things go wrong has a surprisingly strong influence on mood and health.

Consider the following situation. Your mate has just walked out on you. How would you describe the major reason for the breakup of the relationship?

Now, consider how your reason reflects your view of the problem, yourself and others. Do you explain the event as something *stable* ("I always screw up my personal relationships") or *unstable* ("It's a transient, one-time event")? If your explanation is stable, you are likely to link it with past failures and expect the same dismal results in the future.

Then consider whether your reasons are *global* ("I'm incapable of doing anything right; I am completely unlovable") or *specific* ("I'm unlovable because I'm so moody and picky"). The more global the explanations, the more likely you will expect bad things to happen in all areas of your life.

Finally, do your reasons tend to be *internal* ("It was all my fault. My lover did everything possible to keep the relationship going") or *external* ("My mate had significant problems and was very moody")? Again, internal explanations reflect and reinforce self-blame and lower self-esteem.

When bad things happen, as they will, pessimists explain the causes in *stable, global, internal* terms ("It's going to last forever, its going to affect everything I do, and it's all my fault"). At the same time, should something good happen to a pessimist, the event is discounted as *unstable, specific, and external* ("It won't last, it won't change my life, I was just lucky").

Most people, of course, wouldn't want to be caught dead being pessimistic, and might feel even less inclined to think this way after reading this book. On the other hand, we may not realize that many of our attitudes are negative or can lead to pessimism.

Most of us, for instance, don't necessarily believe that we look on the bad side of events. Yet when confronted with an uncontrollable bad event we will offer up a litany of subtle explanations that reflect our enduring, global, and self-centered view of the world.

This tendency toward creeping pessimism is to some degree a reflection of the brain's attempt to organize and simplify the world. Believing that things are stable and constant and revolve around the self brings order and stability—but at considerable cost to health and happiness.

In one study, a pessimistic explanatory style predicted which college students would report more sick days and more visits to the doctor. Another long-term study tracked members of the Harvard classes of 1939 through 1944. In 1946, the men responded to questionnaires about their experiences in World War II. Their responses held clues to what their state of health would be some thirty years later.

For example, one soldier reported that "Giving orders was sometimes very hard, if not impossible, because I always had this problem of dealing with men under me, even later in the war and when I had the appropriate rank." Recognize the tell-tale signs of pessimistic thought—the global, stable, and internal explanation of the problem? Contrast that with the following more optimistic narrative: "During the war I was occasionally bored, because anyone who's ever been on a ship is bored to tears."

Overall, men who explained negative events with stable, global, and self-centered reasoning at age twenty-five were less healthy later in life than men who believed their troubles were due to short-lived factors outside themselves. Belief seemed to affect health most strongly at age forty-five, approximately twenty years after the assessment.

Does pessimism also put us at risk of early death? Several researchers pored through the sports pages of *The New York Times* and *The Philadelphia Inquirer*. They analyzed the quotes of all the Baseball Hall of Fame players who played between 1900 and 1950. The pessimists, who said their success was short-lived and due to "luck," lived significantly shorter lives than did the optimists.

Optimism may also favorably affect our immune function. Comparisons of blood samples from optimists and pessimists revealed a better ratio of "helper" to "suppressor" lymphocytes, suggesting that the white blood cells of optimists may be more effective in defending the body against tumors. Also, a study of patients with advanced breast and skin cancer revealed that a joyful attitude and optimistic style were the strongest psychological predictors of how long the patients would remain cancer-free before the disease returned.

Of course, we aren't claiming that optimistic attitudes are the only determinants of who stays well and who gets sick. The role of optimism and pessimism in physical illness seems to depend on the stage and type of disease. If a truck hits you, it probably doesn't matter much what you think. If the magnitude of your cancer is overwhelming, your psychological outlook may help you cope, but is unlikely to influence your survival. On the other hand, if your cancer is marginal or if an illness is just beginning, your psychological state may be critical.

A reflexive optimism is, for America in particular, a major cultural trait: As they rate the future, Americans overwhelmingly believe that the present is better than the past, and project that the future will be better still. When interrogated about their own outlook, most healthy college students stated that for them there would be four times as many probable future positive events than negative experiences.

Americans respond so unremittingly to optimism that a content analysis of presidential candidates' speeches shows that voters are likely to pick the most optimistic-sounding contender. The only recent exception was 1968, when Richard Nixon beat Hubert Humphrey. The ever optimistic Humphrey was burdened by a disastrous war and a chaotic political convention. He then came from fourteen points behind in the polls to lose by only one point. Presenting good feelings yields votes as well as health!

Optimism "is an inclination to anticipate the best possible outcome," according to Webster's Unabridged Dictionary. To redefine it psychologically: optimism is the tendency to seek out, remember, and expect pleasurable experiences. It is an active priority of the person, not merely a reflex that prompts us to "look on the sunny side." For some of us, optimism is learned after encountering serious difficulties, while others are brought up to emphasize the positive.

All optimists expect good things to happen, but for different reasons. Some may attribute it to their talents or skills, others to ongoing good fortune, while still others to the benevolence of God. Whatever the reason, optimists, expecting to be pleased, fill their minds with positive thoughts and their lives with positive experiences. It is this increase in positive feeling that crowds out negativity and seems to improve health.

An optimistic frame of mind reshapes the stories we tell ourselves about our past, present, and future. Optimism involves memory: we selectively remember positive events at the expense of negative ones. It involves our current situation: we actively highlight the more promising aspects of the present. It involves the future: looking to a promising tomorrow with an eye toward what can be done instead of what can't happen. People who are positive feel hopeful, not helpless, concerning their future.

An optimist feels challenged by the future and its difficulties, and believes that he or she can control the environment. An optimist believes that the world is coherent and that individual actions can make a significant difference. In general, optimistic men and women are passionately engaged in the world and believe in their own abilities. They have a fair measure of self-worth. They feel that they matter. And they appear to live longer, healthier lives.

On the other hand, pessimistic thinking undermines healthy pleasures and a healthy life. You pay for it twice: first, it feels bad to be glum about future prospects, and second, it costs you in health.

So it is not so much reality that causes stress and illness, but the stories we tell ourselves about reality. And we can learn to turn pessimistic stories into healthier, more optimistic ones.

11

. . . .

Telling Yourself a Good Story

We often bet our lives on the stories we tell ourselves about the world, but rarely hear them while they are being told. Try to listen carefully to your continuous internal monologue. We are constantly talking to ourselves, describing what is happening, what is going to happen, and what should happen. Perhaps as you're reading this book you may hear a stream of internal commentary that says something like this: "This is a really fascinating book! It makes me feel good just reading about how enjoying myself is one of the best ways to improve my health. The authors are brilliant and write so clearly." Or perhaps your internal narrative runs more along these lines: "This book is stupid. The last point about optimistic people being healthier is just wishful thinking. It's so annoying. All those silly things about getting a massage or smelling roses."

We all tell ourselves a story about what we are experiencing. It is that story which largely shapes how we feel and act. We maintain the world as it exists by our "automatic stories." If we know that our story of the world—whether positive or negative, optimistic or pessimistic, realistic or illusory—controls our life, we can choose to rewrite the unpleasant elements.

Sometimes our stories aren't healthy and need to be rescripted. When the stories are very scary, depressing, or constricting, a person may seek help from family, friends, or professional therapists. Fortunately, it is possible to change our stories. We can learn to observe how negative self-talk critically influences how we perceive and respond to external events.

For example, have you ever met an old high school friend and suddenly felt very sad? The reaction was so quick that you thought your friend caused this feeling. But there were hidden thoughts—part of your internal monologue—that connected the meeting with your feelings of sadness.

By listening in, you may have heard yourself say, "He was always popular and successful. He probably won't even remember my name. We won't have anything in common. I don't think he ever liked me. It's been twenty years since I've seen him. I've accomplished nothing in my life since then." And so it goes. The internal story, not the meeting with the friend, evokes the sad feelings. As it turns out, this internal narrative may be completely fictitious. By examining your self-talk, you can begin to question the underlying irrational beliefs which shape your responses and mood. And by reframing how you think about events, you can shift into a more positive mood.

Eliminating negative, pleasure-blocking stories is important for health and happiness. During difficult times, most people's automatic pessimism gets stronger and stronger until it takes command. Cognitive therapist Gary Emery points out a scene from a Woody Allen movie which was originally titled *Anhedonia*—the inability to experience pleasure—but was later renamed another annie title.

You may have seen the movie *Annie Hall*. One scene is a good illustration of automatic negative thinking. In this scene, [the couple] nervously meet for the first time. They make awkward small talk, which you hear on the sound track. Meanwhile, under each is a subtitle of what they're really thinking—ideas such as, "Why did I say that? I can't believe I'm such a jerk." Their automatic thoughts keep the couple anxious. And this type of automatic thinking keeps you depressed.

Eavesdropping on Your Internal Stories

Many of us seem to get the old adage wrong. We accentuate the negative and eliminate the positive.

Changing to a more optimistic frame of mind begins with becoming aware of negative self-talk. Here's how it might work: One person's story is that you must *always* be loved by everyone, show perfect control, and be good at everything. Because these are unreachable goals, the person often feels a failure, no good and demoralized.

Because we tend to tell ourselves that we'll be happy only if we can perform perfectly, our efforts are usually self-defeating. Thus our negative beliefs are reinforced. Some typical stories are: "In order to be happy, I have to be successful in whatever I undertake, or be accepted (liked, admired) by all people at all times," or "If I make a mistake, it means that I'm inept."

And we tell ourselves that we should always be generous, dignified, unselfish; the perfect lover, friend, teacher, student, spouse; able to endure any affliction with composure; capable of finding a quick solution to every problem; always happy and serene; always at peak efficiency.

You might recognize some of these internal stories. Or perhaps your self-talk is driven by such ideas as "Anything that is unknown or uncertain makes me fearful or anxious," "It is easier to avoid life's difficulties and responsibilities," "Anger is bad and destructive," "You need to protect most people from the truth," "When people disapprove of you, it always means you are a bad person."

Let's see how negative ideas color our thoughts. Try recalling a stressful situation that made you feel extremely angry, sad, fearful, or anxious. Now try playing back the scene in slow motion, frame by frame, and see if you can recall some of the automatic thoughts you had that triggered the emotion. Often it is difficult to track past events, so you might try keeping a diary for a few days. Record the situation as precisely as you can—just the facts, not your interpretations. Then list the feelings you had: anger, sadness, frustration, disappointment, and so on. Finally, write down all the automatic thoughts that circulated in the back of your mind: the concerns, worries, explanations, judgments, and rationalizations.

For example, if you are watching television and begin to feel sad, listen in. Perhaps your inner voice is saying something like: "All I do is sit around all day wasting my time. I'm a failure. I haven't done anything with my life."

Questioning Pessimistic Stories

Once you have some good examples of negative self-talk, you can begin to explore ways to change it. Pessimistic stories are usually off the mark. But how can we know this? The key is questioning the basis of the negative ideas, exposing the irrational ones, and offering alternative, healthier story lines.

Here's an interchange between Aaron Beck, a pioneer in cognitive therapy, and his frightened patient. The therapist asks questions which expose his client's pessimistic thoughts.

> *Scared:* I have to give a talk before my class tomorrow and I'm scared stiff.
>
> *A.B.:* What are you afraid of?

Scared: I think I'll make a fool of myself.

A.B.: Suppose you do . . . make a fool of yourself. . . . Why is that so bad?

Scared: I'll never live it down.

A.B.: Never is a long time. . . . Now look here, suppose they ridicule you. Can you die from it?

Scared: Of course not.

A.B.: Suppose they decide you're the worst public speaker that ever lived. . . . Will this ruin your future career?

Scared: No. . . . But it would be nice if I could be a good speaker.

A.B.: Sure it would be nice. But if you flubbed it, would your parents or your wife disown you?

Scared: No. . . . They're very sympathetic.

A.B.: Well, what would be so awful about it?

Scared: I would feel pretty bad.

A.B.: For how long?

Scared: For about a day or two.

A.B.: And then what?

Scared: Then I'd be O.K.

A.B.: So you're scaring yourself just as though your fate hangs in the balance.

Scared: That's right. It does feel as though my whole future is at stake.

A.B.: Now somewhere along the line, your thinking got fouled up . . . and you tend to regard any failure as though it's the end of the world. . . . What you have to do is get your failures labeled correctly—as failure to reach a goal, not as disaster. You have to start to challenge your wrong premises.

After the patient gave his talk, Beck reviewed his client's notions about failure.

A.B.: How do you feel now?

Scared: I feel better . . . but I was down in the dumps for a few days.

A.B.: What do you think now about your notion that giving a fumbling talk is a catastrophe?
Scared: Of course, it isn't a catastrophe.
A.B.: What is it then?
Scared: It's unpleasant, but I will survive.

The best way to expose and get rid of pessimism is to ask good questions. This is essentially what cognitive therapists do: ask questions that make their clients think more clearly. After you have written down some examples of your own negative self-talk, try asking some of these questions.

Am I thinking in all-or-none terms?: "I'm completely ugly and everyone else is beautiful." Just about everything exists in degrees and on a continuum. Watch out for words like "all," "nothing," "totally," and "completely."

Am I assuming every situation is the same?: No two situations are completely the same. Each time, you have the choice of responding differently. Does your self-talk reflect overgeneralizing and global conclusions? Look for words like "always" and "never" as tip offs.

Am I confusing a rare occurrence with a high probability?: One mailman reported this thought: "They'll probably fire me for missing three days of work." But when was the last time they fired anyone at the post office?

Am I assuming the worst possible outcome?: "If my project idea is rejected, my entire career is down the drain." Do you tend to assume the worst by imagining catastrophic scenarios? Consider the worst thing that could happen. Would it truly be a catastrophe?

Am I overlooking my strengths?: In almost every situation we display elements of weakness and strength. Do you ignore your positive attributes?

Am I blaming myself for something that was beyond my control?: "I gave a party and it rained. It's my fault." Accepting personal responsibility is reasonable only when dealing with something you can reasonably influence.

Am I expecting perfection in myself and others?: Do you really think that people should never make mistakes? If you do, you are always going to fail and always going to be disappointed in others. Give everyone, including yourself, some leeway to be fallible. It's part of being human. Why waste your energy criticizing yourself for your mistakes? Better to use that energy to your advantage. Mistakes can be opportunities to learn and grow when you don't paralyze yourself with self-blame. If you drop an egg, make an omelet; don't blame yourself for being clumsy.

How could I have handled this situation differently?: List three alternative ways you could explain the event to yourself. How would each of these alternatives make you feel?

What difference will this make in a week, a year, or ten years?: Will anyone remember (let alone care) in ten years that you made a stupid remark at a party or had dandruff on your sweater? We often believe that our mistakes will be frozen forever in others' minds.

WRITING down alternatives to gloom allows us to weigh them and develop a better perspective. It takes practice. It may take writing down as many as fifty situations with alternative thoughts before you can do it in your head.

Gary Emery gives this account of a recently divorced woman.

> After being turned down for a job interview, her automatic [pessimistic] thoughts were, "I'm no good. I'll never find a job. I'm just not as good as other people."
>
> She was able to challenge these thoughts by writing them down and telling herself (on paper): "The fact that I didn't get one job doesn't mean I'm no good. That's a gross overgeneralization. All it means is that I didn't get one job. It's ridiculous to compare myself with others on the basis of a job. Really, it's ridiculous for me to compare myself with others for any reason."
>
> By repeatedly challenging her automatic negative thoughts, she was able to maintain enough encouragement to look for a job until she found one.

Your internal narrative is only a guess as to why something happened. Put your beliefs to the test. By questioning your stories about the world, you can gather information which either supports or discredits your tale. Many of your current ideas are personal contracts that you made with yourself as a child. Maybe your mother told you to give up or share an immediate pleasure (such as a delicious ice cream) with the promise of a bigger, better reward. There's nothing wrong with learning to postpone or share pleasure. But if in the process you begin to make rigid and unrealistic contracts with yourself, such as "Being nice will always earn me a reward," then you are setting yourself up for disappointment.

Challenge those beliefs. An unhappy man might decide to wallpaper his living room. His wife papers one side, and he does the other. He predicts that he will not be as good as his wife at the job. When he finishes the papering, he may point out all the places on his side where the pattern does not exactly match or the seams are slightly off kilter. He may point to the excellent job on his wife's side of the room. By asking himself questions such as those outlined above, his hidden pessimism may become clearer to him. He may see how strict the standards are by which he judges his own work. How trivial the mistakes that he has made are, as well as how he could as easily tell himself an alternative, more optimistic story about his wallpapering efforts. Eventually, this type of feedback may make it possible for him to change his perception of himself and his life.

Or consider this scenario. You work in an advertising company, and after a recent presentation, your boss grumbles something about you "missing the boat." You think immediately: "I'm an all-out disaster. I do everything wrong. I work for hours over that presentation and he doesn't show any gratitude. Why can't I ever write anything well?" You are miserable about it all.

But when your boss likes one of your ideas you say to yourself, "He's just being nice." With one instant impression you cast out the compliment. Screening out favorable remarks and zooming in on unfavorable ones are common faults of the mind. But they are disabling stories. Their price is continual pessimism and an inability to appreciate the good things that happen.

Your explanations aren't really helping. You think everything in life depends on this one presentation or an offhand remark from your boss. All of sudden, everything becomes too clear to you: it's all-or-nothing, black-or-white. You're completely and evermore awful because you think your boss thinks that your presentation was off the mark. Your thoughts escalate this incident into a major catastrophe and you begin to feel that this always happens to you, that you'll never be a good writer, businessman, person, anybody worthwhile. You zoom in on this one situation and, as they say in England, "make a whole meal out of it."

But wait a minute, what happened? Your boss could be

wrong. He could have failed to understand the client's needs and the opportunities as well as you did. Maybe he had an argument with his spouse and he is taking it out on you and your presentation. Even if your presentation wasn't a showstopper, so what? What about all the rest, when you've done so well? Everybody loses sometimes, and your boss will naturally be disappointed for a moment. Does your self-esteem need to rest on such slippery ground? Do you need to focus all your attention on this one incident? After all, people are dying in the streets, others are homeless, still others can't get medical care. Now, just how important in our four billion years of Earth history, among the empires that have risen and fallen, and compared to the problems of nuclear arms, is this one offhand remark from your boss? You can zoom out, too, as well as zoom in.

Healthy Comparisons

As we discussed earlier, the mind works by comparison, and many of us judge ourselves by comparison to others. Such comparisons can be tricky business, leaving you with either a bad case of inferiority or false pride. Yet understanding how to use comparisons in the stories you tell yourself can sometimes make them work better for you.

Many of us look at the lives of the rich and famous with admiration, envy, and jealousy. In comparing ourselves to such idealized standards we often come up short. You may believe that many acclaimed men and women have always had clear sailing, that you're a dumb schmuck because you haven't made millions like Iacocca, or made President as did Reagan, or made sculpture like Giacometti. You need your view of your heros and yourself taken in to the shop for an overhaul.

Consider for a moment how few of the millions of slaving businessmen and businesswomen get to be as famous as

Iacocca. Many artists work for years, producing hundreds or thousands of paintings that are never seen. And many famous writers also produce hundreds of works of which you have only seen the few startling successes. No wonder all of your work seen together may not look as good as does one or two of theirs shown in a museum! Two-time Nobel Laureate Linus Pauling was once asked how he had so many brilliant ideas. He responded, "I just have a lot of ideas, and throw out the bad ones."

We all face problems, failures, and setbacks—even the rich and famous. Here are a few facts to help keep your own problems in perspective.

Did you know that Norman Vincent Peale was so disgusted with the manuscript *The Power of Positive Thinking*, that he threw it in the wastepaper basket? It was saved by his cleaning lady and became an important international best-seller. Everybody feels that they're the only ones to get rejected, and that the famous people we hear about don't have these problems. This misapprehension exists in all of us because we usually read only about the accomplishments of people, not their problems. Nobody writes about the 75,000 book manuscripts that were rejected last year, the two million business pro formas sent back for redrafting, or the millions of marriages in the United States that suffer from daily arguments. So we get biased news, and we compare ourselves with the highlights in the lives a few luminaries.

However, the celebrated women and men of the world weren't and aren't always so successful or perfect: Michelangelo's answer to Pope Julius's complaint that he was taking so long to paint the Sistene chapel ceiling was: "I told Your Holiness I was no painter." Playwright Tennessee Williams was fired by the Gotham Book Mart because he was inept at wrapping packages. Napoleon, Karl Marx, and Marilyn Monroe suffered from hemorrhoids. The *Ecole des*

Beaux Arts, Paris's most prestigious painting academy, turned down Paul Cézanne five times when he applied for entrance.

Lots of famous people have their incompetencies and problems, so should your inability to find your car in the parking lot make you feel like a total incompetent? Sigmund Freud never traveled alone because he didn't know how to read a railroad timetable. Ronald Reagan was rejected for the leading role in the 1964 movie *The Best Man* because "he doesn't look like a President."

You might have picked the wrong stock to invest in, gone to the wrong restaurant, or missed hiring a young executive who is doing so well at the competing firm that she is making life difficult for you. You tell yourself that you're an idiot. But remember that other, quite prestigious executives have made worse errors. Thomas J. Watson, chairman of the board of IBM, said in 1943 "I think there is a world market for about five computers." When Alexander Graham Bell offered Western Union exclusive rights to his "talking machine" for one hundred thousand dollars, Western Union president William Orton turned down the offer with the question, "What use could this company make of an electrical toy?"

It's important to get the real story of how others live, aspire, and fail. To make the right kind of comparisons you need to be familiar with the biographies of people you admire, so you can see how difficult life was for them and that the perfection you demand of yourself is a misleading story.

Another kind of comparison can help restore a healthy perspective to your life. By considering your problems in light of truly monumental disasters, your load may lighten. In the Swedish film *My Life as a Dog*, the young boy Ingemar faces many truly trying moments: his mother succumbs to cancer, he moves to a strange new village, his beloved dog is put to sleep by his guardian. He survives by telling himself the story of Laika, the poor dog sent up in a Soviet satellite. Laika was launched into space with limited provisions, probed and measured for several months until, as Ingemar says, "Her doggie bag ran out." He repeats over and over to himself, "Poor Laika, things could be worse." Sometimes switching your mental yardstick for comparison to much worse outcomes can enhance your appreciation of what you do have.

But sometimes our pleasure-denying stories are deeply hidden and held close to the heart.

Untold Stories: Why Confession Is Good for the Body

I simply couldn't live any longer without telling someone. He was not the father of our ten-year-old-daughter, but he didn't know it. Each time I glanced at our child, each time we played, my happiness was always clouded, always diminished, knowing that he didn't know. Sometimes I could feel the thoughts of betrayal well up inside me. I thought my chest would burst at times. But I kept the secret locked away inside.

On the day I finally told him I felt awful. I couldn't find the words at first, but then they rushed out all at once. It was ugly, but afterwards and since then I have felt a liberating release.

You are probably quite familiar with the claim that confession is good for the soul. But confession is more than a moral issue: it can sometimes be good for the body as well. This may sound somewhat surprising since we've so far made a very strong case for *not* facing up to reality, emphasizing the positive, and ignoring the negative. But shoveling emotional experiences aside and not confronting them has its limits.

The principle is this: If the trauma is minor then it is a healthy pleasure to minimize, ignore, or deny the problem. However, when there is a major trauma it is probably healthier in the long run to face up to it. Confessing may be unpleasant at the moment, but getting it off your chest can clear your mind to enjoy a more pleasurable life, and apparently a healthier one.

We can live our whole life holding a secret close to the chest. We may be afraid of hurting others, so we hold our feelings in. Or we may keep traumatic secrets to avoid shame, embarrassment, or pain. But when the cost of holding in our feelings exceeds the benefit of ignoring the distressing events, we need to shift gears and learn how to remove the negative experiences.

In many lives there are extraordinary traumas, events that can scar one for life. We don't mean ordinary business disappointments, financial setbacks, or the usual marital upsets. The health-damaging secrets are the major traumas like childhood rape, seeing a loved one die in an accident, witnessing a murder, committing a violent crime.

But can holding in such strong feelings—feelings never discussed with anyone—be demonstrably bad for health? Shouldn't we just ignore them? The evidence is that long buried events can undermine health. One survey showed that individuals who experienced traumatic experiences in childhood *and* who had not confided them to others were more likely to develop cancer, hypertension, ulcers, and major bouts with influenza than were people who had either not had traumas or who had confided them.

Men and women who had suffered the death of their spouse due to an automobile accident or suicide found that confiding is good for health. They spoke with others about their tragedies, and in the year following the death, were healthier than those who had not talked with others.

Encouraging people to disclose long-held traumas can measurably improve health. Psychologist James Pennebaker instructed students as follows: "I want you to write continuously about the most upsetting or traumatic experience of your entire life [and] discuss your deepest thoughts and feelings about the experience. You can write about anything you want, but whatever you choose, it should be something that has affected you very deeply. Ideally, it should be about something you have not talked with others about in detail. It is critical, however, that you let yourself go and touch those deepest emotions and thoughts that you have. . . ." Meanwhile, other students simply wrote about trivial daily activities or events.

The students kept these diaries over four days. One student disclosed that while he was in high school he was beaten by his stepfather. After he attempted suicide with the stepfather's gun, the man further mortified him by laughing at his attempt. Another student in a fit of rage accused her father of marital infidelity in front of her mother. This disclosure precipitated her parents' divorce and triggered the daughter's continuing guilt. Yet another student wrote about his feelings concerning the divorce of his parents. His father told him at age nine that he was divorcing the boy's mother because their home life had been disrupted ever since the boy had been born.

Disclosing feelings about such traumas was obviously difficult and emotionally distressing. But getting these secrets off their chest paid off in the long run. When compared to the students who wrote about something neutral like going to the ball game, the ones who confessed an emotionally traumatic event had fewer health complaints, fewer visits to the doctor, and fewer drugs prescribed during the following six months of the study. Importantly, Pennebaker and his colleagues also found improved immune functioning six weeks after the end of the study in students who had disclosed their traumas.

Not only undergraduate students in a psychology experiment benefit from confession. Thirty-three survivors of the Holocaust gave videotaped interviews about their experiences during World War II while skin conductance and heart rate were monitored.

Virtually all these survivors had suffered, many of them in silence, for decades. They had been displaced from their homes and forcibly relocated in ghettos. Many endured random beatings. Most witnessed the deaths of children, close friends, and family members.

Was it better for their health to disclose the most private aspects of their experiences? Those who more freely described their powerful trauma reported fewer health problems. Expressing *both* the facts of the trauma and the emotions seems to be critical for health improvement.

Written, even anonymous, disclosures of thoughts and feelings about traumatic experiences, unpleasant as they might be at the moment, can improve health. And the majority of people seem to appreciate the opportunity to confess. Many said things like: "It made me think things out and realize what my problem is"; "It helped me look at myself from the outside"; or "It was a chance to sort out my thoughts."

So, confessing may be very good for the body. In the mind, a covered over negative event is never finished. People tend to mull over the trauma again and again in their mind; rehearsing what they should have said, what they might have done. Writing about something or confiding in someone may force you to organize your thoughts and feelings about events, revealing hidden biases and unresolved issues. Once it is "out there," you can often distance yourself from the traumatic experience. By "getting it off your chest", you may be able to break the endless recycling of negative thoughts and feelings.

This may be one of the reasons why many religious traditions, social organizations, and self-help groups encourage confession, self-disclosure, and confiding in other people. The act of confession may well enable a person to improve his or her health in a way that had not previously been understood. This may also help explain why people enmeshed in strong social support networks are healthier: These networks may provide greater opportunity for people to confide their difficult experiences. There's now even a hotline confession service in Los Angeles that you can dial up to confess.

Our internal stories can be rewritten, negative themes purged, and optimistic elements highlighted. Spending time on these stories may be one of the highest yielding mental investments you can make.

12

$\cdot$ $\cdot$ $\cdot$ $\cdot$ $\cdot$ $\cdot$ $\cdot$ $\cdot$ $\cdot$ $\cdot$ $\cdot$ $\cdot$ $\cdot$ $\cdot$ $\cdot$

Investing in Yourself

Many of us bet our lives, investing most of our time and attention in getting rich, getting ahead, and getting to the top. And, often, the time, training, and money invested doesn't pay off in terms of happiness and health. Knowing that happiness doesn't come from high status, high income, or the amount of stuff we accumulate might help a bit. But many people may well need to rethink their whole investment strategy. Most of our life can be spent in investments that don't pay off for us, even if they pay off financially.

We need to think more about investing in ourselves in ways that bring meaningful, lasting, and healthy pleasures. Here we invite you to diversify your portfolio by considering excellent investment opportunities in work, play, and hobbies. Did you know that getting an education may be more important to your health than almost anything else you can do? Working hard can be awful if you're doing something that you don't care about, but working late hours may be healthful if you're doing something meaningful. Diversifying investments in yourself can yield huge dividends in terms of a more positive, optimistic outlook and better health.

Enjoying Our(selves)

Most of us like to think of ourselves as one unified person: The same person goes to work, does the gardening, raises children, reads books, and carries on through life's tasks. As it turns out, we are all collections of multiple selves, and the more developed and distinct these aspects of ourselves are, the less vulnerable we are to stress.

Human beings have different selves within us, different minds, different intelligences. The brain was built up in different eras, with different sections developed to operate differently. You can see this when you remember a face but not a name, or when your intellect tells you that something is a good idea but your emotions disagree. Each of us acts differently and is genuinely a different person to lovers than to co-workers, to children and to the police, different to old, close friends and to new business acquaintances. We have a great range of abilities and talents within ourselves, and the more we use them, the healthier we are.

Our different selves act to absorb the blows of life and the hard times. They help us laugh when work isn't going well, they help us maintain some good feelings, even for a moment of relief, when a loved one dies. We need to hedge our emotional bets, to give voice to our different selves, to blot out sorrow and to cheer up the rest of us.

Imagine a woman attorney going through a divorce. If we analyze her personality, we find that her roles as wife and attorney are closely linked. She met her husband at law school and they share the same circle of personal and professional acquaintances. When the divorce hits it shatters the linked selves, her sense of confidence, and her ability to adapt to the stress. The self-doubts, anger, and sadness triggered by the divorce spill over to cloud her career. Her entire life is in turmoil. She has put everything in one basket, and there's nowhere to retreat for solace.

In contrast, consider a woman who has separate identities as wife, lawyer, mother, friend, and tennis player. When faced with a divorce her entire sense of competence, confidence, and enjoyment of the other parts of her life are less likely to be completely devastated. She may still be able to enjoy an intense game of tennis, celebrate the winning of a difficult case as an attorney, or relish intimate moments nurturing her baby.

An innovative study of "self-complexity" finds that men and women who are complex and diverse, whose selves reach out in different directions, suffer fewer signs of life's stresses. They report less depression and fewer foul moods, colds, coughs, stomach pains, headaches, and muscle aches than their less complex counterparts.

The more we diversify our investments in ourselves, the more resistant we are. Many of us sell our(selves) short. Some identify with their careers, others with their role as a parent. Whether you cultivate a garden or a new friendship or care for a pet or a plant, developing variety can make you healthier and less vulnerable to setbacks.

In trying times it is more likely you can find solace within. You can activate a different, separate, area of your life which is satisfying, fulfilling, and the source of positive feelings. This positive feeling, say in the middle of grief over a loved one or the loss of a job, is neither sinful nor counterproductive. The positive mood may help you deal better with the difficulty. Focusing on areas of success and competence ("Despite my marital problems, I am still a good parent") can buffer the ill effects of stress.

Get a Head

It always struck us how long-lived were our professors. Al G., an old friend, was professor emeritus when we entered

graduate school, 70 years old at the time. For years we
continued to talk over ideas and work, hardly noticing that
he was getting on in years. He died when he was ninety-
four. This is not unusual. Harvard professors, for example,
are in the top 1 percent of oldsters in the United States. It
can't be the food, the pay, or the exercise, we can tell you.
So many well-educated women and men living so long
made us wonder about how worthwhile an investment education is for a person. (It is advantageous for society to
invest this way as well. The costs of education are small
compared with the benefits to the person in health as well
as productivity.)

Paralleling the great improvement in health and longevity
is the increased education of most individuals. While popular attention focuses on the problems and inadequacies of
our schools and the lowering of IQ scores, we overlook the
great rise in both literacy and education that has taken place
in the last fifty years. More men and women today are
educated about the world and know more about what is
going on than ever before.

The amount of education seems to correlate with improved health and resistance to disease—even more powerfully than some of the highly publicized risk factors like
high cholesterol, smoking, high blood pressure, or obesity.
For example, a 1984 study appearing in the *Irish Medical
Journal* compared the different risk factors for heart disease
and concluded that:

> The results confirm a strong association between educa-
> tion and cardiovascular disease which is not entirely ex-
> plained by differences in age, cigarette smoking, diastolic
> blood pressure, weight or plasma cholesterol. *Indeed, on
> the basis of the logistic analysis, the independent effect of education
> on cardiovascular disease is as strong as the effects of smoking,
> blood pressure, weight and cholesterol combined.*

The more education, the *less* disease. Workers with the least education in this study had four times the rate of heart disease compared with those with doctorates. So, studying history and mathematics and above all, literacy, all seem to relate to better health. It isn't that those better educated make more money, either. A study comparing American men and women with *equal incomes,* shows that subjects with postgraduate degrees are two and a half times more likely to have good health than subjects with no education, and are twice as likely to be in good health than those with an eighth-grade education. And they not only report good health, but live longer as well.

It isn't those highly-stressed, highly publicized, sedentary Type A executives who drop dead in great numbers from cardiovascular diseases, but the hardworking, uneducated physical laborers. And it isn't only heart disease, as in the Irish study, that is affected. Blood pressure drops with more education. Many more uneducated blacks are hypertensive than more educated ones. And with increasing levels of education, rates of kidney disease drop, accidents decline, and all cancers drop dramatically (except for breast cancer, perhaps due to less breast feeding among highly educated women).

This isn't just another minor statistical relationship, significant only to researchers, where risk changes by a bit, affecting only one in a million. Consider Maria and Lydia, each 25 years old. Lydia has two years of college, while Maria dropped out of school in the 6th grade. Their incomes are equal, family histories comparable, but Lydia can expect to live fully 10 years longer than Maria. By comparison eliminating all cancer deaths would add less than two years to life expectancy.

What happens when people get educated? Of course they can read safety warnings and the instructions on their prescription labels. They can read the best health advice and learn of impending health risks and opportunities to improve health. But this is hardly the whole story, although it is certainly a part. There is, we believe, a direct link between good health and knowing what is going on around us, understanding how economic and social forces operate to affect one's life, and, in general, understanding how things work.

Education offers a sense of the world, much as in ancient cultures stories and myths helped make the world seem more coherent and less threatening. If you know that lightning is followed by thunder, you won't get upset twice. If you know that downturns in the economy affect your business, you can plan accordingly, with less worry. If you get chest pains during the flowering of acacia, you can either avoid exposure to the plant or, at least, not panic. If you know there is a flu going around, you can care for yourself and, if you get it, avoid worrying about the cause. If you know that most other people, even famous and accomplished individuals, have had great difficulty in setting up their careers and have failed at new projects, you will be less pessimistic. Your comparisons are healthier and allow you to keep heart and expect better things in the face of adversity.

There's also a sense of mastery and competence that derives from having the benefit of an education. Education helps us see events in the world as coherent, so that we can avoid panic. And the healthy pleasures of literacy and knowledge can boost self-esteem and optimism, and, as we've seen, seem to pay off in better health and longevity.

So, pay more attention, if you have not already done so, to increasing both your formal and informal education. You might decide to enroll in night school to better your knowledge of the world and perhaps gain that training you lacked. Or you might have always wanted to know more about French, medieval history, Japanese, computers, or religion.

You have a lot of time, perhaps, ten years worth of extra time in your life, to do it.

News from the Work Liberation Front

You want to do it morning, noon, and night. You do it in all sorts of odd places. You have on occasion, performed it on airplanes, while watching television, in the back seats of cars, even in the bedroom.

You simply love to *work*. Hard work pervades your life. But does it ruin your health? Is all this hurry bad for your heart? Should you love work less?

Working, like cholesterol and salt, has received too much bad press. Type A people, as they are called, supposedly are those men and women who watch television programs, read trade journals, and eat dinner all at the same time. They make calls from their car while having a "pre-breakfast" meeting with three other people who commute with them. (Lyndon Johnson watched three television networks at once, even in the middle of meetings. He had three television sets in his bathroom.)

Type A behavior is popularly thought to be an aggressive, incessant struggle to achieve more and more in less and less time, and if required, to do so against opposing forces. Other symptoms include ardent pursuit of one's goals and a pressing time urgency, often called "hurry sickness."

But the idea that passionate pursuit of work is harmful has caused many of us to worry that we are too attached to something we love. In one of his more pragmatic moments, Sigmund Freud recognized that the important things in life are love and work. Wouldn't it be ideal to combine the two?

The good news is that working hard, meeting deadlines, and doing several things at once like going over papers while watching the football games do *not* kill us. It is our *attitude* toward work and toward others that is important. If you are constantly pushing to gain dominance and subjugate others, then you may well be in trouble, especially if you can't control your urges.

But if you are working hard to create something worthwhile, or to build up something important, or to serve other people, then there is no great risk to you. If you need to rush to save a poor family from unjust foreclosure, this is not necessarily a heart-blocking reaction. The test should be whether you can work hard and then stop when you need to, or whether this incessant activity is controlling you. We're not singing the praises for compulsive workaholics, but rather making room for legitimate, hard work as a healthy pleasure.

Working Well

Loving work may well have protective effects. Dissatisfaction with work lowers resistance to disease, while job satisfaction seems to have fortifying properties. People report low job satisfaction as one of the greatest sources of unhappiness. It is associated with high rates of anxiety, depression, psychosomatic symptoms, and coronary heart disease. Furthermore, a study of several hundred volunteers revealed that work satisfaction and feelings of happiness were better predictors of longevity than *health habits*.

While most people work for the money, and many for the social contact, others find work itself intrinsically satisfying. What makes it more likely that a job will be satisfying?

Most people like to have a clear, identifiable task to complete, and they like to feel that the work they are doing has a significant impact on the lives of others. They don't like to work in the dark—literally and figuratively. They hope to get positive feedback when they have done a good job.

Using a variety of skills and talents is also important for many. But perhaps the greatest asset of a healthy, satisfying job is the feeling of autonomy and control.

Though the typical image of an executive is that of a highly stressed individual, making difficult decisions under constant pressure, it is not the boss but the lower-level workers who suffer the most mental and physical damage from work stress. Job strain results when we have insufficient control over our work situation to be able to deal with the level of demands placed on us. A bus driver may be held to a schedule that is virtually impossible to meet due to traffic congestion; the output of a cashier, computer operator, or assembly line worker is monitored, but they feel powerless to control the flow of work. One study showed that men whose jobs combine high psychological demand with little control over their work face two to three times the risk of heart attack than do sales people, professionals, executives, and other workers with lower demand or higher decision latitude in their work. Risk from job strain is equivalent to the risk of heart disease faced by smokers or by those with elevated blood cholesterol levels.

Unmanageable job demands include having to produce too quickly or facing excessively heavy workloads or conflicting demands. Having control includes choosing how to perform your job, being able to make decisions on your own, and being able to take part in decisions that affect you. Even seemingly small things like whether you can decide to take a break, make a personal telephone call, or run an errand significantly influence your sense of control and personal freedom at work.

Job dissatisfaction can result from underload as well as overload. Insufficient job variety or complexity causes boredom and depression. Without meaningful challenges at work and the opportunity for skills and esteem to grow, many workers become demoralized. When there isn't a good fit between the individual's needs, abilities, and aspirations and job demands and rewards, frustration develops.

Fortunately, some companies are redesigning the work environment to reduce job strain. Workers are given more freedom (and responsibility) in decision making. Assembly lines in which a worker spends the entire day installing one small part are yielding to work teams. In some auto factories, for example, teams are responsible for assembling an engine, front end, or the entire vehicle. Teamwork, skill variety, and self-pacing replace the lockstep, cog-in-the-great-industrial-machine mentality. Workers can then see how their efforts fit into the larger product. Some managers are also finding that distributing decision-making authority to front-line workers can improve the quality of the product as well as the work environment. Many women and men seem to work more effectively when they have some say over what they do and how they do it.

Unfortunately, many of us don't find such freedom or stimulation and can't change our jobs. Less than half of us are satisfied with our jobs, and nearly 70 percent of us would not keep our present job if it were financially unnecessary for them to work.

So what can you do if you face a hectic, demanding job with little opportunity for personal control? You can try to focus on small things that you can control. You can approach your boss with some suggestions on how to modify his demands or increase your control and active participation. You can consider a different job or gaining new skills to equip yourself for other, less straining, more satisfying work. But for many, these suggestions simply won't help. This makes it all the more important that you cultivate sources of satisfaction in life outside of work. For example, some people who are dissatisfied with their jobs find great pleasure in leisure activities and community involvement. You may need to shift your attention to private events in life that can give you satisfaction and solace, like hobbies.

Riding Your Own Hobby Horse

A search of the medical literature on the relationship between hobbies and health again reveals the pathological focus of medicine. Scores of studies exist regarding the health hazards of various hobbies and leisure activities: lead poisoning in painters and potters, higher cancer rates in amateur ham radio operators, skin conditions in gardeners. There is even some mention of how various diseases can interfere with hobbies. More pages are devoted to describing the hobbies of doctors, dentists, and nurses than how intense involvement in a hobby can be good for the mental and physical well-being of patients and people.

John is crazy about woodworking. He has set up a small workshop in his basement and during every spare hour (and some not so spare) you can find him working away on some project, completely absorbed in the task. He loves every stage of woodworking: from selecting just the right piece of wood to shaping the pieces to fit perfectly, to putting on the final coat of finish to bring out the subtle highlights in the wood. He proudly shows you a chair which took him well over eighty hours to craft. If you give him a chance, he'll gladly talk for hours about the new skills and techniques he learned while making the chair.

John is not paid for this work. The thought of selling his beloved chair never even occurs to him. He does it purely because he enjoys it. His hobby is like a retreat, a place to escape, an island of satisfaction. Within his workshop he discovers sources of self-confidence and self-mastery.

Having something you love to do, not for the pay of it, but just for the sake of it, is the essence of recreation. Whether it be sports, collecting material objects (art, stamps, or wine) or experiences (birds sighted, trains ridden, places traveled), or even recreational shopping, some kind of hobby seems an essential complement to healthy work.

13

. . . .

Indulging Yourself

The dictionary definition of *indulgence* is "to gratify or satisfy a desire." That's simple enough, we could all live with that. Unfortunately, for many the idea of indulgence has taken on a moral tone, and people often feel that to indulge in pleasurable pursuits is to sin or to waste time.

But pleasing yourself with special treats from time to time is vital to a healthy, satisfying life. This is especially true in modern life, where for many the opportunities for pleasure in work or other daily routines are scarce.

Modern life has taken much away from us. Especially important is the real and lasting relationship between our actions and their outcomes. A craftsman can see his or her triumphs and mistakes in wood and stone: If he or she does well, rewards can follow. Farmers can live or die by the choices they make: Do we pick or wait for a rain? Some do go under, but it is their own choices and mistakes that get rewarded or thrashed.

Now, it's not so clear. Your company can go out of business. Your division can get merged into another and you be let go. The whole country can go out of a business (like making television sets or cameras). There's nothing you can do about it.

Many people work from dawn to dusk and find little room

for sensual enjoyment or mental pleasure. (Not too many accountants actually delight in having all the columns of numbers match perfectly, or finding the divisional sales up over last year in some part of the country they've never been to.) There's often little to get your teeth into. For many their entire business can rise and fall on international economic tides over which they have little control.

So, we need to surround ourselves with little rewards that mean something to us, that we can keep separate. Whether it be a sip of wine, a shopping spree, a well-deserved vacation, a vigorous laugh, or a satisfying cry—such small indulgences can brighten and enliven our lives. Consider the following sampler of special treats. You can probably think of many other such healthy pleasures in which to indulge. Speaking of special treats, let's start with chocolate.

Chocolate: The Divine Decadence

For many, chocolate is the epitome of indulgence. You may give some to a lover as a symbol of your affection. You may make an urgent, midnight run to a neighborhood store to secure some when no other food, sweet or sour, will satisfy the craving. The Aztecs believed chocolate was a gift from the gods—and if you are one of the millions of chocolate lovers today you'll agree.

And yet, there is a dark side to chocolate. A friend of ours once went to a doctor for a check-up. He was asked if he had any food cravings. He sheepishly admitted a hankering for chocolate, but added that he tried to keep this passion in check because after indulging he often felt sluggish. The doctor smiled and replied, "Guilt." That comment thankfully cured him of his regard of chocolate as a guilty pleasure.

Yet chocolate somehow has gotten a decidedly bad reputation. It is said to add to your girth, clog your arteries, rot your teeth, and provoke pimples. While chocolate may not qualify as a leading health food, recent studies indicate that it is not evil incarnate, either.

For example, the old adage "eat it today, wear it on your face tomorrow" is simply not true. Studies in which chocolate was force-fed to patients have repeatedly failed to show that it either causes or aggravates acne.

There is also good news from the Tooth Fairy and dental researchers. Chocolate contains substances that appear to protect tooth enamel and help prevent tooth decay. Not that chocolate is endorsed by the American Dental Association as a preventive measure, at least not yet. But it seems to produce fewer cavities than other, nonchocolate sweets.

We all know that chocolate is high in saturated fats. However, cocoa butter, unlike other saturated fats such as dairy butter, palm oil, and coconut oil, does not jack up blood cholesterol by much. The principal fat in cocoa butter, stearic acid, actually may lower cholesterol levels. Unfortunately, the "good" saturated fat accounts for only some of the fats in chocolate. Nearly a third of the fat content is palmitic acid, which raises cholesterol levels. So as researcher David Kritchevsky commented, "I'd say chocolate lovers can now cut their guilt quotient. My standard advice remains what it has always been: Moderation, not martyrdom."

No one knows for sure why chocolate holds a special attraction for us, though theories do exist. It may be the caffeine content, which acts as a stimulant; or the generous doses of theobromine, which stimulates the muscles more than the brain.

One exciting theory speculated that chocolate contains phenylethylamine (PEA), a stimulating, mood-elevating brain chemical. In 1979 Michael Liebowitz and Donald Klein, psychiatrists at Columbia University, speculated that a craving for chocolate represented an attempt to raise brain levels of PEA. Since PEA is naturally produced during periods of elation such as those experienced while falling in love, perhaps chocolate cravings are really an attempt to duplicate the lover's "high." Unfortunately, PEA in food doesn't make it to the brain. In her book *Chocolate: The Consuming Passion*, Sandra Boynton dismisses this theory on other grounds: "Clearly it is not the lovelorn sufferer who seeks solace in chocolate, but rather the chocolate-deprived individual who, desperate, seeks in mere love a pale approximation of bittersweet euphoria."

Perhaps it's the flavor of chocolate itself that explains our obsession. Cocoa is a complex blend of over five hundred flavor components—more than twice as many as are found in the simpler treats of strawberry or lemon. Chocolate is also rich in volatile compounds that waft up the back of the throat to tickle the nose with fruity, earthy, malty, and floral scents. And then there's the velvety, melt-in-your-mouth feeling of chocolate as it transforms from a solid to liquid at just body temperature.

Tantalizing though these theories are, they're not as tantalizing as chocolate itself. Perhaps this gift of the gods will—and should—remain one of the sweet mysteries of life.

The Case for Wine (and Alcohol)

"A votre santé"— With glasses raised, people in every language and of every culture celebrate long life and good health with an alcoholic drink. Yet the medical view of alcohol consumption is decidedly dismal. Liver damage, impaired nutrition, depressed immunity, peptic ulcers, gastritis, and inflammation of the pancreas are all common in heavy drinkers.

Large amounts of alcohol can damage the brain and dull the senses, destroy heart muscle, and raise blood pressure. Alcohol use is associated with cancer of the mouth, esophagus, and liver, and possibly with lung, breast, prostate, and pancreatic cancer. Mothers who drink heavily are likely to give birth to babies suffering from mental retardation, stunted growth, and facial abnormalities. Alcohol increases the risk of deadly mishaps: from car accidents to drownings, from burns to falls. Sexual performance in men suffers with alcohol ingestion. As one of Shakespeare's characters observed, drink "provokes the desire but it takes away the performance."

The litany of disasters and disorders linked to alcohol is admittedly sobering: in large doses, booze is certainly harmful to many. But as a small, daily pleasure, alcohol has surprising health benefits. Nearly two-thirds of Americans drink alcohol, while fewer than 10 percent ever develop problems due to their drinking. The toasts to good health, therefore, may be closer to the truth than one might suspect.

People who drink *moderately* may live longer, healthier lives than either heavy drinkers, which is not surprising, or teetotalers, which is quite surprising. Moderate means approximately one to three drinks per day. (A twelve-ounce can of beer, a four-ounce glass of wine, and a mixed drink all contain more or less the same amount of alcohol, and count as one drink.)

One for the Heart

Moderate drinkers have less blockage of their coronary arteries, suffer fewer heart attacks, and face less risk of death from heart disease than do abstainers or heavy drinkers. In a landmark study, Arthur Klatsky and his associates found that moderate drinkers were only 40 percent as likely to be hospitalized with a heart attack than were total abstainers. In a subsequent investigation, they found the lowest overall death rates among those who averaged one to two drinks per day. Nondrinkers and people consuming three to five drinks per day had a 50 percent greater mortality rate, while heavy drinkers (six or more drinks daily) top the list with double the death rate of light drinkers. Most of the deaths among the heavy drinkers were due to cancer, cirrhosis, accidents, and lung problems—not heart disease.

The Honolulu Heart Study found that ex-drinkers had the highest rates of heart attack (fifty-six cases per one thousand), followed by teetotalers (forty-four cases per one thousand). Moderate drinkers had the lowest incidence, at (thirty cases per one thousand). In an editorial accompanying the publication of this study, a researcher with the Framingham Heart Study wrote: "It is encouraging to note that not everything one enjoys in life predisposes to cardiovascular disease. There is nothing to suggest, for the present, that we must give up either coffee or alcohol in moderation to avoid a heart attack."

Does the type of alcoholic beverage make a difference? The evidence slightly favors wine. Those countries that prefer wine tend to have the lowest rates of cardiac fatalities. Women who drink wine have a lower risk of a heart attack than those who drink beer or liquor. But beer is helpful, too: the lowest incidence of heart attacks in the Japanese men of the Honolulu Heart Study was among beer drinkers. (Results of other studies indicate that the type of alcohol makes little difference.)

However, no matter what the drink, the harms and benefits of alcohol critically depend upon the dose consumed. This idea was noted more than two thousand years ago by the mythical Greek, Eubuleus, as he commented:

> Three bowls only do I mix for the temperate; one to health, which they empty first, the second to love and pleasure, the third to sleep. The fourth bowl is ours no longer but belongs to violence; the fifth to uproar, the sixth to drunken revel.

While it is not clear how large these "bowls" of drink were, in modern terms the safest range appears to be up to about three drinks per day.

You might wonder whether you can save up your daily ration and consume the entire week's allotment in one drunken weekend. The answer appears to be *no*. There is higher incidence of blockage of coronary arteries in people who binge. Alcohol protects only with *moderate, regular consumption*.

Just how moderate alcohol contributes to healthier hearts is not known, but current evidence favors one, not for the road, but for the heart.

An Appetite for Wine

For centuries the ability of wine to stimulate the appetite has been extolled. For those who are underweight, such as the frail, elderly, or ill, the appetite-stimulating properties of wine can be a boon. One study of undernourished hospitalized patients revealed that a small glass of dry wine taken before meals boosted food intake by as much as 60 percent and body weight by 12 percent in as little as three months of "treatment."

However, for obese people, drinking has been a "no-no." The concern is excess calories: A beer may contain one hundred fifty calories and a sweetened mixed drink two hundred to three hundred. Fortunately, the dieter need not be overly concerned with an occasional drink. With only a drink or two a day, obese people seem to naturally decrease food intake to partially compensate for the calorie increase. Hence, there is less change in overall calorie intake or in weight from drinking than might be expected.

Alcohol may even *boost* the metabolic rate and burn off some of the excess calories. In a study at Stanford University, middle-aged overweight men recorded everything they ate or drank over seven days. The drinkers, who averaged approximately two drinks per day, did consume more calories than their nondrinking counterparts. However, the drinkers did not gain weight as expected. The imbibers' metabolic rates increased by some 13 percent on average after one drink, thereby burning off some of the excess calories from the drinks.

The boost in metabolism nullified from half to more than all the surplus alcohol calories in the men imbibing up to three drinks per day. Some people would then gain only half the weight, while some would actually lose weight from drinking. The researchers' conclusion: Moderate alcohol use may not be as fattening as traditionally believed.

Wine *with* meals may even decrease the amount we eat. One group of obese patients was served three four-ounce glasses of dry red table wine thirty minutes before meals, a second group drank the wine only with the meal, and the third group downed the wine at bedtime. The greatest weight loss occurred in the people who drank the wine along with their meals.

A Social Solvent

The hostile, staggering drunk; the physically abusive alcoholic; the pathetic drunk isolated in a fog of inebriation—such images of the psychological devastation due to alcoholism usually dominate our view. Moderate drinking, however, may produce some happier psychological effects. Many people report reduced anxiety and improved mood after consuming small amounts of alcohol.

The effectiveness of alcohol as a social lubricant is well illustrated in a study of elderly residents in a nursing home. Two months after the hospital staff began offering an afternoon beer to the geriatric patients, the number of them who could walk on their own increased from 21 percent to 74 percent (though how straight wasn't specified). Social interaction tripled, and the percentage of patients taking Thorazine, a strong tranquilizer, plunged from 75 percent to zero.

Moderate amounts of alcohol may even stimulate altruism. Psychologist Claude Steele and colleagues found that college students who had had a few drinks were more likely than nondrinking peers to offer help to a fellow student with a dull, tedious task. The alcohol appears to dissolve inhibitions, including those that restrain compassion and altruism. Indeed, alcohol, in the right amounts at the right time, may be the "milk of human kindness."

Fortunately, you don't have to drink alcohol to derive most of the psychological benefits—you just have to *think* you are drinking alcohol. Studies show that when people drink tonic water but *think* they are consuming a vodka-laced drink, their mood and behavior changes in line with their expectations. If they think that alcohol makes people less inhibited, more relaxed, sexually aroused, and more sociable, then that's what happens. On the other hand, if they down a glass of vodka and tonic but believe it to be alcohol-free, none of these expected changes occur. Both types of responses appear to depend more on the contents of the drinker's mind than on the contents of the glass.

The Risks of Moderation

So far the evidence seems to favor those who indulge in moderate drinking. The risks of one or two drinks per day on average seem minimal, while the benefits are probable. Recently, however, there have been reports that the consumption of as few as three alcoholic drinks *per week* is linked with a significant increase in the risk of women developing breast cancer. However, other studies of women and breast cancer have found no association at all. In addition, no one has come up with a plausible biological explanation for how drinking alcohol could lead to cancer in breast tissue. This is quite a different situation than that of the proven cancer-causing effect of cigarette smoke on lung tissue. Also, unlike cigarettes, where smoking more increases the risk, higher doses of alcohol—more than one drink per day—do not seem to further increase the risk of breast cancer.

So the link between *moderate* alcohol use and breast cancer is far from proven. Even if there is a slight increase in the risk of breast cancer, the benefits of a significant reduction in heart disease greatly outweigh the possible risk of cancer.

If you drink moderately, should you stop? Probably not, unless you show signs suggesting you may have a problem controlling your drinking (see "Are You at Risk?," below). If you don't enjoy a daily drink or two, should you start? Not necessarily. Alcohol may not be your cup of tea. It's a personal choice, and you may find other, more enjoyable ways to improve your health.

Are You at Risk?

1. Do you have the following symptoms after drinking: stomach pain, nausea, heartburn, fatigue, weakness, frequent headaches, insomnia, or depression?
2. Do you need to drink in the morning to start the day?
3. Do you ever do things while drinking that you regret afterward?
4. Do you black out or forget what happened during a drinking episode?
5. Do you have trouble stopping drinking when you want?
6. Do you have five or more drinks daily?
7. Are your friends or family concerned about your drinking?
8. Does your drinking interfere with your family relationships or work?
9. Do you drive under the influence?
10. Do you have a family history of alcoholism? (Alcoholism is four to five times more prevalent in offspring of alcoholics. Whether this is due to a genetic predisposition or to social factors is not known.)

If you answered yes to any of these questions, drinking alcohol may be an unhealthy pleasure for you. If you answered yes to more than three questions, an alcohol problem is very likely. Seek professional counseling or contact your local Alcoholics Anonymous chapter.

Born to Shop

For many people, shopping is their favorite hobby. They endlessly prowl the malls in search of juicy bargains. When suitable prey is spotted they quickly pounce on it, wrap it up, and drag it home, where it is shared, displayed, or devoured. Sounds like the remnants of the hunting-gathering behaviors that sustained our early ancestors.

Today, shopping is more than a matter of survival. Recreational shopping has emerged as a favorite pastime. The average adult—woman or man—spends approximately six hours every week shopping. And not just for necessities. Over half of all purchases are made on impulse. One survey of mallgoers found that fewer than 25 percent had come there in pursuit of a specific item.

Shopping, like so many other pleasures, can be healthy in moderation. It can dispel boredom, lift the spirits, quell loneliness, and provide the backdrop against which we can live out our fantasies. Some shop for sport, searching for a great bargain, bartering when permitted, and celebrating when they make a killing. The "high" that comes from finding "just what you were looking for," or even a good deal on something you weren't, has been likened by some veteran shoppers to the effect of a drug.

Many head for the malls to find the company of others. The shopping center has replaced the town square as a gathering place. They stroll up and down the shop-lined promenade, refreshing acquaintances and, on occasion, making new ones. It's a safe haven: where else can you safely walk the streets at night in most cities? The mall has also recently become a choice indoor exercise facility for many seniors. For some, it's an escape from loneliness. Most avid shoppers are single, widowed, or divorced.

Shopping can also provide relief from boredom. Seeking out the hottest fashion, the latest model car, the newest record, or a fruit just come into season can satisfy some of our hunger for novelty. Wandering about the mall can be an escape, a mini-vacation that distracts you from worries and concerns.

Of course, there is a dark side to recreational shopping: On just the other side of the street from shopping for fun and enjoyment lies compulsive shopping. The afflicted relentlessly roam the stores, and now, the channels of the television shopping networks, in search of something to fill the void, to make them whole, all the while racking up an enormous consumer debt. They are trapped in the search for happiness through the acquisition of material things—a hopeless mission as we've seen. It's here we encounter the millions of people cutting up their credit cards, and Debtors Anonymous, a life-saving self-help group for compulsive spenders.

Fortunately, compulsive shopping, like so many other addictions, is the exception, not the rule. Most of us can safely and enjoyably indulge in shopping and reenact this hunt in modern dress. But sometimes we need more than a quick shopping trip to rejuvenate—we may need to take serious time off.

Time Off for Good Behavior

Perhaps you feel bored with the usual routine and want some fresh stimulation. Or perhaps you are a bit overwhelmed by the stresses and strains of daily life and just want to escape to a quiet spot for some well-deserved rest.

You need a vacation, a chance to invigorate yourself. A vacation can be the breeding ground for some of life's healthiest pleasures, and a good investment in yourself.

Vacations, of course, mean different things to different people. They can provide a rare opportunity for recapturing those uncluttered and free moments of childhood, when playful learning about the world and about the self was the only real necessity. A vacation can lead to a rediscovery of the body, of forgotten physical skills, of social charms; perhaps it can even lead to a different attitude toward the life left at home.

Some Good Excuses to Take a Vacation

Rest and Relaxation: While a vacation is certainly not a panacea for all that ails you, most people report relief from mental and physical stress. In one study, findings showed that a vacation reduced fatigue, digestive problems, insomnia, and loss of interest in sex by half. Headache pain plunged to only 3 percent, compared to 21 percent before the vacation. A survey of people on holiday in Brampton Island near the Great Barrier Reef found a marked drop in physical symptoms by the fourth or fifth day of vacation.

The first few days are usually devoted to the process of unwinding, gradually letting go of the tensions and routines of daily living. Not until the third or fourth day is there a real separation from the routine and full participation in the new experiences offered by the vacation. It is our birthright to have some free time, to wander, to explore, to play, and to rest. Doing "nothing" and just hanging out is a vital part of self-renewal.

Family Togetherness: Why not take a vacation to get to know your children better or to visit friends and relatives? When both spouses are working outside the home and relatives are scattered all over the country, vacations sometimes provide the only opportunity for families to spend more than a few hours together. Shared experiences and adventures, even when they are difficult, form the type of valued memories which draw people closer together and reinforce a sense of connectedness.

Meeting New People: Whether you travel to a distant exotic land or just beyond your own backyard, a vacation can be an opportunity to meet individuals with very different backgrounds, experiences, and views. Spending time with new and different people can enrich your own understanding of life, bringing a fresh perspective on your own habits, beliefs, and values. Sometimes chance meetings on a vacation can lead to lasting friendships.

Adventure: Thrillseekers roam the globe in search of new challenges: climbing a mountain, rafting a raging river, trekking to exotic, inaccessible villages. In contrast to the predictability of everyday life, such adventures offer unexpected delights. Adapting to such challenges and testing yourself against a new environment can be refreshing and can improve your self-esteem.

Self-Discovery: For some, a vacation may be more of a personal, internal adventure. Many self-seekers want to be alone to solve personal problems or simply enjoy themselves. Solitude is not a luxury—it is a periodic necessity.

Self-Indulgence: Perhaps one of the most compelling reasons to take a vacation is to pamper yourself. Most people work hard and are generally frugal. We all deserve to taste the fruits of our labor with a chance to splurge, to live it up, to fulfill our dreams, to be treated well and made to feel important. For some, this means a dream vacation in a luxury resort where every whim and fancy can be indulged. To others, it means a shopping spree in Florence, Paris, or Hong Kong, or perhaps bargain-hunting in some offbeat outdoor marketplace. Others prefer to travel off the beaten path to distant, exotic lands.

Unfortunately, many of us end up taking guilt trips instead of vacation trips. The thought of doing something indulgent for ourselves is so repugnant that either we never plan a special vacation or have serious second thoughts before or even during the trip.

Freedom: The essence of a vacation is the freedom to do what you want when you want. With so much of our time in the workaday world structured, disciplined, and controlled, a vacation offers the freedom to explore our own wishes and fantasies. For a brief moment we may escape the time pressures of the modern era and rediscover the joy of a less regulated lifestyle.

The Art of Vacationing

Reviewing the "excuses" above may help you clarify what you really want from a vacation and then help you choose the right type of respite. Perhaps you need adventure, risk, or breathtaking views to lift you out of the doldrums of your normal routine. On the other hand, your internal doctor might prescribe a slow-paced, relaxing sail to a tropical island.

When you return, try to plan a slow re-entry. Allow yourself a day or two when you return to settle into your home, sift through accumulated mail, or to call friends and relatives with the first wave of vacation stories before plunging into the usual work or school routine. Allowing a smooth transition will give some of the memories a chance to solidify.

Recalling previous vacations, their successes and disappointments, may also help you better understand your needs and plan your next holiday. Perhaps lessons can be learned from others' vacation experiences. Consider the conclusions drawn from a survey of over ten thousand readers of *Psychology Today* magazine.

> Those who enjoyed their vacations most tended to relish excitement and adventure, to enjoy meeting other people, and to not be overconcerned with comfort and convenience. They had traveled extensively during childhood and have learned from that experience how to enjoy vacations. They are more energetic than others, and not especially cautious. Finally, they look forward to their vacations with excitement or relief; they seem better able to wind down soon after they leave work, to feel vibrant when away, and, paradoxically, to look forward to returning.
>
> But they do not necessarily regard vacations as more important than work. . . . Thus, they do not seek a leisure-filled life, but a better *balance* of time between work, personal growth, and family.

Laughing Matters

When was the last time you laughed really hard? You know, a hearty, sidesplitting belly laugh, the kind that suddenly grasps you and sends you spinning, reeling out of control in a breathless euphoria? When was the last time your laughter reverberated in endless ripples, flooding your mind with a delicious ecstasy, erasing all memory of the inciting cause of laughter, leaving you laughing without reason? Not the controlled laughter of social amiability or the bitter laughter of scorn, ridicule, contempt, or cruelty; but a positive, health-affirming, joyful mirth.

The Bible proclaims "A merry heart doeth good like a medicine." Court jesters tended the emotional needs of monarchs. King Henry VIII was often relieved of his sadness by his favorite fool, Will Somers. Queen Elizabeth I was regularly amused by her jester, who "cured her melancholy better than all her physicians." But modern science is just beginning to confirm what the ancients pronounced. Laughter can sometimes be good medicine. And perhaps "He who laughs, lasts."

The scientific definition of a laugh is "a psychophysiological reflex, a successive, rhythmic, spasmodic expiration with open glottis and vibration of the vocal cords, often accompanied by a baring of the teeth and facial grimaces." But this gruesome description fails to explain the purpose of this uniquely human "happy convulsion."

Hearty laughter is a genial exercise of the body, a form of "inner jogging." A robust laugh gives the muscles of your face, shoulders, diaphragm, and abdomen a good workout. With convulsive or sidesplitting laughter, even your arm and leg muscles come into play. Your heart rate and blood pressure temporarily rise, breathing becomes faster and deeper, and oxygen surges throughout your bloodstream. A vigorous laugh can burn up as many calories per hour as brisk walking or cycling. In theory, you could stay in shape by lying on the sofa watching, say, the *Bill Cosby Laughout Tape*.

While laughing itself may be arousing, the afterglow of a hearty laugh is positively relaxing. Blood pressure may temporarily fall to below pre-laugh levels, your muscles go limp, and you bask in a mellow euphoria.

It Only Hurts When I Don't Laugh

During a hearty laugh your brain orchestrates a melody of hormonal rushes that rouse you to high-level alertness and may numb pain. Some researchers speculate that laughter triggers the release of endorphins, the brain's own opiates; this may account for the pain relief and euphoria that accompany laughter. Norman Cousins nursed himself back to health from a crippling arthritic condition, in part by watching reruns of *Candid Camera* and movies by the Marx Brothers. He claimed that ten minutes of belly laughter had "an anesthetic effect and would give me at least two hours of pain-free sleep."

Controlled studies suggest that laughter can, indeed, raise pain thresholds. Student volunteers listening to twenty minutes of Lily Tomlin joking about Alexander Graham Bell were far less sensitive to pain that their peers who listened to a dull lecture titled "Ethics and the Sociology of Peer Review."

There's even a hint that laughter may put your immune system in a better humor. Watching a humorous videotape of Richard Pryor temporarily boosted levels of antibodies in saliva that help defend against infections like colds. The immune enhancement only lasted an hour, but those subjects who reported using humor frequently as a way of coping with life's stresses had consistently higher baseline levels of these protective antibodies. So it may be necessary to laugh often.

The Importance of Not Being Earnest

Laughter is an invigorating tonic that heightens and brightens mood, releasing us from tensions, pretensions, and constraints. It usually arises from the sudden perception of incongruity between what we expect and what we see. Humor offers a healthful perspective on ourselves and the world. Psychologist Gordon Allport suggested, "I venture to say that no person is in good health unless he can laugh at himself, quietly and privately, noticing where he has overreached, [where] his pretensions have been overblown or pedantic. He needs to note when he has been hoodwinked, too sure of himself, too short sighted, and above all, too conceited." Laughter is an affirmation of our humanness.

Laughter, or at least humor, may also be an effective antidote to adversity. When confronted with a threatening situation, animals have essentially two choices: to flee or to fight. Humans have a third alternative: to laugh.

By seeing the humor in a stressful situation, we may be able to diffuse the threat and divert physiological arousal into merriment. When we laugh, we simply cannot be thinking about what's troubling us. Humor allows us to distance ourselves from a threat, short-circuiting the often paralyzing feelings of anxiety and helplessness. And there is some experimental evidence to support this. Levels of the stress hormones epinephrine and cortisol predictably fell when experimental subjects watched for an hour a comic pummeling a watermelon with a mallet and performing other ridiculous antics.

People who like humor, who liberally use humor in their lives, and who are themselves funny are less likely to suffer distress when confronted with negative life events. For example, imagine sitting at a table on which an old tennis shoe, a drinking glass, and an aspirin bottle have been placed. Now make up a three-minute comedy routine describing the objects on the table in as humorous a manner as you can. Research shows that the wittier the monologue you are able to produce, the less likely you are to become tense, depressed, angry, fatigued, or confused when confronted with stressors in your life.

Laughter can free us to detach and consider problems along new, creative lines. After viewing funny movies people tend to solve problems with more ingenuity and innovation. Think of the satisfying laughter that follows a sudden perception of the truth, the undeniably real, the candid, the world as it is, in a world usually veiled by pretense and misrepresentation. Custom and civilization urge upon us the conventional, the usual, the regular, the customary, the decorous, and the logical. Laughter is a celebration of the unconventional, the unusual, the irregular, the indecorous, the illogical, and nonsensical.

Not that all laughter is high-minded. Humor can discharge hostile, cynical, and resentful feelings. However, better through humor than through violence and physical aggression.

Healthy humor is a universal social balm, "breaking the ice," building trust, and drawing people together into a common state of well-being. Nothing sweeps away individual inhibitions like a rolling tide of laughter. A laugh can provide a face-saving way to express anxieties, fears, and other hidden emotions to others. Some experts even theorize that the baring of teeth in a smile or laugh says to others that while I may have teeth, I will not bite—a nonverbal sign meaning "it's safe, you may relax."

Yet how different are the laughs of people. What we find funny and how we laugh reflects our tastes, sympathies, and personalities. Some people belly laugh or let out booming, volcanic guffaws, complete with thigh-slapping. Others giggle, titter, snicker, or laugh tight-lipped covering their mouths. Still others seem to laugh with their eyes. What we laugh at and how we laughs is very expressive of our character. How a society deals with humor says a lot about that society as a whole.

Most of us don't take laughter seriously enough. Too often, laughter is regarded as child's play. To be adult is to be hardworking, responsible, and serious. We need to revive our natural sense of humor. If laughter is as contagious as it is said to be, then let's start an epidemic. Or perhaps we need doctors by the thousands to prescribe regular doses of humor. Though this Great Laughter Cure may not be a panacea, it is reassuring to learn, in these days of painful and expensive medical therapies, that laughter is medicinal and the only side effects are pleasurable.

There are many ways in which you can indulge yourself in humor. You can use it to help control your mood. Take liberal doses of funny movies, joke books, and the amusing antics of comedians. Laugh at other people's jokes: they'll feel better and like you more. Collect cartoons and jokes you enjoy from books, newspapers, and magazines. Share these with friends, colleagues, and family. Use humorous exaggeration to help see things in perspective. Jokingly expand a situation into mock life-and-death proportions.

Find a humorous motto and repeat it to yourself when you get in a stressful situation. For example, "Soon as you get to the top of the ladder, you'll discover it's leaning on the wrong wall." When you hear a new joke, tell it to at least five other people, preferably ones who haven't heard it. Can't laugh? Smile. Can't smile? Fake it.

Not-So-Idle Tears

"Tears, idle tears, I know not what they mean," lamented poet Alfred Lord Tennyson as he pondered why people cry. On the face of it, all this sobbing, bawling, weeping, and tearing makes little sense. Yet, recent evidence suggests that the tears produced by emotional crying may help the body release stress and dispose of toxic substances. It may seem strange to think of crying as beneficial. Yet most people say that "a good cry" makes them feel better, even when they're not crying tears of joy.

The belief that weeping has positive effects is ancient. More than two thousand years ago, Aristotle theorized that crying cleanses the mind of suppressed emotions by a process called catharsis—the reduction of distress by releasing the emotions. Many of us attend movies and plays that we know beforehand are tearjerkers. And we delight in the experience.

The vast majority of people report that crying improves mood and offers a welcome release of tensions. New evidence establishes some intriguing differences between the chemical content of tears triggered by emotional experiences and those provoked by irritants such as onion juice. The results of one study showed that emotional tears, experimentally elicited by viewing a sad movie, contain more protein than tears induced by irritants. Tear researcher William Frey contends that emotional crying is an eliminative process in which tears actually remove toxic substances from the body, helping to restore physiological and emotional balance.

Emotional tears also appear to contain endorphins, ACTH, prolactin, and growth hormone, all of which are released by stress. So crying may "cleanse the mind" in a much more literal sense than even the catharsis theorists imagined.

If shedding tears does serve a stress-reducing, excretory function, what are the consequences of suppressing our tears? Consider the strong prohibitions against crying, especially for men. In our society, men cry only one-fifth as often as women. Apparently men take very seriously the admonition, "Big boys don't cry." Big boys, however, for a variety of reasons also live shorter lives on average than their weeping female counterparts. Is there a connection between tears and longevity?

At least one study of men and women with peptic ulcers or colitis showed that they were less likely to cry, compared to their healthy peers. Also, the dry-eyed patients were more likely to regard crying as a sign of weakness or loss of control. While the research on psychoactive substances in tears is just beginning, there is reason to think that emotional tears may be important in the maintenance of physical health and emotional balance.

Intentionally indulging yourself is vital to maintain a level of pleasure often lost in today's hurried lifestyle and unnatural surroundings. Of course, indulgence and sensuality can get out of hand. Therefore, we must attend not only to ourselves but to others around us, especially those less well off. The benefits of helping others are surprisingly strong for us as well. A combination of minor self-indulgence and real selflessness, as we'll soon see, seems to contribute most to health and happiness.

14

. . . .

Selfless Pleasures

It was God who said, in the book of Genesis,
"It is not good that man should be alone."

Up to now, we've described many solitary, perhaps even selfish, practices to balance the sensual poverty and mental pessimism of much of modern life. Still, simply and selfishly increasing personal joy isn't the entire saga of healthy pleasure, because people don't really exist as individuals at all. All our lives are bound together. Individuals and society develop and thrive together. We're primed to live cooperatively, and to touch and nourish others in many ways. We evolved to find great pleasure in helping others. So being self*less*—caring about and working for others—can be healthy for oneself as well as others.

Consider how strongly we feel the pain of separation and apartness.

It was unendurable. I saw my buddies die each day in fighting but after a while I could stand it. I was captured and tortured and after a while I could stand it. But I couldn't stand even a few days of this.

This prisoner of war wasn't describing extreme physical torture or sustained starvation. He was recounting his experience of solitary confinement in the Korean war, a torture more difficult to endure than any other he described.

Each of us needs other people to complete ourselves and enliven us. We become ill when we're apart from others, and become healthier when we're involved in helping others. Joined in groups, joined in associations, relationships, teams, or companies, we become part of something beyond ourselves, something larger, something safer, something stronger than any of us alone. In part, it's because humans aren't complete human beings living solo.

This chapter offers suggestions why you should take seriously, as important, practical advice, concepts like "love your neighbor as yourself" and "when one person suffers, we all suffer." These aren't archaic and abstract principles, merely to be learned by rote in church or school. These ideals, common to almost all societies and religions, tell us something important about what it means to be human. They tell us that connecting with and helping others, being part of the human organism or social body, are genuine healthy pleasures.

The Social Body

Human beings are social animals and find being alone very difficult. Our individual bodies share in a living social body, and the health of each of us depends on our social connectedness. This view is in sharp contrast to the usual medical view of people as discrete and separate, with diseases that can be treated mainly with medication, surgery, or health regimes aimed at the individual.

However, our physiology does not stop at the skin, nor does our health. Consider the heart: Feelings of hostility and isolation of oneself from others appear to damage the heart. Self-centered people who feel *apart from* others, not *a part of* a larger social body, are more likely to succumb to heart disease. Disruptions of relationships with other people can profoundly disrupt health, which accounts for the spikes of illness after the loss of a loved one or after moving to a new city or country.

Men and women form social relationships, whether to spouses, friends, companies, societies, or even pets. In ancient times these social groups enhanced health in many practical ways: bringing up offspring, hunting and gathering, and cooperating against predators. But our connection with others is still vital; it is physical and tangible. Human society is a living organism, a social body, in its own right. Powerful evolutionary forces operating over millions of years have shaped it.

Human babies are born very early in their development, resulting in the longest infancy in the animal kingdom. A colt can get up and run within hours of birth; a kitten or a puppy can manage on its own within three months. But we are born helpless and remain so for years. Without bonding and ongoing care, we would all die. So our social dependency begins at our very beginnings and is a matter of life and death from birth on.

The comparative immaturity of human infants means that relatively little of our behavior is programmed by reflexes at birth. More of our learning is shaped by our almost umbilical connection with society. Our mind, our character, our outlook are molded by contact with others. Without a strong social connection, we're unfinished animals. And we suffer when the link to others is broken.

In adulthood we are still dependent on others, but in a more elaborate way. We look to the stabilizing cooperative network of society for food, shelter, the production of goods, and information.

Organized groups can accomplish what no individual can. Through cooperative efforts cities grow, land is farmed, and industry and technology develop. All this depends on our language ability, which binds us in a way different from that of any other animal. Language connects individuals into a larger society in which their own chances to survive improve.

There seems to be some channel, deep inside us, that transmits these social needs. Maybe this is what happens when the immune system declines when the person's attachment to the social body is ruptured, as in widowhood or in grief. And a solid connection to the larger social group, even to humanity as a whole, may have the opposite result: improved resistance helps the person remain a more valuable, connected group member. The unit of survival is not just the individual, but the species.

This may be one reason why almost all societies emphasize the same virtues, and why there is such stress in most religions upon caring for others, upon being generous to others, and upon serving others. Doing so is not only helpful to the entire community but to the health of the donor. Even *watching* others help seems to help us. When students at Harvard University watched a film of Mother Teresa tending to the sick and dying of Calcutta, their immune functioning improved. Even men and women who consciously showed no sympathy for Mother Teresa responded with enhanced immunity.

Marriage: Why Can't a Man Be More Like a Woman?

The health benefits of social contact can be clearly seen in marriage. For most people marriage is the primary connection with others and, as it turns out, the most beneficial, especially for *men*. Married men live longer, have fewer illnesses, and appear happier. Married *women* don't do as well, possibly because the status of women in society at large is still unequal. So one major principle for health seems to be: either be a woman or marry one.

However, this one-sided benefit of marriage has its costs: married men react more strongly to the loss of their wives than do women to the loss of their husbands. Death rates for widowers are more than three times higher than widows' after the loss of a spouse.

This happens because men and women form different types of connections with others, at least in our culture. Male friendships are rarely lifelong. Instead, men have school chums, fishing buddies, and work associates— friendships specific to different circumstances. What is important is that men usually don't form strong emotional ties in these friendships, and often don't have a close confidant outside of their marriage. Women operate differently. They often keep lifelong ties with friends of their youth and with their families, and have more close, long-lasting confidants, whom they tend to keep even after marriage. It is this strong emotional tie that seems to ensure health: In one study, people who felt loved were 1.7 times less likely to have heart trouble than those who didn't.

To return to the dissolution of marriage: there is an immediate physiological reaction to the loss when a spouse dies. But since women are more likely to have other strong social bonds and people with whom to confide and share feelings than are men, they are less vulnerable to the loss and less likely to suffer, at least in terms of health, from the trauma of bereavement. For men, the risk of illness following divorce is probably magnified due to the loss of their *only* confidant. There's no one to express pain with, to grieve with, to connect with, to care for.

These social bonds bond health. People who are single, separated, divorced, or widowed are twice as likely to die prematurely than those who are married. They also wind up in the hospital for mental disorders five to ten times as frequently. Heart disease, cancer, depression, tuberculosis, arthritis, or problems during pregnancy occur more in those with few social ties.

These connections between human beings are subtle ones, perhaps not as visible as an artery or a nerve, but just as vital. We don't perceive the unseen hand of others in society, but it operates all the time: a mile runner needs another racer to set the pace that will break the record; bicyclists never set records alone.

In areas with great family instability, many illegitimate children, and single-parent families, there are higher death rates from stroke and high blood pressure. Each time the unemployment rate increases by 1 percent, 4 percent more men and women commit suicide, and 2 percent more die of cirrhosis of the liver or cardiovascular disease. People even commit suicide more readily when they read that someone famous has done so: after Marilyn Monroe died, the rate went up 12 percent. People with few close friends die faster than those with close emotional ties, and people who feel they have someone they can turn to, who feel loved, have lower incidence of coronary artery disease.

The Joys of Parenting

The bond between parent and child is perhaps stronger than any other. Yet we can think of scores of reasons, some health-related, *not* to have children. They take up an enormous amount of time: many say that raising a child is easily more demanding than a full-time job. It's very expensive: Some estimate the cost of raising a child from birth to college at several hundred thousand dollars. Even childbirth is risky, at least for mothers. But both parents can get sick from their offspring; most parents with school-aged children battle cold after cold given them by their young ones. Also, parents can lose a child to illness or accident, a crushing blow to anyone's health and mental stability.

Given all this, it is a wonder than anyone chooses to have children. Some say we are biologically programmed to have sex, and children are just the byproduct. But to us children represent the essence of healthy pleasure. They provide adults with a needed excuse to play, to act and talk silly, and to appreciate once again the small sensual pleasures in life. Just watching a child smell a flower for the first time or dance to a new tune reminds us of our own potential for joy. With children, there is no delayed gratification or sense-less mental barriers to healthy sensuality.

Children also give us a sense that we matter, that we are needed. They force, or should we say, invite us to look outside ourselves. The constant care and feeding of a child is as close to selflessness as most of us get. As they develop, children prompt us to think ahead to what the world will be like for the next generation. They connect us to a seamless human progression, and their growth can be an optimistic affirmation of the future. Though raising children certainly can be a hassle, some of the most intense pleasures in life come from being a parent.

There is even some evidence of the double payoff in parenting of feeling good and better health. In at least one study, married couples with children lived longer than childless couples.

The Pet Prescription

Our strong connection to others even extends to animal companions, who for many are just like another child in the family. However, as a pet-owner you can get clawed, scratched, or bitten. You can contract rabies, ringworm, or lung disease. You might, therefore, wonder why over one-half of American homes have one or more pets. One reason is that, contrary to the bad news with regard to pet-associated diseases, owning a pet can be good for your health. Among people who suffer a heart attack, pet owners have one-fifth the death rate of the petless. Since most people don't walk their pet fish or lizards as they do their dogs, the benefits don't lie in increased exercise. But talking over the day's problems with your cat, confiding problems or sorrows with your golden retriever, or just looking at fish swimming in their tank, as we've seen, can lower blood pressure.

Pets prescribe health in several ways. First, through the sense of responsibility experienced by pet owners, who may have an added incentive to survive in order to continue to care for their animal companions, who depend so completely on them. Second, having a pet provides moments of pleasure and solace in hard times, and a pet's compelling needs can interrupt our bad times. When the dog has to go out, out goes an ongoing argument, too. The pleasure cancels the negativity. Third, pets help connect us to the larger world outside ourselves, so, prescribing a pet may at times work better than prescribing a pill. Pets, along with other interests, shift attention outside ourselves and absorb some of our stresses, and provide a launching pad for positive feelings, which triumph.

Alone or Lonely?

Most of us use the words *alone* and *lonely* interchangeably. But there are times when we want to sit alone in solitude, away from the noisy life with others. This isn't loneliness. And there are times when we're with a large group, but feel alone in their midst, maybe even because of all those around us. If alone always means lonely, then we should feel less lonely when more people are around. And, as we grow older, we should feel more and more lonely as friends die and leave us. But the opposite is true. Young people, who have many contacts, are the most lonely; and the older we get, at least until loved ones die, the less lonely we are likely to be. Why? Looking at this may yield some clues to reducing loneliness. Of course, there are some social factors in loneliness. It is highest in the uneducated, unemployed, and poor. But the most important factor is our comparisons; the match between our desire and our current world. Young people are hopelessly romantic. They seek the ideal mate, friend, job, and future. A popular young man may find that none of his friends comes up to his standards. The illusions of youth are almost those of the depressive: Nothing is good enough; there's always dissatisfaction. Mr. or Ms. Right is never there. So we discount who *is* there.

But as we age, our expectations change. We realize that perfection exists only in our minds, not in life, and that others have their faults as do we. We tend to focus more on the positive, connecting with what we can in other people. Comparisons change; we can become grateful for what they have and are happier with what we have in life.

According to major surveys, lonely people are dissatisfied with everything—living arrangements, number and quality of friends, work and sex lives. And this loneliness, is certainly neither healthy nor a pleasure. But you can change your loneliness.

Making a Good Connection

It is the quality of your intimate relations that defeats loneliness, not just the number of your friends. People can feel profoundly alone in the midst of hundreds of acquaintances if they aren't close to anybody. So it's important to have people you can depend on in life and important to invest yourself in these relationships. Unless the relationship is extremely destructive, it's often worth the hassle of putting up with someone who is a pain if you are really close to him or her. And remember, the best way to have friends is to be a friend. Don't expect perfection from others and don't lose contact with people because they do something you don't agree with. We have multiple selves, and, as no one faces reality, no one faces another person fully. We connect parts of ourselves to different parts of each other, and our illusions with respect to life and people often interfere. Lighten up on others—you're more connected to them than you may believe.

Make sure that you have close confidants in your life. It may be a clergyman, an old friend, a mentor, or a lover, but make sure there are people in your life with whom you can share your problems and difficulties. If your mate is your only confidant, you should begin to take seriously the lesson of married men and women: Act more like a woman and have confidants outside the primary relationship. They're important in keeping you connected and stable if your lover is away, if he or she dies, or if you split up. Like multiple selves, you can't keep all your feelings in one basket. You need a place to go emotionally, always.

Heartbreaking Hostility

Q: How many self-centered people does it take to screw in a light bulb?

A: One. He holds it still while the world revolves around him.

The social world speaks to our bodies, and we reply. Our health and happiness lie in this vital conversation. People who cut themselves off from others, who focus almost exclusively on themselves, and who harbor hostile feelings toward others seem to be at particular risk for heart disease.

Hostility is a continuing animosity that accumulates in response to minor incidents. Friends may note that a person outwardly expresses concern regarding others, while preoccupied with his or her possessions, insurance, pension, social status, income, investments, and more, and displays more anger than appropriate about nearly everything. Those people with the most hostility show the most blockage of their coronary arteries.

We're not arguing for a nice-guyism type of approach: Anger can serve a useful function, goading us out of unproductive life situations. It is necessary to express such feelings from time to time to get what we need, to drive obnoxious or threatening people away, or to "clear the air."

But hostility as a way of life puts us at risk. There is a strong sense of self-involvement underlying hostility. A person who thinks of himself or herself as better than others in many ways is vulnerable to anyone who confronts such claims. Hostility may be a strategy for coping with such challenges by saying, "Who do you think you are to challenge me like this!" To the self-involved, almost any event can be viewed as a personal threat: the turn of the stock market, the prospects for one's company, and the daily difficulty in a marriage. Individuals who think that everything is theirs—*my* wife, *my* kids, *my* company, *my* car, *my* neighborhood, *my* church—have a lot of territory to defend.

Those who are hostile use more self-references in conversation; they use the words *me, my, mine,* and *I* more frequently. The "mine" expression is the aspect of the self that claims ownership—"That's my money!" When we begin to look at the world through these eyes, a viewpoint usually considered egocentric, there are consequences within the brain and the heart. Heart attack survivors are usually less self-involved than those who die from a heart attacks. Blood pressure reactions to challenges are higher, too, in self involved individuals. The self-centered, hostile person tears his heart out because he or she is likely to have intense reactions to stress. Such a person responds to everything as a challenge and mobilizes to face it.

Self-centered, hostile people set themselves apart from the world rather than see themselves as a part of it. They have seceded from the social union, and cut themselves off from the life-sustaining give-and-take of social intercourse. The result may literally break their hearts.

The antidote is selflessness. It connects us to others and dampens the threats of many different situations. If we focus on the welfare of others, then we gain a more stable, less disturbing view of life's changes and shocks. And being connected with others may also shelter us from illness.

Selfish Altruism

"Afterwards I always feel calm but energized. It gives me a warm glowing feeling. An almost physical sensation in my chest."

"I was hesitant at first, but now I can hardly live without it. It's what gives my life meaning."

"I find it relieves my arthritis pain better than any medication."

"It gives me a chance to forget myself."

You might think these people are describing some gratifying sensual experience or a drug "high." Actually, these are comments from hospital volunteers describing their feelings about helping others. In addition to benefiting those they help, volunteers report a kind of "helper's high," and at times euphoric sensation that accompanies their efforts. In one survey of volunteers, nine out of ten reported that they are as healthy or healthier than others their own age.

Attention outside of ourselves, whether it be to other people, a pet, a plant, or a natural scene, or to a religious, philosophical, or political cause, seems to be important to health. Like other healthy pleasures, forgetting ourselves seems to both feel good and pay off in terms of better health. It might be that one aim of the religious emphasis on service has been to keep the helpers healthy. Attention to the larger group, away from a constant focus upon ourselves, is something we should not neglect.

This is the central message of most self-help groups. Leaders of Parents Without Partners tell potential new officers, "The more you put into PWP, the more you get out of it." It is lore in Alcoholics Anonymous that those who help other alcoholics help themselves to stay sober. This idea has been dubbed the "helper-therapy principle" by those who study how people get better. And it's a principle that, if applied to our own lives, may protect us from getting ill in the first place.

There has been a lot of research in the past few decades with respect to social ties and health, showing that those rich in friends live longer. Perhaps the most startling finding of all this work is from a large study in Tecumseh, Michigan, which followed 2,700 people for close to ten years. Those men who did regular volunteer work had death rates two and one-half times lower than those who didn't. However, there was little or no reduction in death rate for women. This happens, perhaps, because most pre-liberation women already had ample opportunity to take care of others without additional voluntary work.

Being in control and having a choice is crucial to the health benefits of giving. If you are forced to help, for whatever reason, you may not benefit. Those who must care for sick loved ones for long periods often report more, not less, stress and illness. People caring for a family member with Alzheimer's disease also have been found to have depressed immune function. But when the caring is voluntary, we seem to get as much, or more, than we give.

Why Helping Others Helps You

How do compassion, charity, and generosity benefit us? We receive the benefits of helping others through a number of the psychological mechanisms described in this book. It's important to embrace the insights of Alcoholics Anonymous and other self-help organizations. In these organizations, sensitivity to others is the final key to a healthy, meaningful life. There is little research evidence to back these claims, but what there is is positive. Among twenty volunteers at a Catholic college in rural Pennsylvania who volunteered as helpers, those who helped face-to-face benefited more than those who did administration. But even the latter fared better than those who didn't help at all. So the more contact we have with others, the better for us. We need to meet the people we help, see their lives, connect with them.

Most of us feel uncomfortable seeing someone else's pain or misfortune. You may, by helping others, relieve your own distress and prevent pleasure-denying guilt feelings.

Helping others also removes us from the sequences of difficulties and problems we live in. By focusing on someone else's problems, we get a break from our own family, financial, and work hassles.

We can get a special kind of attention from those we help. This sincere gratitude can be very nourishing. Like the impoverishment of sensuality, we lack healthy doses in our lives of genuine appreciation and heartfelt thanks for our good actions. Most of us need such thanks from others, and need to feel that we matter to someone.

Helping others also changes our mental comparison in many healthy ways. Most of our judgments about ourselves come from comparing ourselves to a small, select group of people in our lives. Helping others, especially those most needy, brings us into contact with new people and can help us refocus our frame of reference. For example, when we help someone who is less capable, we may well grow to feel more competent ourselves. Teaching someone to read or learn a craft can remind us of our own skills and strengths. Often, our assessment of how financially secure or how healthy we are is limited to a comparison with few people. But associating with those who are poorer or less able allows us to get a more comprehensive perspective. You're probably not so poorly off as you might think. You can see all that you have, materially, socially, and physically, that you take for granted. And be grateful for what you do have.

There are also probably direct effects of helping others on one's physiology, as observing Mother Teresa tending the unfortunate seems to boost immune function. Caring for others may break the stranglehold that hostile self-centeredness has on your heart. Scientists don't understand all of this yet, but certain feelings can surely have important effects. Compassion and empathy refocus our attention and consciousness outside ourselves, and the feelings of warmth and unconditional attention that we might give to others come back to us.

Why not give it a try? You can easily find time to spend an evening every other week teaching someone to read or visiting someone in the hospital. If you're more of an entrepreneur, why not start a community self-help operation such as a soup kitchen, an association to help refurbish vacant homes for the homeless, or a political group that will lobby to get more homes built. If you're rich, remember that an excess of money doesn't really help you. Instead of paying that last bit in taxes, a donation can help restore sight to a child, nourish a pregnant mother who lacks the means, or house a refugee. This will give you better value for your donation than buying the latest high-tech high-resolution television to replace your current set. If you have secretarial, accounting, or administrative skills, many helping organizations could use your talents. Even if you're relatively unskilled, surely you can find some way to help. You can begin to tap into a healthy feedback loop: When you help others, your mood and their mood improves. And when people feel better, they are more likely to help others. Why not start a chain reaction?

WE hope these selfish reasons for helping others get you started. But they are only a start. If you help others because you feel you will be condemned otherwise, you won't benefit. If you are helping because you've just read that it is good for you, it probably won't be. If you're helping to gain attention, wealth, or fame, you may achieve that, but not much more. If your generosity is *calculated* to benefit you, you're likely to get shortchanged.

Healthy altruism comes from the understanding that you and those around you are part of the same human community or social body. When one person suffers or is deprived, all of us are affected. It is for this reason that religions counsel generosity and service to others. The human community is strengthened and the server, too, benefits.

It is important, even vital, to be able to connect with other people and to be part of life in general; our lives, our health, and our destiny are connected with that of others. *The great surprise of human evolution may be that the highest form of selfishness is selflessness.*

15

· · · · · · · · · · · · · · · · ·

Healthy Pleasure Points

Oscar Wilde wrote that "simple pleasures are the last refuge of the complex." They are more than an oasis in life: They may be the best defense against illness and way to lengthen life.

This book offers a unique kind of advice for a healthy life. The focus is not on the latest, most elaborate health program or medical miracle, but on the commonplace, simple pleasures that can improve mood and sustain health. The pleasures are many, they are varied, and they are life-giving— from cultivating a garden to implanting of an optimistic outlook; from downing hot chilis to sinking pessimism, from the heat of a sauna to the warmth of caring for others. Such simple acts have health benefits in many cases greater than the latest diet, workout routine, or wonder drug.

It is important to regain lost pleasures, because each of us comes into the world unaware of the changes in the world before us. The natural world that sustained us throughout evolution is fast disappearing from our lives. We are the first generation to lose touch with the world that made us: In the last century we've changed the environment more than at any time in history, and many of the connections between life-enhancing elements inside us and life outside are cut off. Farmland is disappearing, the oxygen supply is being depleted, and pleasurable outdoor activities have nearly vanished for the urban majority. The sun is something in the background, and the seasons seem only to appear in advertising campaigns, invisible as we sit in our air-conditioned or heated cars or trains for hours on the way to work. This may not be the world we want to live in, but we do.

Our lives have become impoverished, and we need to pay more attention to our real sources of pleasure. Often our connection with outside life is lost in the minutiae of the day, and we need a reminder to get back to doing what's vital and central to us, with the new knowledge that doing so will benefit us.

As we said at the beginning, this is a book about making a lasting and real change. We think real change can come about because the actions we suggest are easy to do and pleasurable, except, of course, for getting tough problems off your chest. While all the advice may sound simple, beware of rejecting it because it all seems too easy.

WE realize that all disease is not determined by a lack of healthy pleasures. In fact, sometimes, disease and illness can undermine our ability to pursue and experience pleasure. Some people, despite following all the advice offered here, will still find themselves sick. But to foresake our natural endowment—the inborn health-promoting aspects of pleasure—seems a waste.

Many of us need to regain something lost in the progress of modern life and lost as we grow from child to adult—the ability to appreciate and celebrate simple joys. Children seem to be able to totally immerse themselves in daily activities; they learn by playing. As adults we tend to overload our pleasures with delight-defeating meanings. Parties and social gatherings, once the source of fun, become battlefields for social anxieties and obligations. A massage triggers thoughts of work not being done and guilt for time "wasted." We need to personally and culturally reclaim our birthright: the ability to enrich our lives through pleasure.

Pleasure begets pleasure, which enhances mood, which benefits health. The feedback system within us amplifies an increased vitality and enjoyment. Suppose you do a little exercise, like walking 10 minutes. You feel better, your mood brightens. These small mood changes help you think more positively about other actions. You feel more hopeful, can plan the future better, and may even increase your immunity to disease.

After a while, the small changes add up. Each one makes it possible for us to do more, and do it more easily. Changing your internal story makes it possible for you to relax, which might make it possible for you to feel better about yourself when you get a reprimand at work, so you avoid self-blaming, depressing tendencies. Don't discount the value of surprise. One innovative study found that people who were given unexpected food (cookies) were more likely to help others. And we know that in helping others we also help ourselves. And so, the cycle of pleasure, good mood, good acts, and good health rolls on.

The key, of course, is getting on the pleasure cycle. There are many different venues to choose from: exercise, relaxation, education, helping others, pets, hobbies, laughter, shopping, and more.

And you'll discover many more pleasures we haven't even thought of. You'll recognize the healthy ones by the way they make you feel—the improved mood, total absorption in the activity, sense of timelessness, and loss of self-consciousness.

Some modern pleasures don't bring health, of course. Our world may lack many natural delights, but there is no shortage of places to buy fatty foods, cigarettes, and drugs. Not everything that feels good is good for us anymore. And what

The alerting effects of naps in sleep-deprived subjects. *Psychophysiology* 1986; 23(4):403–408. Carey B: In praise of napping. *Hippocrates* March/April 1988; 49.

page 120 Trichopoulos D, Tzonou A, Christopoulos C, Havatzoglou S, and Trichopoulou A: Does a siesta protect from coronary heart disease? *Lancet* August 1987; 2:269–70.

page 120 Wingard DL and Berkamn LF: Mortality risk associated with sleeping patterns among adults. *Sleep* 1983; 6(2):102–107. Kripke DF, Simons RN, Garfinkel L, and Hammond EC: Short and long sleep and sleeping pills: Is increased mortality associated? *Archives of General Psychiatry* January 1979; 36:103–16.

page 121 Krueger JM and Karnovsky ML: Sleep and the immune response. *Annals of the New York Academy of Science* 1987; 496:510–16. Moldofsky H, Lue FA, Eisen J, Keystone E, and Gorczynski RM: The relationship of interleukin-1 and immune functions to sleep in humans. *Psychosomatic Medicine* 1986; 48(5):309–18.

page 121 Horne J: *Why We Sleep.* New York: Oxford University Press, 1988.

page 121 Oswald I: Sleep as a restorative process: Human clues. *Progress in Brain Research* 1980; 53:279–88.

page 121 Perhaps the greatest health benefits of being well-rested come from the prevention of accidents. More than 20 percent of car accidents involve sleepy drivers. A committee of scientists from the Association of Professional Sleep Societies recently sounded the alarm with respect to major catastrophes in the early hours of the morning due to human errors.

The most serious United States incident in a commercial nuclear power plant occurred at 4 a.m. on March 28, 1979, at the Three Mile Island plant unit 2 reactor in Pennsylvania. Between the hours of 4 and 6 a.m., shift workers failed to recognize the loss of core coolant water resulting from a stuck valve. Although a mechanical problem precipitated the incident, it was chiefly this human error of omission and the subsequent flawed corrective action that caused the near meltdown of the reactor later that morning. . . . Perhaps most disturbing is the fact that the nuclear plant at Chernobyl is officially acknowledged to have begun at 1:23 a.m. as the result of human error.

. . . The recent report of the Presidential Commission of the Space Shuttle Challenger Accident did cite the contribution of human error and poor judgment related to sleep loss and shift work during the early morning hours. In describing the substantial sleep loss experienced by senior managers at Marshall Space Flight Center before the evening teleconference with Morton-Thiokol on January 27, 1986, the report stated that the decision to launch "should have been based on engineering judgments. However, other factors may have impeded or prevented effective communication and exchange of information." The effect on managers of irregular working hours and insufficient sleep "may have contributed significantly to the atmosphere of the teleconference at Marshall." Certain key managers had obtained less than 2 hours sleep the night before and had been on duty since 1:00 a.m. that morning. The report noted that "time pressure, particularly that caused by launch scrubs and turnarounds, increased the potential for sleep loss and judgment errors."

Mitler MM, Carskadon MA, Czeisler CA, Dement WC, Dinges DF, and Graeber RC: Catastrophes, sleep, and public policy: Consensus report. *Sleep* 1988; 11(1):100–109.

page 122 Hales D: *How to Sleep Like a Baby*. New York: Ballantine, 1987. Hales D: *The Complete Book of Sleep*. Reading, MA: Addison-Wesley, 1981. Coates TJ and Thoresen CE: *How to Sleep Better*. Englewood Cliffs, NJ: Prentice-Hall, 1977.

page 122 Roth DL and Holmes DS: Influence of aerobic exercise training and relaxation training on physical and psychological health following stressful life events. *Psychosomatic Medicine* 1987; 49:355–65.

Chapter 9. ". . . And the Pursuit of Happiness"

page 127 The Eda LeShan quote is from Dennis Wholey's *Happiness* (New York: Ballantine Books, 1988).

page 131 In assessing happiness, different investigators use a variety of rating scales. Some are 4-point, some 5, some 7, some 9, some 11. For the sake of clarity, we have converted all the results into this standard 9-point scale so that unmatched studies are readily comparable. Some minor inaccuracies might result from this, but standardizing the scale greatly clarifies unrelated studies.

page 132 Comparison processes span everything from judgments of primitive sensations (e.g., heaviness and heat) to social status. Sensations are always louder, softer, brighter, dimmer, warmer, colder, greener, or redder than other stimulation.

Adaptation, too, is a common way in which the mind makes the world constant. Estimate the weights of objects between 2 and 6 ounces; a 1-pound object will seem "heavy," whereas it would seem "light" if you were judging 3- to 6-pound objects.

We calculate against a standard based on information experienced in the past. So, alike conditions could be pleasurable or painful depending on the previous "adaptation level." We adapt to noises and to pollution and don't even notice because compared to our standard things haven't changed. You travel to New York in the summer and say, "It's so humid." And the reply is, "You shoulda seen it yesterday."

page 133 See, too, Festinger L: A theory of social comparison processes. *Human Relations* 1954; 7:117–40.

page 133 The lottery winner study is by Brickman P: Adaptation level determinants of satisfaction with equal and unequal outcome distributions in skill and chance situations. *Journal of Personality and Social Psychology* 1975; 32:191–98.

page 135 General evidence on the psychology of happiness can be found in Argyle M and Henderson M: *The Anatomy of Relationships.* New York: Penguin Books, 1985; and Argyle M: *The Psychology of Happiness.* London: Methuen, 1987.

page 136 The section on the finances of happiness is based on a discussion in *The Psychology of Happiness* by M. Argyle.

page 137 Milan Kundera's *The Unbearable Lightness of Being* (New York: Penguin Books, 1986) is the source of the position we challenge, although we are great fans of his writing in most other respects.

page 140 The quote is again from Dennis Wholey's *Happiness* (New York: Ballantine Books, 1988).

page 140 Ed Diener and colleagues have developed the understanding about the need for many moments of happiness, rather than the great peaks. Larsen RJ, Diener E, and Cropanzano RS: Cognitive operations associated with individual differences in affect intensity. *Journal of Personality and Social Psychology* October 1987; 53(4):767–74.

page 142 The dollar bill study is recounted in Isen AM: Affect, cognition, and social behavior. In Wyer RS and Srull TK (eds.): *Handbook of Social Cognition,* vol. 3. Hillsdale, NJ: Erlbaum and Company, 1984; 179–236. The wisdom of the common expression "Have a nice day" takes on new significance: smiling brings about an external feedback system—others will be more likely to smile and a happier time will be had. However, the act of smiling may well also create the same kind of *internal* feedback system in which the smile actually stimulates further good feelings. So, small events such as petting the dog, gardening, telling ourselves a good story, or watching a funny movie might have much more profound effects than we might imagine.

page 144 The work of the German psychologists Strack and Schwartz has greatly added to our understanding of the psychology of happiness. Strack F, Martin LL, and Stepper S: Inhibiting and facilitating conditions of the human smile: A nonobtrusive test of the facial feedback hypothesis. *Journal of Personality and Social Psychology* May 1988; 54(5):768–77. Kommer D, Schwarz N, Strack F, and Bechtel G: [Mood and social information processing in depressive disorders]. *Z Klinical Psychology, Psychopathology, and Psychotherapy* 1986; 34(2):127–39.

In this experiment, subjects were asked to think about different kinds of past events: positive or pleasant, negative or unpleasant in the past. They then rated points on a scale from 1 to 11 at their current level of satisfaction and happiness. A positive past event caused happiness to be rated 6.23, but a negative past event rated 7.23!

page 146 Another study in Germany confirmed the result. In this study, good moods were induced by asking people to think about pleasant or exciting events. These investigators tested the mood-altering effect of weather conditions, the quality of the room, or whether the subjects' team had won a match. The results again showed that unpleasant weather had a very negative effect on mood, a pleasant room had a very positive effect on mood, and an unpleasant room as well, and the carry-over effect from a sports event was surprisingly high.

Chapter 10. The Optimism Antidote

page 149 For an excellent review of the importance of illusion and the relationship between depression and perception of reality, see Taylor SE and Brown JD: Illusion and well-being: A social psychological perspective on mental health. *Psychological Bulletin* 1988; 103(2):193–210.

page 153 For an in-depth exploration of the costs and benefits of illusions and denial, see Bresnitz S (ed.): *The Denial of Stress.* New York: International Universities Press, 1983; and Goleman D: Denial and hope. *American Health* December 1984; 3:54–61.

page 153 Psychologist Richard Lazarus comments on the necessity of illusions in our psychological economy:

The fabric of our lives is woven in part from illusions and unexamined beliefs. There is, for example, the collective illusion that our society is free, moral and just, which, of course, isn't always true. Then there are the countless idiosyncratic beliefs people hold about themselves and the world in which they live—for example, that we are better than average, or doomed to fail, or that the world is a benign conspiracy, or that it is rigged against us. Many such beliefs are passed down from parent to child and never challenged. Despite the fixity with which people hold such beliefs, they have little or no basis in reality. One person's beliefs are another's delusions. In effect, we pilot our lives in part by illusions and by self-deceptions that give meaning and substance to life.

Lazarus R: Positive denial: The case for not facing reality. *Psychology Today* November 1979; 44–60.

page 154 An excellent work on the biological necessity of denial is Goleman D: *Vital Lies, Simple Truths: The Psychology of Self-Deception.* New York: Simon & Schuster, 1985.

page 154 Denial can interfere with asthmatic patients taking appropriate action at the onset of symptoms to prevent severe asthmatic attacks. Staudenmayer H, Kinsman RA, Dirks JF, Spector SL, and Wangaard C: Medical outcome in asthmatic patients: Effects of airways hyperreactivity and symptom-focused anxiety. *Psychosomatic Medicine* 1979; 41:109–18.

page 154 Cohen F and Lazarus RS: Active coping processes, coping dispositions, and recovery from surgery. *Psychosomatic Medicine* 1973; 35:375–89.

page 155 Hackett TP, Cassem NH, and Wishnie HA: The coronary care unit: An appraisal of its psychological hazards. *New England Journal of Medicine* 1968; 279:1365–70. Hackett TP and Cassem NH: Psychological management of the myocardial infarction patient. *Journal of Human Stress* 1975; 1:25–38. Levine J, Warrenberg S, Kerns R, Schwartz G, Delaney R, Fontana A, Gradman A, Smith S, Allen S, and Cascione R: The role of denial in recovery from coronary heart disease. *Psychosomatic Medicine* 1987; 49:109–17.

page 156 For a review of the role of hope in therapeutic relationships, see Bruhn JG: Therapeutic value of hope. *Southern Medical Journal* 1984; 77:215–19.

page 157 Mills M, Mimbs M, Jayne EE, and Reeves RR: Prediction of results in open heart surgery. *Journal of Religion and Health* 1975; 14(3):159–64. Mason RC, Clark G, Reeves RB, and Wagner B: Acceptance and healing. *Journal of Religion and Health* 1969; 8:123–30.

page 157 Schmale A and Iker H: The affect of hopelessness and the development of cancer: I. Identification of uterine cervical cancer in women with atypical cytology. *Psychosomatic Medicine* 1966; 28:714–21. Schmale A and Iker H: Hopelessness as a predictor of cervical cancer. *Social Science and Medicine* 1971; 5:95–100. Goodkin K, Antoni MH, and Blaney PH: Stress and hopelessness in the promotion of cervical intraepithelial neoplasia to invasive squamous cell carcinoma of the cervix. *Journal of Psychosomatic Research* 1986; 30(1):67–76.

page 157   The words we use can reflect our degree of hope and may signal who is more likely to have cancer. Researchers analyzed interviews with women before the biopsy results for cervical cancer were known. They looked for certain key words such as "dark", "disgusting", "difficulty", "conflict", "cancer", and "tense", which suggested a mental state of hopelessness. Other marker words such as "desire", "eager", "expect", "longing", "wish", and "yearn" reflected a more hopeful attitude. Again, the more hopeless women were more likely to have biopsies showing cervical cancer. For details on how words may signal cervical cancer, see Spence D: The paradox of denial. In Bresnitz S (ed.): *The Denial of Stress*. New York: International Universities Press, 1983.

page 157   Rodin J: Aging and health: Effects of sense of control. *Science* 1986; 233:1271–76.

page 157   Increasing sense of control can pay off in health. In one bold experiment, elderly residents were given increased control with simple changes such as choosing their meals, determining when the phone would ring in their rooms, or how the furniture should be arranged. They were also asked to select a house plant and to take care of it. These may seem like trivial changes, but the increased sense of responsibility and control made them happier, more active, more alert, and most dramatically, lowered their death rate by 50 percent over eighteen months, compared with residents who did not have the experience of increased control. Langer EJ and Rodin J: The effects of choice and enhanced personal responsibility for the aged: A field experiment in an institutional setting. *Journal of Personality and Social Psychology* 1976; 34:191–98; and Rodin J and Langer EJ: Long-term effects of a control-relevant intervention with the institutionalized aged. *Journal of Personality and Social Psychology* 1977; 35:897–902.

page 157   Stern GS, McCants TR, and Pettine PW: Stress and illness: Controllable and uncontrollable life events' relative contributions. *Personality and Social Psychology Bulletin* 1982; 8(1):140–45.

page 157   Pennebaker JW, Burnam MA, Schaeffer MA, and Harper DC: Lack of control as a determinant of perceived physical symptoms. *Journal of Personality and Social Psychology* 1977; 35:167–74.

page 157   Laudenslager ML, Ryan SM, Drugan RC, Hyson RL, and Maier SF: Coping and immunosuppression: Inescapable but not escapable shock suppresses lymphocyte proliferation. *Science* 1983; 221:568–70. Their review article is: Maier SF and Laudenslager M: Stress and health: Exploring the links. *Psychology Today* August 1985; 44–49.

page 158 Bennett HL, Benson ER, and Kuiken DA: Preoperative instruction for decreased bleeding during spine surgery. *Anesthesiology* 1986; 65(3A):A245.

page 159 Gravelle K: Can a feeling of capability reduce arthritis pain? *Advances* 1985; 2:8–13. Lorig K, Laurin J, and Holman H: Arthritis self-management: A study of the effectiveness of patient education for the elderly. *The Gerontologist* 1984; 24:455–57. Lenker S, Lorig K, and Gallagher D: Reasons for the lack of association between changes in health behavior and improved health status: An exploratory study. *Patient Education and Counseling* 1984; 6:69–72.

page 160 For a discussion of self-efficacy theory developed by Albert Bandura, see Bandura A: Self-efficacy mechanism in human agency. *American Psychologist* 1982; 37:122–47. For a review of perceived self-efficacy applied to smoking cessation relapse, pain experience and management, control of eating and weight, success of recovery from myocardial infarction, and adherence to preventive health programs, see O'Leary A: Self-efficacy and health. *Behavioral Research and Therapy* 1985; 23:437–51.

One study documented physiological changes related to changes in people's belief in their competence. Catecholamine secretion, chemical substances released in response to stress, was measured in twelve women who had a spider phobia. The level of catecholamine secretion was related to the women's perception of how well they thought they could cope with a spider (looking at one, putting a hand in a bowl with one, and allowing a spider to crawl on her hand).

The higher the perceived capability to deal with the stressful encounter, the less stress and the less chemical secretion. When the sense of capability was enhanced with regard to the tasks which aroused the phobic reactions, secretion also dropped. So beliefs in one's capability reflect in improved physiology. Bandura A, Taylor CB, Williams SL, Mefford IN, and Barchas JD: Catecholamine secretion as a function of perceived self-efficacy. *Journal of Consulting and Clinical Psychology* 1985; 53:406–14.

page 161 The findings of the Manitoba Longitudinal Study on Aging are reported in Mossey JM and Shapiro E: Self-rated health: A predictor of mortality among the elderly. *American Journal of Public Health* 1982; 72:800–807. Another study of seven thousand adults in

Alameda County in California confirmed the importance of the way a person views his health. Men with poor self-rated health were 2.3 times more likely to die than those who saw their health as excellent. For women the difference was five times greater. The importance of self-reported health remained even when health behaviors (smoking, drinking, and exercising), social ties (marriage and contacts with friends), and psychological state (happiness and depression) were controlled for. Kaplan GA and Camacho T: Perceived health and mortality: A nine-year follow-up of the Human Population Laboratory cohort. *American Journal of Epidemiology* 1983; 117:292–304.

page 162 Scheier MF and Carver CS: Optimism, coping, and health: Assessment and implications of generalized outcome expectancies. *Health Psychology* 1985; 4(3):219–47. Scheier MF and Carver CS: Dispositional optimism and physical well-being: The influence of generalized outcome expectancies on health. *Journal of Personality* June 1987; 55(2):169–210. Scheier MF, Weintraub JK, and Carver CS: Coping with stress: Divergent strategies of optimists and pessimists. *Journal of Personality and Social Psychology* December 1986; 51(6):1257–64. Strack S, Carver CS, and Blaney PH: Predicting successful completion of an aftercare program following treatment for alcoholism: The role of dispositional optimism. *Journal of Personality and Social Psychology* September 1987; 53(3):579–84.

page 164 For a discussion of why (and how) some people seem to remain healthy in the face of stress, see Antonovsky A: *Unraveling the Mystery of Health*. San Francisco: Jossey-Bass, 1987.

page 164 You can get something of the flavor of the hardy personality from this profile:

A small, neat man in his mid-50's, Chuck L. introduced himself as someone who enjoys solving problems. In the company, his specialty is customer relations, even though he was trained as an engineer. His eyes light up as he describes the intricacies of investigating customer needs and complaints, determining the company's service capabilities and obligations, formulating possible solutions to disputes that appear fair to all parties, and persuading these parties to agree. He thinks customer relations work is more demanding as the company streamlines and approaches reorganization. Asked in a sympathetic manner whether this is making his job unmanageable, he notes an increase in stress but adds that the work is becoming all the more interesting and challenging as well. He assumes that the role he plays will become even more central as the company's reorganization accelerates. He looks forward to this and has already formulated plans for a more comprehensive approach to customer relations.

Chuck doesn't seem to neglect family life for all his imaginative and energetic involvement at work. He married in college, and the couple has two grown children. His wife has returned to school to finish a college degree long ago interrupted. Although her absence from the home causes Chuck some inconvenience, it is clear that he encouraged her. He is full of plans about how he can preserve a close home life. Should he find too much time to himself, he imagines he will get involved in useful community activities.

In the past, Chuck's family life has hardly been uneventful. His daughter's two-year-old son died; then her husband divorced her, and she returned home for a year. This was a difficult time not only for her but for Chuck and his wife, who felt their daughter's pain and sense of failure in a very personal way. Chuck describes the long talks they had. Although he mentions their crying together, it is also clear that he was always searching for a way, a formula, to relieve mutual pain. He encouraged his daughter to pick up the pieces of her life, learn from what had happened, and begin again. He tried to help his wife see that she had little responsibility in what had happened and that it was not the end of the world. He told himself the same thing. This difficult time, in his view, drew the three of them closer together.

Maddi SR and Kobasa SC: *The Hardy Executive: Health Under Stress*. Homewood, Illinois: Dow Jones-Irwin, 1984. Kobasa SC: Stressful life events, personality and health: An inquiry into hardiness. *Journal of Personality and Social Psychology* 1979; 37:1–11. Kobasa SC, Maddi S, and Kahn S: Hardiness and health: A prospective study. *Journal of Personality and Social Psychology* 1982; 42:168–77. Kobasa SC and Puccetti MC: Personality and social resources in stress-resistance. *Journal of Personality and Social Psychology* 1983; 45:839–50.

Some people take advantage of their mental capabilities for improving frame of mind and boosting immunity. In one study, hardy executives who didn't get sick had a strong *commitment* to self, work, family, and other important values, a sense of *control* over their life, and the ability to see change in their life as a *challenge* rather than a threat. This complex of positive beliefs is called hardiness.

Maddi and Kobasa have developed "hardiness induction groups," which encourage commitment, control, and challenge. Group members learn to focus on their bodies and mental sensations in response to stressful situations. They ask themselves questions such as, "What's keeping me from feeling terrific today?" This focusing increases optimism.

People are also encouraged to think about a recent stressful episode and imagine three ways it might have been worse and three ways it could have gone better. In addition, group members are given ideas of what to do when they come face to face with a stressor they cannot avoid or control, such as the death of a spouse or a serious illness. They refocus on another area of life in which they can master a new challenge and restore their sense of control and competence. They might learn a new skill, such as swimming, or offer their services in tutoring.

It seems to work. Eight high-stress, hypertensive executives attended eight weekly group sessions. At the end, their hardiness scores rose, they reported fewer symptoms of psychological distress, and their blood pressures were lower when compared to an untreated control group. So, it is possible to develop this sense of optimism.

page 166 For a popular account of optimism and health, see Silver N: Do optimists live longer? *American Health* November 1986; 50–53; and Trotter RJ: Stop blaming yourself. *Psychology Today* February 1987; 21(2):31–39. For the original research, see Seligman ME, Castellon C, Cacciola J, Schulman P, et al.: Explanatory style change during cognitive therapy for unipolar depression. *Journal of Abnormal Psychology* February 1988; 97(1):13–8. Peterson C and Seligman ME: Explanatory style and illness. *Journal of Personality* June 1987; 55(2):237–65. Nolen-Hoeksema S, Girgus JS, and Seligman ME: Learned helplessness in children: a longitudinal study of depression, achievement, and explanatory style. *Journal of Personality and Social Psychology* August 1986; 51(2):43. Alloy LB, Peterson C, Abramson LY, and Seligman ME: Attributional style and the generality of learned helplessness. *Journal of Personality and Social Psychology* March 1984; 46(3):681–87. Peterson C and Seligman ME: Causal explanations as a risk factor for depression: Theory and evidence. *Psychology Review* July 1984; 91(3):347–74. Peterson C, Bettes BA, and Seligman ME: Depressive symptoms and unprompted causal attributions: Content analysis. *Behavior Research and Therapy* 1985; 23(4):379–82. Raps CS, Peterson C, Reinhard KE, Abramson LY, and Seligman ME: Attributional style among depressed patients. *Journal of Abnormal Psychology* April 1982; 91(2):102–108.

Chapter 11. Telling Yourself a Good Story

pages 173–179 Cognitive therapy has begun to prove itself the major contribution to changing ideas and behavior. Aaron Beck is the prime exponent, although there are others: Beck A: Cognitive therapy: Nature and relation to behavior therapy. *Behavior Therapy* 1970; 1:184–200. Beck A and Bohnert M: Ideational components of anxiety neurosis. *Archives of General Psychiatry* 1974; 31:319–25. Beck AT: *Cognitive Therapy and the Emotional Disorders.* New York: International Universities Press, 1976. Beck AT: *Depression: Causes and Treatment.* Philadelphia: University of Pennsylvania Press, 1972. Beck AT: Thinking and depression. *Archives of General Psychiatry* 1963; 9:324–33. Beck A, Rush AJ, Shaw B, and Emery G: *Cognitive Therapy of Depression: A Treatment Manual.* New York: Guilford Press, 1979. Ellis A: *Reason and Emotion in Psychotherapy.* New York: Lyle Stuart, 1962. Ellis A: *Growth Through Reason: Verbatim Cases in Rational-Emotive Psychotherapy.* Palo Alto: Science & Behavior Books, 1971. Emery G: *Getting Un-Depressed* (updated edition of *A New Beginning*), New York: Simon & Schuster, 1988.

page 180 The comparative effectiveness of various forms of therapy is discussed in Frank JD: Therapeutic components shared by all psychotherapies. In Harvey JH and Parks MM (eds.): *Psychotherapy Research and Behavior Change.* Washington, DC: American Psychological Association, 1981.

page 182 The difficulties and pains of many famous people are recounted in *Not a Good Word About Anybody*, by Jane Goodsell (New York: Ballantine Books, 1988).

page 183 Pennebaker JW: Confiding traumatic experiences and health. In Fisher S and Reason J (eds.): *Handbook of Life Stress, Cognition, and Health.* New York: John Wiley & Sons, 1988. Pennebaker JW, Kiecolt-Glaser JK, and Glaser R: Disclosure of traumas and immune function: Health implications for psychotherapy. *Journal of Consulting and Clinical Psychology* 1988; 56(2):239–45. Pennebaker JW, Hughes CF, and O'Heeron RC: The psychophysiology of confession: Linking inhibitory and psychosomatic processes. *Journal of Personality and Social Psychology* 1987; 52(4):781–93.

Chapter 12. Investing in Yourself

page 189 Linville PW: Self-complexity as a cognitive buffer against stress-related illness and depression. *Journal of Personality and Social Psychology* 1987; 52(4):663–76.

Patricia Linville, a psychologist at Yale University, tested the protective effects of self-complexity. She had people categorize various aspects of themselves: their roles, relationships, and activities, as whether they were outgoing, playful, competitive, and imaginative. From this she contructed a measure of self-complexity—that is, how complex and distinct was the picture each person created of themselves. She also measured the number of life stresses the people experienced, including personal and family disruptions, financial woes, career setbacks, and the like.

In the two weeks following the initial survey, those people who scored higher in self-complexity were considerably less likely to suffer mental and physical symptoms in the face of life stresses. They reported less depression, foul moods, colds, coughs, stomach pains, headaches, and muscle aches than did their less complex counterparts.

page 191 For a discussion of the impact of education level on death rates, see Sagan LA: *The Health of Nations*. New York: Basic Books, 1987. And Kitagawa E and Hauser P: *Differential Mortality in the United States*. Cambridge, MA: Harvard University Press, 1973. National Center for Health Statistics and P.W. Ries, *Americans Assess Their Health: United States, 1978*. Vital and Health Statistics, series 10, no. 142. Washington, DC: U.S. Government Printing Office, 1983. Mulcahy R, Daley L, Graham I, and Hickey N; Level of education, coronary risk factors, and cardiovascular disease. *Irish Medical Journal* 1984; 77 no. 10: 316–18.

page 195 Sales SM and House J: Job dissatisfaction as a possible risk factor in coronary heart disease. *Journal of Chronic Disease* 1971; 23:861–73.

page 195 Palmore E: Predicting longevity: A follow-up controlling for age. *The Gerontologist* 1969; 9:247–50.

page 195 Lohrer BT, Noe RA, Moeller NL, and Fitzgerald MP: A meta-analysis of the relation of job characteristics to job satisfaction. *Journal of Applied Psychology* 1985; 70:280–89.

page 195 Argyle M: *The Psychology of Happiness*. London: Methuen, 1987.

page 196 Karasek R, Baker D, Marxer F, Ahlbom A, and Theorell T: Job decision latitude, job demands, and cardiovascular disease: A prospective study of Swedish men. *American Journal of Public Health* 1981; 71(7):694–705. Alfredsson L, Karasek R, and Theorell T: Myocardial infarction risk and psychosocial work environment: An analysis of the male Swedish working force. *Social Science & Medicine* 1982; 16:463–67. Karasek RA, Theorell T, Schwartz JE, Schnall PL, Pieper CF, and Michela JL: Job characteristics in relation to the prevalence of myocardial infarction in the U.S. Health Examination Survey (HES) and the Health and Nutrition Examination Survey (HANES). *American Journal of Public Health* 1988; 78(8):910–18.

Chapter 13. Indulging Yourself

page 201   Rinzler CA: *The Book of Chocolate*. New York: St. Martins, 1977.

page 201   Weil A and Rosen W: *Chocolate to Morphine: Understanding Mind-Active Drugs*. Boston: Houghton Mifflin, 1983.

page 202   Paolini VJ and Kashket S: Inhibition by cocoa extracts of biosynthesis of extracellular polysaccharide by human oral bacteria. *Archives of Oral Biology* 1985; 30(4):359–63.

page 202   Reynolds EC: The prevention of sub-surface demineralization of bovine enamel and change in plaque composition by casein in an intra-oral model. *Journal of Dental Research* 1987; 66(6):1120–27.

page 202   Roach M: More reasons to love chocolate. *Hippocrates* 1988; 2(5):18–21. (Material here adapted in part from this article.)

page 202   Schuman M, Gitlin MJ, and Fairbanks L: Sweets, chocolate, and atypical depressive traits. *Journal of Nervous and Mental Disease* 1987; 175(8):491–95.

page 202   Liebowitz MR and Klein D: Hysteroid dysphoria. *Psychiatric Clinics of North America* 1979; 2(3):555–75.

page 203   Karoum F, Nasrallah H, Potkin S, Cuang L, Moyer-Schwing J, Phillips I, and Wyatt RJ: Mass fragmentography of phenylethylamine, m- and p-tyramine and related amines in plasma, cerebrospinal fluid, urine, and brain. *Journal of Neurochemistry* 1979; 33:201–12.

page 203   Boynton S: *Chocolate—the Consuming Passion*. New York: Workman Publishing, 1982.

page 203   Eckardt MJ, Hartford TC, Kaelber CT, et al.: Health hazard associated with alcohol consumption. *Journal of the American Medical Association* 1981; 246(6):648–66.

page 204   Darby WJ: The benefits of drink. *Human Nature* 1978; 1(2):30–37.

page 204   Klatsky AL, Freidman GO, and Siegelaub AB: Alcohol consumption before myocardial infarction: Results from the Kaiser-Permanente epidemiological study of myocardial infarction. *Annals of Internal Medicine* 1974; 81:294–301. Klatsky AL, Freidman GO, and Siegelaub AB: Alcohol and mortality: A ten-year Kaiser-Permanente experience. *Annals of Internal Medicine* 1981; 95:139–45.

page 205   Yano K, Rhoads GG, and Kagan A: Coffee, alcohol and risk of coronary heart disease among Japanese men living in Hawaii. *New England Journal of Medicine* 1977; 297:405–409.

page 205 Marmot MG, Shipley MJ, Rose G, and Thomas BJ: Alcohol and mortality: A U-shaped curve. *Lancet* 1981; 1:580–83.

page 206 Gruchow HW and Levin EW: Drinking patterns and coronary occlusion. *Primary Cardiology* November 1981; 129–37.

page 206 It was thought that alcohol increases levels of HDL cholesterol in the bloodstream. This is the so-called "good" cholesterol that is linked to lower heart disease risk. However, drinking alcohol increases apolipoprotein A1, a protein attached to HDL cholesterol, which helps clear cholesterol out of the bloodstream and prevents arteries from clogging. In one study, a beer-a-day diet caused apolipoprotein A1 levels to jump nearly 7 percent while it fell by 4 percent in abstainers. Since apolipoprotein levels are strongly linked with heart disease risk, even small increases fueled by as little as a beer a day can have significant protective effects. Moore RD and Pearson TA: Moderate alcohol consumption and coronary artery disease: A review. *Medicine* (Baltimore) 1986; 65(4):242–67.

page 206 Some investigators have reservations about the protective effects of moderate alcohol consumption. Moderate drinking may actually be more common among those in higher socioeconomic status, which may account for their better health. Many (though not all of the studies) did not control for smoking or exercise and some did not distinguish between lifelong teetotalers and ex-drinkers. The ex-drinkers may have given up drinking for health reasons, which makes it appear that nondrinkers have greater risk than moderate drinkers. Eichner ER: Alcohol versus exercise for coronary protection. *American Journal of Medicine* 1985; 79:231–40. Shaper AG, Philips AN, Pocock SJ, and Walker M: Alcohol and ischaemic heart disease in middle aged British men. *British Medical Journal* 1987; 294(6574):733–37.

page 206 Forkner DJ: Should wine be on your menu? *The Professional Nutritionist* 1981; 14(2):1–3. Irvine DO: Influence of tannic, tartaric and acetic acid upon olfactory acuity. *American Journal of Digestive Diseases* 1953; 20:17–21. Vilter RW: Nutritional problems in surgical patients. *Postgraduate Medicine* 1964; 36:34–38. Goetzl FR: A note on the possible usefulness of wine in the management of anorexia. *The Permanente Medical Foundation Bulletin* 1950; 8:72–86. Camargo CA, Vranizan KM, Dreon DM, Frey-Hewitt B, and Wood PD: Alcohol, calorie intake, and adiposity in overweight men. *Journal of the American College of Nutrition* 1987; 6(3):271–78.

page 207 Kastenbaum R: *Alcohol and Old Age.* New York: Grune

& Stratton, 1980. Steele CM, Critchlow B, and Liu TJ: Alcohol and social behavior II: The helpful drunkard. *Journal of Personality and Social Psychology* 1985; 48(1):35–46.

page 208   Marlatt GA and Roshsenow DJ: The think-drink effect. *Psychology Today* December 1981; 60–93.

page 208   There have been reports that as few as three alcoholic drinks per *week* are linked with a 50 percent increase in the risk of women developing breast cancer. This figure has been greatly misinterpreted. For example, some people thought this meant that the risk of getting breast cancer was 50 percent in women who drank moderately—a gross overestimate.

Further, since the lifetime risk of all women for developing breast cancer is 9 percent (one in eleven), some people incorrectly concluded that drinkers run a lifetime risk of 14 percent. The problem with this interpretation is that the 9 percent figure refers to the lifetime risk for *all* women, so it already includes those who drink moderately. The 9 percent lifetime risk figure is also misleading when applied to adult women who have not already developed breast cancer. The actual risk of a woman developing breast cancer between the ages of forty and sixty is closer to 3.3 percent. Therefore, even if the newly reported risk figures for drinking women are correct, the risk of a woman drinking moderate amounts of alcohol only increases to about 4.3 percent—much less alarming than the 14 percent figure often quoted.

Willet WC, Stampfer MJ, Colditz GA, et al.: Moderate alcohol consumption and the risk of breast cancer. *New England Journal of Medicine* 1987; 316:1174–80. Schatzkin A, Jones DY, Hoover RN, et al.: Alcohol consumption and breast cancer in the epidemiological follow-up study of the first national health and nutrition examination survey. *New England Journal of Medicine* 1988; 316:1169–73. Webster LA, Wingo PA, Layde PM, and Ory HW: Alcohol consumption and risk of breast cancer. *Lancet* September 24, 1983; 723–26. Harris RE and Wynder EL: Breast cancer and alcohol consumption: A study in weak associations. *Journal of the American Medical Association* 1988; 259(19):2867–71. Longnecker MP, Berlin JA, Orza MJ, and Chalmers TC: A meta-analysis of alcohol consumption in relation to risk of breast cancer. *Journal of the American Medical Association* 1988; 260(5):652–56.

page 209   Are You at Risk? adapted from various alcoholism screening questionnaires. Selzer ML, Vinokur A, and van Rooijan L: A self-administered short Michigan Alcholism Screening Test (SMAST). *Journal of Studies on Alcohol* 1975; 36(1):117–26. Powers JS and Spickard A: Michigan Alcoholism Screening Test to diagnose early alcoholism in a general practice. *Southern Medical Journal* 1984; 77(7):852–56.

page 210   Morris B: Born to shop. *Wall Street Journal* article reprinted in *San Jose Mercury News,* September 27, 1987.

page 210   Rook DW: The buying impulse. *Journal of Consumer Research* 1987; 14:189–99.

page 211   Shapiro SA and Tuckman AJ: *Time Off: A Psychological Guide to Vacations.* New York: Doubleday, 1978.

page 212   The study of tourists at the Great Barrier Reef is found in Pearce PL: *The Social Psychology of Tourist Behavior.* Oxford: Pergamon, 1982.

page 212   Padus E: *The Complete Guide to Your Emotions and Your Health.* Emmaus, PA: Rodale Press, 1986.

page 215   Rubinstein C: *PT's* survey report on how Americans view vacations. *Psychology Today* May 1980; 13:62–76.

page 216   Brody R: Anatomy of a laugh. *American Health* November/December 1983; 43–47.

page 216   Long P: Laugh and be well? *Psychology Today* October 1987; 28–29.

page 216   Cousins N: *Anatomy of an Illness as Perceived by the Patient: Reflections on Healing and Regeneration.* New York: Bantam, 1979. Cogan R, Cogan D, Waltz W, and McCue M: Effects of laughter and relaxation on discomfort thresholds. *Journal of Behavioral Medicine* 1987; 10(2):139–44.

page 217   Dillon KM, Minchoff B, and Baker KH: Positive emotional states and enhancement of the immune system. *International Journal of Psychiatry in Medicine* 1985–86; 15:13–17.

page 218   Berk LS, Tan SA, Nehlsen-Cannarella SL, Napier BJ, Lewis JE, Lee JW, Fry WF, and Eby WC: Laughter decreases cortisol, epinephrine, and 3,4–dihydroxyphenyl acetic acid (DOPAC). Abstract, Society of Behavioral Medicine, 1988.

page 218   Dixon NF: Humor: A cognitive alternative to stress? In Sarason IG and Spielberger CD (eds.): *Stress and Anxiety* (Vol.7). Washington, DC: Hemisphere, 1980. Lefcourt HM and Martin RA: *Humor and Life Stress: Antidote to Adversity.* New York: Springer-Verlag, 1986.

page 219   Blumenfeld E and Alpern L: *The Smile Connection: How to Use Humor in Dealing with People.* Englewood Cliffs, NJ: Prentice-Hall, 1986.

page 220   Borquist A: Crying. *American Journal of Psychology* 1906; 17:149–205. Frey WH, DeSota-Johnson D, Hoffman C, and McCall

JT: Effect of stimulus on the chemical composition of human tears. *American Journal of Ophthalmology* 1981; 92(4):559–67. Fry WH: Not-so-idle tears. *Psychology Today* January 1980; 91–92.

Chapter 14. Selfless Pleasures

page 222   For an excellent recent review of the evidence relating social support and health, see House JS, Landis KR, and Umberson D: Social relationships and health. *Science* July 1988; 241:540–45. Cohen S, Syme SL (eds.): *Social Support and Health*. New York: Academic Press, 1985. Also see Broadhead WE, Kaplan BH, James SA, Wagner EH, Schoenbach VJ, Grimson R, Heyden S, Tibblin G, and Gehlbach SH: The epidemiological evidence for a relationship between social support and health. *American Journal of Epidemiology* 1983; 117:521–37. Berkman L and Syme SL: Social networks, host resistance, and mortality: A nine-year follow-up study of Alameda County residents. *American Journal of Epidemiology* 1979; 109:186–204.

page 223   For a more complete discussion of the evolution of the social body, see Ornstein R and Sobel D: *The Healing Brain*. New York: Simon & Schuster, 1987. For a highly readable discussion of our earliest ancestors, see Johansen D and Edey M: *Lucy: The Beginnings of Humankind*. New York: Simon & Schuster, 1981; and Leakey R and Lewin R: *Origins*. New York: E.P. Dutton, 1977.

page 224   The critical role of early attachment is discussed in Bowlby J: *Attachment and Loss*, Vols. 1, 2, 3. New York: Basic Books, 1969. Also see Ainsworth MDS: *Infancy in Uganda*. Baltimore: Johns Hopkins University Press, 1967. Ainsworth MDS, Blehar M, Waters E, and Wall S: *Patterns of Attachment: A Psychological Study of the Strange Situation*. Hillsdale, NJ: Lawrence Erlbaum, 1978.

page 225   For a discussion of the differences in social relationship between men and women, see Longino CF and Lipman A: Married and spouseless men and women in planned retirement communities: Support network differentials. *Journal of Marriage and the Family* 1981; 43:169–77. For a study of the differential effects of divorce on mental health problems in men and women, see Gerstel N and Riesman C: Social networks in a vulnerable population: The separated and divorced. Paper presented at the American Public Health Association Meetings, Los Angeles, CA, November 4, 1981.

page 227   Brenner MH: Importance of the economy to the nation's health. In Eisenberg L and Kleinman A (eds.): *The Relevance of Social Science for Medicine*. Dordrecht, Holland: D. Reidel Publishing Co., 1980.

page 228   Kobrin FE and Hendershot GE: Do family ties reduce mortality?: Evidence from the United States, 1966–1968. *Journal of Marriage and the Family* 1977; 39:737–45.

page 228   Beck A and Katcher A: *Between Pets and People: The Importance of Animal Companionship.* New York: Putnam, 1983. Katcher A and Beck A (eds.): *New Perspectives on Our Lives with Companion Animals.* Philadelphia: University of Pennsylvania Press, 1983. Fitz-Gerald FT: The therapeutic value of pets. *Western Journal of Medicine* 1986; 144:103–105. Friedmann E, Katcher A, Lynch JJ, and Thomas SA: Animal companions and one-year survival of patients after discharge from a coronary care unit. *Public Health Reports* 1980; 95:307–12.

page 232   Rosenman RH, Brand RJ, Jenkins CD, Friedman M, et al.: Coronary heart disease in the Western Collaborative Study: Final follow-up experience of eight and one-half years. *Journal of the American Medical Association* 1975; 223:872–77. Friedman M and Rosenman R: *Type A Behavior and Your Heart.* New York: Alfred A. Knopf, 1974. Friedman M and Ulmer D: *Treating Type A Behavior and Your Heart.* New York: Alfred A. Knopf, 1984.

page 232   Dembrowski TM, MacDougall JM, Eliot RS, and Buell JC: Moving beyond Type A. *Advances* 1984; 1:16–26.

page 232   For a current look at anger and hostility in cardiovascular disease, see Chesney M and Rosenman RH (eds.): *Anger and Hostility in Cardiovascular and Behavioral Disorders.* Washington, DC: Hemisphere Publishing Corp., 1985.

page 232   For a thorough review of self-involvement and heart disease see Scherwitz L, Graham LE, and Ornish D: Self-involvement and the risk factors for coronary heart disease. *Advances* 1985; 2:6–18. Also, Scherwitz L, McKelvain R, Laman C, et al.: Type A behavior, self-involvement, and coronary atherosclerosis. *Psychosomatic Medicine* 1983; 45:47–57.

page 233   Kohn A: Beyond selfishness. *Psychology Today* 1988; 22(10):34–38. Luks A: Helper's high. *Psychology Today* 1988; 22(10):39–42. Luks A and Growald E: *American Health* March 1988. Panksepp J: The psychobiology of prosocial behaviors: Separation distress, play and altruism. In Zahn-Waxler C, Cummings EM, and Iannotti R (eds.): *Altruism and Aggression: Biological and Social Origins.* New York: Cambridge University Press, 1986. Staub E: A conception of the determinants and development of altruism and aggression: Motives, the self, and the environment. In Zahn-Waxler C, Cummings

EM, and Iannotti R (eds.): *Altruism and Aggression: Biological and Social Origins.* New York: Cambridge University Press, 1986.

page 234   Gartner A and Riessman F: *Self-help in the Human Services.* San Francisco: Jossey-Bass, 1977. Hurley D: Getting help from helping. *Psychology Today* January 1988; 22(1):63–67.

page 234   House JS, Robbins C, and Metzner HL: The association of social relationships and activities with mortality. *American Journal of Epidemiology* 1982; 116:123–40.

Chapter 15. Healthy Pleasure Points

page 240   Being in a good mood seems to increase our willingness to help others. See Isen AM and Levin PF: The effect of feeling good on helping: Cookies and kindness. *Journal of Personality and Social Psychology* 1972; 21:384–88.

Index

expectations and, 5–7, 30–
31, 127–130
food for, 91–93
and guilt, 201
and health, 4–7, 239–243,
248
human desire for, 3–4
mental channels of, 32
"minimum daily require-
ment" of, 37
and mood, 142–143
in preindustrial times, 9–13
self-indulgence and, 200–
201
sensual channels of, 31–32
simplicity and, 238–239
work as barrier to, 11–13
"Power lunch," 96
Power of Positive Thinking, The,
181
Psychoneuroimmunology, 250

Reagan, Ronald, 6, 180, 182
Relaxation
as anxiety source, 117
and immune system, 251
methods of, 271–272
techniques for, 117–118
"Runner's high," 108

Salt, 14, 19–20
Saunas, 46–48
and resistance to infection,
47
Scheier, Michael, 162
Seasonal Affective Disorder

(SAD), 49–52
in children, 257
"reverse," 257
Self, sense of, 189–190, 284
Self-efficacy theory, 279–280
Self-indulgence, 200–201
and vacations, 213–214
Serotonin, 95, 97
and diet, 266
Set point, 88
and exercise, 94
Sex
and health, 76–78, 79–81
and smell, 73–76
substitutions for, 80
and well-being, 14
Sexual dysfunction, 14
Sexually transmitted diseases,
14
Shopping, as a healthy pleasure, 210–211
Sleep, 119–123
biological need for, 121–122
and immune system, 121
lack of, and accidents, 273–
274
and life expectancy, 120–121
Smell
and love, 73–76
mechanisms of, 66
and memory, 66–68
sense of, 65–66, 82–83
subliminal sense of, 71–73
Smiling, 276
Social connectedness, 223–225
altruism and, 233–237
and heart disease, 224
and immune system, 27, 225